Let's Take the Kids!

Let's Take the Kids!

Great Places to Go in New York's Hudson Valley

*Including the Catskills, the Capital Region,
the Adirondacks, Lake George, the Berkshires
& Cooperstown*

Revised Edition

JOANNE MICHAELS

The Countryman Press
Woodstock, Vermont

Cover illustration by Charles Forsman, www.chuckmcbuck.com
Maps by Paul Woodward, © The Countryman Press
Book design and composition by Eugenie S. Delaney

Published by The Countryman Press, P.O. Box 748, Woodstock, VT 05091
Distributed by W. W. Norton & Company, Inc., 500 Fifth Avenue, New
York, NY 10110
Printed in the United States of America

Let's Take the Kids!
978-0-88150-938-0

10 9 8 7 6 5 4 3 2 1

To Erik, my favorite traveling companion and fellow adventurer
both in life and on the road

Contents

▼▲▼▲▼▲▼

Acknowledgments

▼▲▼▲▼▲▼

I t is impossible to thank everyone who helps in creating a travel book; for every tourism department head who answers a question, there are scores of office and administrative people who provide additional assistance, source material, and suggestions. So, a heartfelt thanks to everyone I spoke to throughout the region on my travels, and an extra-special thanks to the county tourism directors for their enthusiasm during my research and writing, particularly Kim Sinistore and Lydia Ruth (Westchester County), Heather Duke (Rockland County), Val Hickman and Dee Kraft (Putnam County), Susan Cayea (Orange County), Roberta Lockwood (Sullivan County), Lisa Berger (Ulster County), Nancy Lutz (Dutchess County), Ann Cooper (Columbia County), Nancy Petramele (Greene County), Patty Cullen (Delaware County), Greg Dixon (Saratoga Springs), Joanne Conley (Warren County), and Deb Mussman (the Berkshires). Patrick Del Rosario at Windham Mountain, Jessica Pezak at Hunter, Donna Blaney at Boscobel, and Tony Lanza and Blake Killin at Belleayre were generous with their time.

This book would have taken a lot longer to produce and would have been a lot less fun to write without the suggestions and patience of my editor/publisher, Kermit Hummel. He was always willing to listen and was extremely responsive to any roadblocks encountered during the course of the publishing process. Managing editor Lisa Sacks, whose tenacity and organizational skills helped me tie up any loose ends and frustrating details, was responsible for capably overseeing the publishing process. No author creates a book alone and both Kermit and Lisa were enormously helpful from beginning to end.

I am grateful to artist Charles Forsman, who created an inspired book cover—a critical task that was executed beautifully. Eugenie Delaney conveyed the spirit of the book with her imaginative interior design, and I appreciated Eric Raetz's meticulous attention to detail as he copyedited the manuscript.

Dr. Joseph Appel's advice regarding the medical emergencies parents might be confronted with on a trip and how best to handle such situations is greatly appreciated.

And, of course, Erik Michaels-Ober was always willing to travel with me throughout the region, acting as the final arbiter of taste for this project in its first two editions. Now living in California, his excursions on research trips for this new edition have been limited, but his thoughtful suggestions have been invaluable.

Introduction

▼▲▼▲▼▲▼

T raveling with children is an art: No matter how many trips you have taken on your own, once you put a car and a kid together, there is a whole new world to take into account. Food, travel time, boredom, and rest stops must now all be considered and planned for, especially when you are heading for unfamiliar territory outside of your hometown. Since the first edition of this book appeared in 1990, I have answered literally thousands of questions about what to do with the kids outside the New York metropolitan area. Children will be enchanted by the variety of experiences to be found upstate. Rich with culture, history, and even some magic, the region has captured the imagination of writers, artists, and visitors alike for over three centuries. This is the land of Rip Van Winkle, and what child wouldn't want to stop by the bridge where Ichabod Crane outran the Headless Horseman? (You can visit the bridge in Tarrytown, Westchester County.) Revolutionary War battles are still fought at the Old Stone Fort in Schoharie, and on an unbearably hot summer day remember that the caves at Howe Caverns remain a refreshing 52 degrees year-round.

This book is not meant to be comprehensive: It's not an encyclopedia. The attractions and activities selected for inclusion were chosen for their appeal to young travelers. The places featuring outdoor activities are those that are appropriate for people traveling with children: Hiking and biking areas are flatter and geared toward the beginner or novice. Historic sites included are those that contain exhibits of interest to most youngsters. Occasionally, a resort is listed; just about all of these places have children's programs. Additionally, they offer an alternative way to explore a large area for travelers who want to stay in one place for a few days or a week at a time.

Let's Take the Kids! is organized by county and provides travelers with a tourism "loop" around the region. The counties follow the Hudson River northward, then west through the Catskills, north again to the capital district and Saratoga, and (finally) reaching the lower Adirondacks. For the Massachusetts section, the Berkshires have been given their own chapter. It would take at least a week to ten days to follow the New York loop in its physical entirety—and you couldn't possibly see all of the sights in this time. But you can use the book to plan day and weekend trips, as well as longer vacations—a fact that should appeal to teachers and scout leaders as well as parents.

For each of the 16 geographical sections covered in the book, the county tourism Web site is provided. You can go online to check out accommodations and restaurants before you depart as well as search listings of seasonal special events. Major annual celebrations and parades are noted in the entries for each site, but details about a variety of workshops, talks, and "happenings" (and their exact dates) are best found on Web site calendars.

When planning any excursion, be mindful that winter may be over in your neck of the woods, but often the snow doesn't melt until well into April in parts of northern New York State. Pack accordingly and remember to dress in layers.

This book was written from a car traveler's point of view, but you can get around certain areas by bus and train. If you want to plan a trip by train, call AMTRAK, 1-800-USA-RAIL, for information; for bus transportation to the Catskills and Adirondacks, call Adirondack Trailways, 1-800-858-8555. Both train and bus lines offer children's fares.

I have spent my entire life (outside of a dozen years which included college and living and working in Manhattan) in the region covered by this book, and was the editor-in-chief of *Hudson Valley* magazine for several years before writing a guidebook to the Hudson Valley and Catskill

Mountains that has been in print for 23 years and seven editions. I remember many wonderful years exploring the area with my family and friends. Of course, things have changed since I was a child (for the better, in many cases) and I hope that a new generation of travelers will enjoy discovering the wonder and magic of this diverse region as much as I have loved rediscovering it year after year—both as a parent, and while researching the best places to go for my travel books.

Before You Hit the Road . . . a To-Do List

The following thoughts evolved out of my experiences during trips throughout upstate New York and the Berkshires, and while these tips may not solve all your travel concerns, I wish I had thought about most of them before I set out on my excursions away from home!

Map out your route ahead of time. I traveled thousands of miles during my research trips, and much of the area is rural. One of the easiest things to do before you leave is to call ahead. Although I try to keep the material in this book up to date, activity times and locations do change on occasion—especially for annual events and festivals. The telephone numbers provided here will put you in touch with someone at the business or site.

While the views are beautiful in this part of the world, you will find that sometimes, especially in the off-season, there are not many places to stop for restrooms or snacks. I advise making certain that there are several larger villages and towns on your itinerary; they nearly always have a restaurant or diner with public bathrooms. Finding such an oasis in a tiny hamlet on a Sunday evening can often be difficult and uncomfortable for everyone in the car.

I heartily recommend that you think about taking some of the older side roads, instead of the newer highways and interstates. It is easier to stop if the kids see something of moving interest—like cows or sheep—and there are often clean, quiet picnic stops along such routes as well.

Take along a good supply of snacks for the drive. Unless you and the kids are thrilled with fast-food chains, bringing snacks will do three things: allow you to cut down on travel time (especially during summer lunch hours, which can be busy); help you stay within a travel

Skiing is a great family activity.

budget (most food is overpriced at special events); and let you pack nutritious items for the kids. Don't forget to add a damp washcloth or wipes and a roll of paper towels to make cleanup easier.

Keep a collection of small toys and coloring books in the car. This will keep even the youngest child happy for some of the time on a long drive, especially in areas where there is not much to look for out the windows. I found that kids enjoy drawing pictures of what it is they are going to see: horses, houses, trains, or boats.

Dress the children in layers of clothing. Much of the upstate region is mountainous, and wide temperature ranges can be expected year-round. Summer temperatures can go from the 90s or higher in the afternoon to the low 50s at night; spring and fall may range from the 70s to the 30s, particularly in the Adirondacks and the western part of the region covered here. Winter can bring below-zero temperatures and windy conditions. Don't forget hats and boots (sneakers are fine for dry, warm days, but not for mud and ice). If you are planning to spend time out in the fields picking fruits and vegetables at one of the many farms, bring hats, long-sleeved shirts, comfortable shoes, and sunscreen. River trips are always very windy, so bring along hooded sweatshirts, scarves, and hats—even on a balmy spring day.

Make sure each activity is appropriate for your child's age. Because many places in this book are historic, there are some things you have to consider before you go, especially with very young children. Some sites are geared for all ages, and they allow kids to explore and participate in special hands-on areas; other sites are for looking only—while kids are welcome, they are not allowed to touch anything. While I have tried to make this clear in each of the entries, if you are unsure about the appropriateness of a site for your children, call before you go and ask before you pay.

Find out about a tour before plunging ahead. You know your child best, and while a certain five-year-old might enjoy a 30-minute tour, another one may be tired after 10 minutes. Most sites will allow adults who are not taking a tour to wait outside with children without charging them admission or will charge a reduced admission; if this fee isn't displayed at the ticket office, ask about it. Even if your child is well behaved and takes a tour, you may want to schedule a stop afterward at an amusement park or a nature center where kids are encouraged to participate in the activities. This prevents associating history with boredom, and lets parents see some adult-oriented sites on the outing.

If you are taking a group of children, bring along enough adults to keep the group supervised properly. Many small sites are understaffed, and it is more pleasant for other visitors if your group is well behaved and stays together with the guide. If you are bringing more than six children to a site, it is wise to call before you go; some limit the number of visitors who can be accommodated and require special group reservations and fees.

During the winter months, always call before you go. Outside of ski areas, many sites close down in the winter season (usually November through March) or offer limited hours at this time of year. The flip side is that many smaller sites will make special arrangements for a group in the off-season if they have enough advance notice. Parks and recreation areas are notorious for not listing winter hours in their brochures; if you like to spend time outdoors in the winter, call the park and ask about their hours before you set out. Often Web sites do not have the most up-to-date information either!

Some Advice from the Author

For your convenience. the entries included in *Let's Take the Kids!* contain telephone numbers. Please call in advance to make sure the site you intend to visit is open on the day and at the time you are planning to go. Keep in mind that during the winter months many sites reduce their hours. Additionally. some Web sites aren't updated frequently and may not contain current information. I strongly suggest that you check out the days and hours of operation before hitting the road. The last thing you want to do is disappoint the kids!

Protect yourself and your family against Lyme disease. Lyme disease is a critically important consideration when you are traveling with kids in a rural, wooded area. This tickborne infection has spread throughout the upstate New York and Berkshire regions (it is particularly a problem in Dutchess and Columbia counties). If you are planning to hike or camp in wooded areas, check with your doctor or the local health department for information about this disease. Make sure you and your children wear long sleeves, tuck pants into socks, and check exposed areas of the skin for ticks at the end of the day. Dogs and cats can carry the ticks as well. Deer ticks are smaller than others and it is often difficult to see them on the skin. No matter how appealing it may seem, it is best not to allow children to roll around on the grass in these places (a sight I often see when I travel to parks and historic sites with beautiful picnic areas).

Prepare for emergencies. Dr. Joseph Appel, a pediatrician with Pine Street Pediatrics in Kingston, New York, suggests that parents create their own first-aid kit rather than purchase one that is prepackaged. Those that are ready-made are often more expensive and contain items most people probably wouldn't use. He says, "When our family goes on a trip, we take acetaminophen (Tylenol), simple cold remedies, antibacterial ointment, adhesive bandages, and syrup of ipecac for infants."

In an emergency medical situation that occurs miles away from home, most people might not think of calling their primary care doctor.

Dr. Appel emphasizes that this is exactly what parents should do. "In almost all situations," he says, "there is time to wait for a call back from your doctor or pediatrician." In this way, you can explain the problem to your family doctor before making any medical decisions. "Use your primary doctor as a broker for the system," explains Dr. Appel. "I have had phone calls from Paris, Los Angeles, and other remote places." In his experience, there are many medical conditions perceived as emergencies that can be taken care of over the telephone.

If you are unable to reach your primary care doctor, Dr. Appel believes it is best to contact a local physician rather than relying on emergency room personnel. (Emergency rooms are not usually staffed by primary care physicians, but rather with specialists who are not always comfortable with children.) Dr. Appel suggests locating such a doctor by talking to locals whose judgment you trust, or by calling the emergency room and obtaining the names of local pediatricians. If there is a group practice, you may have luck reaching one of the physicians fairly quickly, since groups tend to have more extensive office hours than individual doctors.

Now that you have thought about what could go wrong on your trip, and have prepared for the possibility of such an event—as well as the inevitable minor inconveniences—you are ready to get in the car and start your journey. Don't forget to take this book with you—and enjoy!

WESTCHESTER COUNTY

▼▲▼▲▼▲▼

A lthough Westchester borders New York City, the county is proud of its sixteen thousand acres of parkland and dozens of family-friendly facilities, including historic sites, nature preserves, and bicycle trails. Throughout the year there is an array of children's activities and special events just about everywhere—from sheepshearing at a 17th-century Dutch mill to a toy show at the busy County Center.

The following attractions are just a few of the highlights not to be missed on a visit to the county. **Rye Playland,** one of Westchester's most popular attractions and America's first planned amusement park, has been a family entertainment center since 1928. Three of the original rides are still in operation—the Whip, the Derby Racer, and the Carousel (with its hand-carved horses). Washington Irving described the enchantment of Westchester County in his short stories, immortalizing Tarrytown and the Headless Horseman. A visit to his home, **Sunnyside,** is well worthwhile to see the cozy "snuggery" where Irving wrote *The Legend of Sleepy Hollow.* Another special place to stop when traveling with children is the **Greenburgh Nature Center** in Scarsdale. The youngest travelers will love visiting the indoor live animal museum, containing over one hundred exotic and local animals, and seeing the outdoor barnyard animals and birds of prey

19

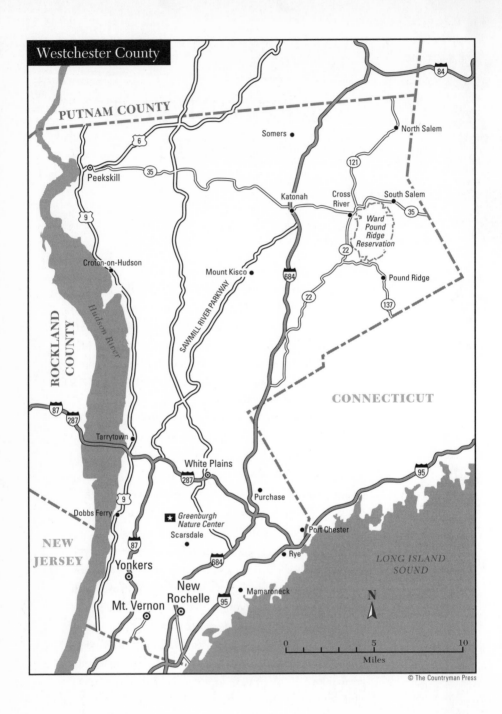

Westchester County

PUTNAM COUNTY

84

6

Somers ●   ● North Salem

35

121

Peekskill

9

Katonah   Cross River   ● South Salem

35

Ward Pound Ridge Reservation

22

Croton-on-Hudson

Mount Kisco ●   684

22   ● Pound Ridge

137

Hudson River

ROCKLAND COUNTY

SAWMILL RIVER PARKWAY

CONNECTICUT

87

287

Tarrytown ●

White Plains

287   95

9   Purchase ●

Dobbs Ferry ●

NEW JERSEY

★ Greenburgh Nature Center
Scarsdale ●   ● Port Chester

87

Yonkers   Rye ●   LONG ISLAND SOUND

684

New Rochelle   ● Mamaroneck

Mt. Vernon   95

N

0   5   10
Miles

© The Countryman Press

GREENBURGH NATURE CENTER

aviary. Don't leave without taking a self-guided nature tour. Older children and parents will particularly enjoy a stop at **Stone Barns** with its organic farm, state-of-the-art greenhouse, and fantastic stone buildings—all formerly owned by the Rockefeller family.

Make sure to check for special events on the county's Web site before leaving on a trip to Westchester. Some of the best annual family events include the **White Plains Cherry Blossom Festival** in Tibbits Park in May; the **Great Hudson River Revival** at Croton Point Park in June; and the **Pinkster Festival** at **Philipsburg Manor** (a cross-cultural celebration welcoming spring), also in June. November brings the **Family Turkey Scavenger Hunt** at the **Greenburgh Nature Center.** December's candlelight tours of the county's historic sites add a festive dimension to the holiday season for visitors of all ages.

For further information, contact: **Westchester County Office of Tourism,** 222 Mamaroneck Avenue, Suite 100, White Plains 10605, 914-995-8500, 1-800-833-WCVB, www.westchestertourism.com.

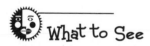 What to See

MUSEUMS AND HISTORIC SITES

Hudson River Museum and Andrus Planetarium. 511 Warburton Avenue, Yonkers 10701; 914-963-4550; www.hrm.org. Open year-round. Call for information on group rates. Admission.

The museum, housed in an old mansion, offers an array of science exhibits and programs; most are family-oriented. Hudson Riverama, a permanent teaching gallery about the Hudson River, simulates the river's habitats and geographic areas with realistic scenic designs, interactive experiences, multimedia technology, aquariums, and a scale model of the river. Teachers should note that special tours and workshops are available, but reservations are required. There is also the unique **Red Grooms Bookstore,** a colorful shop where art, magic, and books come together for people of all ages.

The **Andrus Planetarium,** which adjoins the museum, is home to a state-of-the-art Zeiss M1015 Star Machine, a powerful scientific tool that can project thousands of stars and planets onto the planetarium's 40-foot dome ceiling. A quadraphonic sound system makes the planetarium the perfect setting for multimedia programs, which provide the chance to see stars, comets, constellations, and galaxies up close. Explanatory narratives accompany the shows and fit the season of the year and the age of the audience, from kindergarten to college. The planetarium also sponsors a series of free night observations in the summer in conjunction with local astronomy clubs and even birthday parties.

Facilities: Restrooms, gift shop. Wheelchair and stroller accessible.

Katonah Museum of Art. 134 Jay Street (NY 22), Katonah 10536; 914-232-9555; www.katonahmusem.org. Admission.

This lively teaching museum was founded in 1953 to display art of the past and present as well as to foster arts education. There are exhibits by museum members, annual local studio tours, and changing displays—which may range from fashion designers to Navajo rugs to modern art. Special events, shows, and children's programs are held year-round (check Web site), and the museum is well worth a stop. There is also an outdoor sculpture garden.

Facilities: Restrooms, gift shop. Strollers are easy to maneuver here.

Lyndhurst. 635 South Broadway (US 9), Tarrytown 10591; 914-631-4481; www.lyndhurst.org. Admission.

The term Gothic revival may bring to mind castles, turrets, and crenellations, but it won't prepare a visitor for the wealth and magnificence of Lyndhurst. Built in 1838 for William Paulding, a former New York City mayor, the house and grounds were enlarged by the Merritt family and were later owned by the notoriously wealthy Jay Gould. Many of the furniture, paintings, and decorative accessories are original to the mansion, which was owned by the Goulds until 1961 when it was given to the National Trust. The rooms are sumptuous—each is filled with rare furniture, artwork, and decorative pieces: Tiffany glass and windows are outstanding highlights. Youngsters will enjoy the gardens, a children's playhouse, a conservatory with intricate brick paths, and nature trails that meander among the dozens of different trees (many on the grounds are centuries old), ferns, and plantings. Call ahead to check on scheduled children's programs; the Halloween celebration is a wonderful fun-filled family event.

Facilities: Restrooms, gift shop. Strollers are difficult to maneuver outside of the paved paths.

Neuberger Museum of Art. Purchase College Campus, 735 Anderson Hill Road, Purchase 10577; 914-251-6100; www.neuberger.org.

This is a great place to introduce children to modern art and sculpture. Masterpieces by Avery, Hopper, O'Keeffe, Pollock, and others are displayed in several spacious galleries at this extraordinary teaching museum. There is also an impressive amount of African art, and selections from Nelson Rockefeller's collection of ancient art. An outdoor sculpture area with works by Henry Moore, Andy Goldsworthy, and Alexander Liberman should not be missed. This is one of the county's finest cultural resources, with 16 rotating exhibits every year. The museum offers lectures, workshops, tours, performances, and concerts throughout the year.

Facilities: Restrooms, gift shop, café. Wheelchair and stroller accessible.

St. Paul's Church National Historic Site. 897 South Columbus Avenue, Mt. Vernon 10550; 914-667-4116; www.nps.gov/sapa. Open year-round. Free. Special weekend programs are held five or six times each year; call in advance or check Web site. Groups and school tours are available by reservation. Church tours, leading to the historic 1758 bronze bell and a magnificent view, are occasionally offered.

Construction of the church (which was deconsecrated in 1978) was begun in 1763; the interior has been restored to its 1787 appearance, with interesting high-walled box pews and other decidedly historic features. During the Revolutionary War, it was used as a field hospital, and an exhibition preserves the appearance of the building during the war. The cemetery is one of New York's oldest, with legible headstones dating from 1704. Guided tours explore the historic church, the burial yard, the museum, and the remnant of the town common. Allow about an hour and a half for a tour. The museum features various exhibitions on American and local history, and it includes special scavenger hunts, interactive activities, and historic toys for children.

Facilities: Restrooms, water cooler. The museum is fully wheelchair and stroller accessible.

Philipsburg Manor. 381 North Broadway, Sleepy Hollow 10591; 914-631-8200; www.hudsonvalley.org. Admission (free for children under the age of five). Tours available for students.

Philipsburg Manor was once a late-17th/early-18th-century milling, farming, and trading complex owned by an Anglo-Dutch family of merchants, tenanted by farmers of diverse European backgrounds, and operated by enslaved Africans. The site is of particular historical interest because of the size of the enslaved community and the highly developed nature of this 18th-century commercial property. Featuring a stone manor house, the site also includes a working water-powered gristmill

and millpond, an 18th-century barn, a slave garden, and a reconstructed tenant farmhouse. The grounds are home to cattle, sheep, and chickens. Interpreters dressed in costumes greet the children after they cross the mill bridge. The mill is a crowded, creaky place, full of noise and motion. Children delight as the miller lets in the water to run the great grinding stones that transform wheat and corn into flour and meal (which can be purchased on the spot). The manor house features a number of rooms with touchable reproductions such as beaver pelts, milk buckets, and iron pots. On the farm (depending on the time of day) children can participate in farm chores, thresh wheat, watch a cow being milked, and marvel at the team of oxen as they are hitched to their cart. Colonial food preparation and

At Philipsburg Manor, children are transported back to the 18th century, with costumed guides demonstrating spinning and other crafts common to the era. BRYAN HAEFFELE textile production are explored in the activity center. Special events occur throughout the year. In April, Sheep to Shawl features border collie demonstrations, sheep shearing, wool dyeing, and hands-on activities for children. In May, drummers, dancers, and storytellers contribute to the festive atmosphere of Pinkster, an African American celebration of spring. The Green Corn Festival (Labor Day weekend) brings together Native American storytellers, dancing, and many activities for children—including cornhusk doll making, apple cider pressing, and colonial games. During Legend Weekend (late October), Philipsburg Manor is transformed into a haunted landscape that is "spooktacular" fun for children and adults of all ages.

Facilities: Restrooms, picnic areas, gift shop, café.

Sunnyside. 3 West Sunnyside Lane, Irvington 10533; 914-591-8763; www.hudsonvalley.org. Admission (free for children under the age of five). Children receive creativity totes free with admission. Tours available for students. A reduced-fee, grounds-only pass is available.

Sunnyside was home to author Washington Irving, who described his charming house as being as "full of angles and corners as an old cocked hat." The creator of Ichabod Crane lived and worked at Sunnyside in the 1840s, and this is a fine place to introduce children to American literature. The house stands much as it did in Irving's time, with a graceful carriage drive and wisteria draped over the front door. Inside, costumed guides take visitors through this "cottage," which still has many of Irving's personal belongings, including his writing desk and piano. Although Irving never had children of his own, he did have nieces and nephews living with him, and several of the bedrooms reflect the children who stayed at Sunnyside. Younger visitors who are familiar with *The Legend of Sleepy Hollow* and *Rip Van Winkle* will be fascinated to learn that Ichabod Crane did, indeed, live in the neighborhood (Irving based the character on a neighbor) and that the ghostly hoofbeats are still heard on windy nights along the local roads. Outside the cottage, many walking paths offer lovely views of the Hudson, and there are several outbuildings to visit; the woodshed, the root cellar and milk room, the outhouses, and the icehouse among them. A graceful swan pond, which Irving dubbed the "Little Mediterranean," has picnic tables alongside and is a perfect spot for lunch in the summer. For kids who love trains, there are railroad tracks running next to the Hudson, and

One of the guides at Sunnyside, home of Washington Irving, author of *The Legend of Sleepy Hollow* and *Rip Van Winkle*.

AMTRAK trains can be seen (and heard) shooting by several times a day (earlier trains used to stop and pick up Irving for his trips to New York City). Special events are held throughout the year, and many are especially for children. Past celebrations have included a Strawberry Fest, Independence Day, an ice-cream-making workshop, Apple Time, a 19th-century Thanksgiving dinner, and candlelight tours at Christmas. Teachers should note that there are many workshops for classes, but they have to call ahead.

Facilities: Restrooms, picnic areas, gift shop (with many lovely children's items). Parents with strollers will be fine on the grounds, but the house has some steep staircases; not recommended for wheelchairs. If accessibility is a concern, call ahead to make special arrangements.

Van Cortlandt Manor. 500 South Riverside Avenue, Croton-on-Hudson 10520; 914-271-8981; www.hudsonvalley.org. Admission.

This manor originally consisted of 86,000 acres of land. The main floors of the present manor house were built in 1748; the house remained in the Van Cortlandt family until the middle of the 20th century. The house reflects life in an 18th-century Dutch home. As supporters of the American Revolution, the Van Cortlandts were hosts to such luminaries as George Washington, Benjamin Franklin, and Marquis de Lafayette. Inside the house there is a blend of decorative styles and periods reflecting the history of the family. One impressive item is the fowling gun, a huge firearm that was fired into a flock of birds and reduced hunting time considerably. Outside the gardens beckon flower lovers, and the Long Walk—a brick path that leads to the Ferry House, a nearby inn and tavern—wanders by well-maintained flower beds and herb gardens. Special events are held throughout the year. Animals and Acrobats, over the Memorial Day weekend, examines the birth of the American circus with a number of traditional performers such as jugglers, magicians, fortune-tellers, slack-rope walkers, and musicians. The Independence Day Celebration is complete with military reenactors and a parade through the manor. There is Heritage Crafts over Columbus Day weekend, when children can try their hand at almost 25 vanishing skills like candle making and coopering. The Twelfth Night celebrations, on the December weekends before and after Christmas, are a great time for candlelight tours—and here, the kids get to participate in them. A visit on weekends during the summer months includes several hands-on opportunities for all family members. There is brick making, black-smithing, and a variety of children's games. At the Ferry House (also open for tours), kids will notice the familiar white-clay pipes—they were rented out once, with the ends broken off for each new smoker.

Facilities: Restrooms, picnic areas, gift shop.

Yorktown Museum. 1974 Commerce Street, YCCC Building, Yorktown Heights 10598; 914-962-2970; www.yorktownmuseum.org. Open year-round. Admission is by donation for individuals; there is a small charge for prearranged group tours.

The Yorktown Museum, which contains five exhibit rooms, offers children a chance to look at daily life a century ago through a re-created Colonial two-room house filled with furniture from homes and settlements of northern Westchester's past. One of the best-known rooms is the Small World, where miniature houses and rooms enchant the viewer. The main attraction here is the Marjorie Johnson Victorian dollhouse, which is filled with tiny re-creations of furniture and furnishings. It is 7 feet tall, has 8,000 hand-cut clapboards, a stonework base, and a resident ghost! The Railroad Room contains an operational scale model of the "Old Put" line as it came through Yorktown. Also included are many

Tarrytown

After you finish touring Sunnyside there are a few other places to see in the area. Make a stop at the **village park** on US 9 in the center of Tarrytown. Markets show where Major Andre was captured during the Revolutionary War (he was Benedict Arnold's British contact), and a bridge over the stream where, according to legend, the Headless Horseman carried away Ichabod Crane.

The kids will also enjoy stopping at the **Old Dutch Church**, which was built in the late-17th century and still is used for services. US 9, north of Tarrytown near Philipsburg Manor, on the right; watch for the parking area signs. Call 914-631-1123 for church hours and guided tours of the cemetery. The cemetery, a national historic landmark, contains fascinating old tombstones (many in Dutch), which were decorated in the 17th century. Washington Irving's grave is here, and an old belief holds that the ghost of a headless Hessian soldier haunts the site.

You may want to call ahead for a tour of the **Tarrytown Lighthouse** (follow the signs from the center of town to Kingsland Point Park on the Hudson River. 914-864-7177), which offers displays of logbooks, photos, and furnishings that illustrate what life was like in a lighthouse over the past hundred years. Even if you don't take a tour, the lighthouse and the Hudson River traffic are wonderful attractions for kids. The lighthouse is also the focus of several school- and group-centered tours and workshops; call for schedules and reservations.

photographs and artifacts of the Old Put Railroad. In the Woodlands Room you can sit in a replica of a Mohegan village longhouse, see how corn was ground, and what life was like for the Native Americans of the area. The Tool Room displays tools used during everyday activities in the 18th century. The museum also boasts a library/research room filled with local history and genealogical records. The three annually changing exhibits are displayed in Memory Lane. The museum is small and cozy. A gift shop has a large selection of miniatures, assorted items for the home and garden, and small toys for children.

Facilities: Restrooms, changing areas, gift shop. The building has an elevator and is wheelchair accessible.

OTHER ATTRACTIONS

Greenburgh Nature Center. 99 Dromore Road, off Central Avenue, Scarsdale 10583; 914-723-3470; www.greenburghnaturecenter.org. Admission. Groups welcome by advance reservation.

The Greenburgh Nature Center, a 33-acre oasis in the center of bustling Westchester's greenbelt system, offers a unique opportunity for families to discover nature together. Younger visitors will enjoy the Nature Museum, housed in a former mansion, which contains more than 100 exotic and local animals that can be handled by children, along with aquariums and a greenhouse that contains fascinating plants and a seasonal butterfly exhibit. It's a good place to introduce very young children to the natural world, which at the Greenburgh Nature Center includes short, marked walking nature trails; a pond, rock outcroppings, and glacial boulders; maple sugaring sites; an old apple orchard; and lots of different trees and ferns. There are 58 species of flowering plants here, which makes a spring or summer walk a nice outing for youngsters. Because the property is located along bird migration routes, you might

A demonstration at the Greenburgh Nature Center during one of their popular weekend programs.

GREENBURGH NATURE CENTER

see any of several dozen different songbirds in the woods. Over 30 species, including woodpeckers and nuthatches, can be seen year-round. The center also sponsors children-oriented special events on weekends and has hands-on exhibits. Seasonal holiday camps will keep kids busy with games, walks, and crafts that are nature related. There are seasonal family festivals such as maple sugaring in March, Halloween-themed events in October for both younger and older children, and seasonal fairs with live music on the lawn. The GNC offers

A volunteer shows a red-tailed hawk to captivated visitors at the Greenburgh Nature Center. GREENBURGH NATURE CENTER

a wide array of educational programming and special classes for all ages, from preschool children to senior citizens. The morning drop-in classes offer young children a chance to interact with nature and live animals. Check the Web site for more details. Teachers and other group leaders should ask about the center's special programs geared to preschool, elementary, and upper-level age groups. Nature-related arts exhibits, which appeal to adults and older children, are also held throughout the year.

Facilities: Restrooms, gift shop. The restrooms, first-floor classrooms, and gift shop are wheelchair accessible. The main trail and walkways around the museum are stroller accessible.

Muscoot Farm. 51 NY 100, Somers 10589; 914-864-7282; www.muscoot farm.org. (From I-684, take the Cross River/Katonah exit and follow NY 35 west to the intersection with NY 100. Turn left and drive 1 mile to park entrance.) Open year-round. Free. Group tours available by advance arrangement.

Now run by Westchester County, Muscoot Farm is a 700-acre farm built in 1885. This is a unique chance to visit a model farm of the late-19th century, when technical advances like electricity and indoor plumbing were just being introduced into the area. Younger children will be especially impressed with the multitude of farm life to be seen here. This is a working farm, with horses, cows, chickens, pigs, goats, sheep,

If you are in Somers at Muscoot Farm, you may want to plan a stop at the **Historic Elephant Hotel**, now a town office building, located at the junction of NY 100 and US 202 in Somers; 914-277-4977, free. Built by showman Hackaliah Bailey, who imported the first elephant (called Old Bet) to America in 1805, it now has an exhibit upstairs. The third floor of the building houses a delightful small "circus museum" arranged in five rooms. You will be treated to displays of circus memorabilia, posters, and a miniature big top. This is a stop for those interested in the history of circuses in America, which means just about everyone. There is no wheelchair or stroller accessibility, however.

and ducklings on the grounds. The farm is complete with outbuildings, such as corn-cribs, an outhouse hidden by a grape arbor, a wagon shed with a fine transportation collection of antique wagons and sleighs, and a huge dairy barn. Throughout the farm, interpretive exhibits include tools, housewares, and hardware created in the farm's blacksmith shop. In the summer, the herb garden blooms with plants that were used in cooking and medications, and corn and other crops are still grown and harvested here, so what you see will depend upon the season in which you visit. The emphasis at Muscoot Farm is on "working," so visitors will see farm life in action: Special programs may show the skill needed to be a blacksmith or a beekeeper on a farm, and there are often hayrides to be enjoyed as well. Along with the farm, many acres of park—home to beaver, raccoons, birds, and many wildflowers—can be explored along marked trails.

Facilities: *Restrooms, picnic areas. Strollers can be maneuvered on the paths, but the farm can be muddy and slippery after wet weather.*

BÖHRINGER FRIEDRICH, HTTP://COMMONS.WIKIMEDIA.ORG

Playland. Playland Parkway, Rye 10580; 914-813-7010; www.ryeplay
land.org. (Take exit 19 off I-95.) Different sections of the park are open
year-round although hours vary widely during the season, so call ahead.

A true old-fashioned amusement park and National Historic Site,
Rye's Playland is an architectural gem. Built in 1928, this was the first
amusement park constructed according to a plan where recreational
family fun was the focus. Fortunately, the park's family atmosphere and
art deco style are still here to be enjoyed. Set on the beaches of Long
Island Sound, Playland offers a famous 1,200-foot boardwalk, a swimming pool, gardens, a saltwater boating pond (paddleboats can be
rented), a beach, and (of course) 50 rides and an amusement area. Of
the rides in use, 7 are original; among them are the carousel (with a rare
carousel organ and painted horses), the Dragon Coaster (an unusual
wooden roller coaster), and the Derby Racer (horses zip around a track).
Fireworks and special entertainment, including free musical revues, go

The old-fashioned carousel at Playland is a work of art and a source of delight for
children of all ages.

WESTCHESTER COUNTY TOURISM

The Dragon Coaster has been delivering thrills to Playland visitors since 1929.

WESTCHESTER COUNTY TOURISM

on all summer; in winter, the three ice-skating rinks at Playland are open to the public.

Facilities: Restrooms, picnic areas, restaurant, food concessions. Strollers and wheelchairs can manage in the amusement park.

 What to Do

BICYCLING

Bicycle and Skate Sundays. 914-185-PARK; www.westchester gov.com/parks. From County Center in White Plains to Scarsdale Road in Yonkers, 14 miles round-trip on the Bronx River Parkway; if your family loves bicycling, plan to take part in this activity May through September (except holiday weekends), when the Bronx River Parkway is closed to vehicular traffic.

If you are a bicycle buff and would like to spend a Sunday teaching the kids to ride safely, Westchester sponsors this comfortable and convenient bike path. The parkway is well paved and relatively flat. You bring your own equipment for this ride, but hundreds of people take advantage of the program and all ages participate. The parkway is lined with flowering shrubs and trees in spring and summer. During the autumn months, the rides are a wonderful way to see the foliage while getting some exercise.

Briarcliff Peekskill Trailway. 914-864-PARK. This county-owned linear park runs 12 miles from the town of Ossining to the Blue Mountain Reservation in Peekskill. **North County Trailway.** 914-864-PARK. There are 22 miles of county-owned trail running from Mount Pleasant north to the County line in Yorktown. **South County Trailway.** 914-864-PARK. This 5.2-mile county-owned trail runs from Hastings to

Elmsford. Call and request trail maps for the Bronx River Parkway, North County Trailway, South County Trailway, Briarcliff Peekskill Trailway, and Old Croton Aqueduct State Historic Park, which have free bike paths open year-round. In-line skating is also welcome in these areas.

BOAT CRUISES

Hudson Highland Cruises. Haverstraw Marina, Haverstraw 10927; 845-534-7245; www.commander boat.com. The excursion boat *Commander* offers a three-hour narrated cruise to the Hudson Highlands, leaving Peekskill from Riverfront Park—passing West Point, Fort Montgomery, Garrison, Constitution Island, and the Bear Mountain Bridge. Advance reservations are required.

WESTCHESTER COUNTY TOURISM

Hudson Valley Riverboat Tours. 845-597-7272; www.tahitiqueen.com. Open for weekend and holiday cruises by advance reservation only. This historic refurbished paddle-wheeler, *The Tahiti Queen,* sails on the Hudson from the Charles Point Marina in Peekskill. Northbound cruises pass Bear Mountain and West Point, while southbound cruises pass Croton Point Park.

New York Waterway. 1-800-53-FERRY; www.nywaterway.com. Enjoy special-theme sightseeing cruises up the Hudson River from New York City to Sleepy Hollow to visit Lyndhurst, Kykuit, Sunnyside, and Philipsburg Manor. A two-hour northbound Hudson River tour departs from and returns to Tarrytown on weekends and holidays. Weekend getaway cruises are also available. Call for schedule and reservations.

HORSEBACK RIDING

River Ridge Stable and Equestrian Center. 960A California Road, Eastchester 10709; 914-633-0303; www.riverridgestable.com. Open for both English and Western riding lessons. What makes this a nice stop is that there is a petting zoo on the premises that will enchant the youngest travelers.

ICE SKATING

Edward J. Murray Memorial Skating Center. 348 Tuckahoe Road, Yonkers 10701; 914-377-6469. The center is open for figure skating, speed skating, and ice hockey.

Hommocks Ice Arena. 140 Hommocks Road, Larchmont 10538; 914-834-1069; www.hommocksparkicerink.org. The arena is open daily and offers both figure skating and ice hockey sessions. Call for the schedule.

New Roc City. 33 LeCount Place, New Rochelle 10801; 914-235-6200; www.newroccity.com. This 500,000-square-foot entertainment complex has two ice rinks; a 19-screen theater; a giant-screen IMAX theater; restaurants; and the Sports Plus entertainment center with video, motion simulator, and virtual-reality games for all ages; as well as the Space Shot, a rooftop slingshot thrill ride.

Playland Ice Casino. Playland Parkway, Rye 10580; 914-813-7059; www.ryeplayland.org. There are three ice rinks here; call for a schedule of public sessions. The temperature is always set at a comfortable level at the Ice Casino so that the youngest skaters will not feel too cold!

Westchester Skating Academy. 91 Fairview Park Drive, Elmsford 10523; 914-347-8232; www.westchester.pucksystems.com. The academy has two NHL-size rinks with figure skating, ice hockey, and clinics offered year-round. There are daily public skating sessions.

PARKS

Westchester County is filled with a number of beautiful parks where residents and visitors may bike, hike, and pursue other outdoor recreational activities. More detailed information, as well as special events at the parks, is posted on the Web site www.westchestergov.com/parks.

Blue Mountain Reservation. Welcher Avenue, Peekskill 10566; 914-862-5275. Open year-round.

This lovely county park in northeastern Westchester, originally part of Van Cortlandt Manor, offers a full range of year-round outdoor activities for youngsters. Summer brings lots of action, and groups that want to stay overnight can make arrangements to camp in the rustic lodge (available for rental year-round). There are also trails for hiking, a new playground, extensive picnic areas, and fishing ponds. In winter, the park has excellent cross-country ski trials and fine sledding hills.

Facilities: Restrooms, picnic areas. Restrooms are wheelchair accessible, but strollers are difficult to maneuver here off the paved paths.

Cranberry Lake Preserve. 1609 Old Orchard Street (off NY 22), North White Plains 10601; 914-428-1005. Open year-round.

This beautiful preserve consists of 135 acres of unspoiled wetlands and hardwood forests. The park has a 10-acre pond with trails and boardwalks, so visitors can observe life in an aquatic habitat. You will also find fishing, cross-country ski trails, and hiking. A small lodge offers interpretive programs and seasonal exhibits that the kids will enjoy.

Facilities: Restrooms, picnic areas. Strollers are difficult to maneuver off the paved areas.

Croton Point Park. 1A Croton Point Avenue (off US 9), Croton-on-Hudson 10520; 914-271-3293. Open year-round.

This park is located along the banks of the Hudson River and features a pool, canoe-launching area, recreation hall, and ball fields. The location is ideal for fishing, hiking, and picnicking. Cabins, lean-tos, and facilities for tents and trailers are also available. In mid-June the park is the site of the annual Hudson River Revival Festival, a lively celebration that includes a weekend of live music, an array of food vendors, and family entertainment.

Facilities: Restrooms, picnic areas. Restrooms are wheelchair accessible.

Rye Nature Center. 873 Boston Post Road, Rye 10580; 914-967-5150. Open year-round. A small nature center (under 50 acres), this is a nice stop for those traveling with very young children. The museum has exhibits of local plants and animals, and there are some mini-exhibits about nature. You can take the 2.5-mile walk, described in a guide available at the museum.

Facilities: *Restrooms, picnic areas.*

Teatown Lake Reservation. 1600 Spring Valley Road, Ossining 10562; 914-762-2912. (Take exit 134 off the Taconic, then follow Grant's Lake to Spring Valley Road. Open year-round.) Free.

This 400-acre reservation has marked nature walks and hiking trails, a museum, and outdoor exhibits. Wildflowers are abundant in the spring, and there are a number of stone walls on the property. Kids will enjoy watching the waterfowl and other animals at the large lake. Inside the museum are live exhibits of local plants and animals.

Facilities: *Restrooms, picnic areas.*

Ward Pound Ridge Reservation. NY 35 and NY 121 South, Cross River 10518; 914-864-7317. (From I-684, take Cross River-Katonah exit 6, go east on NY 35 for 4 miles to NY 121 south; turn right and drive to entrance on the left.) Open year-round. Park use charge is rather small. Group rates available; school visits to museum by appointment only. Camping is on a first-come, first-served basis or by advance reservation (two-night minimum), and is allowed in the park's rustic shelters and tent sites.

A 4,700-acre park, Ward Pound Ridge Reservation is both a wildlife sanctuary and education center. It has 35 miles of hiking trails, was designated an Important Birding Area by the Audubon Society, and was also named a Biodiversity Preserve by the Westchester County Parks Department. There are a variety of outdoor activities to be enjoyed here, including hiking, fishing in Cross River, camping, cross-country skiing on marked trails, and sledding in the Pell Hill area. In addition the excellent Trailside Nature Museum features wildlife, nature, and fossil exhibits (including the molar of a mastodon). A honeybee hive vibrates behind glass. Even the youngest children will enjoy participating in the special workshops and events often held at the park and museum. From late February to mid-March, activities include maple tapping programs, in which participants learn the mysteries of sap boiling, and bird walks to see hawks and other wild birds; in other seasons, there are dog shows and Revolutionary War battle reenactments. Just outside the museum is a 0.5-acre wildflower garden, with more than one hundred kinds of wild-flowers—all labeled. Children must be accompanied by an adult in this area. There is also a replica of an Algonquin wigwam.

Facilities: Restrooms, picnic areas. Strollers can manage on the paths and in the museum; if wheelchair accessibility is a concern, call ahead.

Westmoreland Sanctuary. 260 Chestnut Ridge Road, Mount Kisco 10549; 914-666-8448. Open year-round. Free (but fees are charged for some workshops and special events).

While the sanctuary is an active site with more than 15 miles of walking and hiking trails, the special programs at the museum here are the biggest attractions for the younger visitor. A varied offering of classes, hikes, and workshops are held throughout the year, and include building bat houses, birdsong identification walks, Earth Day celebrations, and even a search for the first ferns of spring. The bird-feeder-making workshop will intrigue preschoolers, as will the Sounds Around gatherings in the woods—you listen to the forest sounds with a naturalist who explains what it is you are hearing. A Halloween night hike and party enliven the fall, as does the Fall Festival (third Sunday in October)—complete with sheepshearing, blacksmithing, spinning demonstrations, and petting zoo.

Inside the museum are displays of local animals and plants along with descriptive exhibits about the area's history. It is best to call in advance and find out what is scheduled each weekend.

Facilities: Restrooms, picnic areas. Not recommended for strollers; if wheelchair accessibility is a concern, please call ahead and make special arrangements.

PICK-YOUR-OWN AND OTHER FARMS

Cabbage Hill Farm. 115 Crow Hill Road, Mt. Kisco 10549; 914-241-2658; www.cabbagehillfarm.org. Open year-round. If you have never heard of aquaponics (raising fish and vegetables together), this farm is the place to see it in action. A sustainable farm, greens are grown year-round in greenhouses fed entirely from fish tank water, a by-product of the aquaponics. There are a number of rare and endangered breeds of animals here—including heritage breed sheep and Devon cattle, Narragansett turkeys, and Charlaix sheep. This is an amazing operation that will be particularly interesting to older children.

The programs at Rainbeau Ridge, a sustainable farm in Bedford Hills, give children lots of opportunities to get close to animals.   RAINBEAU BRIDGE

Hilltop Hanover Farm. 1271 Hanover Street, Yorktown Heights 10598; 914-962-2368; www.hilltophanoverfarm.org. Open year-round. This farm, originally owned by the Underhill family, dates back to the 17th century and consists of 187 acres of forest, pasture, and historic buildings. The animals are only one attraction: Visitors will enjoy hiking trails on the property as well.

Outhouse Orchards. 130 Hardscrabble Road, North Salem 10560; 914-277-3188; www.outhouseorchards.info. This is a wonderful place to pick apples in the autumn or shop at the farmstand store where there are fresh vegetables, jams, baked goods, and other fantastic treats.

Rainbeau Ridge. 49 David's Way, Bedford Hills 10507; 914-234-2197; www.rainbeauridge.com. Open year-round. This sustainable farm offers an array of special programs for children that include gardening, cheese making, bread baking, and many more. The Web site has a complete catalog of activities as well as information on their excellent summer camp.

Stone Barns Center for Food and Agriculture. 630 Bedford Road, Pocantico Hills 10591; 914-366-6200; www.stonebarnscenter.org. Open year-round.

This educational center, located on a 4,000-acre property, provides a great opportunity to introduce children to the connection between their food and the natural world. The center is simultaneously a farm, a kitchen, and a classroom. Its mission is to celebrate each of these aspects and involve the community. Where does our food really come from? The center helps children make these farm-to-table connections. There is an

Stone Barns Center for Food & Agriculture offers excellent tours of the large organic farm on the premises. WESTCHESTER COUNTY TOURISM

array of livestock, a sizable organic farm, farmer's market, and more; the Center is a busy place. Educational opportunities including internships, field trips involving hands-on learning, day camp, and extensive programs are all detailed on the Web site.

Stuart Fruit Farm. 62 Granite Springs Road, Granite Springs 10527; 914-245-2784; www.stuartsfarm.com. This is the county's oldest working family farm, operating since 1828, with 200 acres of apple orchards, pumpkin fields, and vegetables. Visitors can pick their own apples and pumpkins in season and take a hayride around the property. Bob Stuart is usually around to answer questions about the farm, a wonderful place to show children how a family business works.

Wilkens Fruit and Fir Farm. 1335 White Hill Road, Yorktown Heights 10598; 914-245-5111; www.wilkensfarm.com. Pick your own apples and peaches in season, and cut Christmas trees too.

THEATER

Emelin Theater. 153 Library Lane, Mamaroneck 10543; 914-698-3045; www.emelin.org. This performing arts center was an unusual gift to

Westchester County from a local businessman; the money for the theater's construction was donated to the Mamaroneck Library. The Emelin, in operation for over 30 years, offers exceptional entertainment in 11 different series including drama, extensive family programs, folk, jazz, holiday performances, klezmer, bluegrass, and films. There is a children's series that runs throughout the year, with most shows offered on weekends. Call for a schedule or check the Web site.

Northern Westchester Center for the Arts. 272 North Bedford Road, Mount Kisco 10549; 914-241-6922; www.nwcaonline.org. There are changing art exhibits, concerts, recitals, and a poetry series here. Art, dance, music, theater, and creative writing classes are offered year-round. Call in advance or check the Web site to get a schedule of activities for children.

Paramount Center for the Arts. 1008 Brown Street, Peekskill 10566; 914-739-2333; www.paramountcenter.org. This restored thousand-seat movie palace of the 1930s offers quality arts and entertainment—ranging from classical to pop music, comedy to drama, art exhibits, and excellent children's programs. The theater's façade contains its original two-thousand-bulb marquee with running chase lights. Call or check the Web site for a schedule.

Westchester Broadway Theater. One Broadway Plaza, Elmsford 10523; 914-592-2222; www.broadwaytheater.com. This is a terrific place to enjoy Broadway-caliber musical revivals in an intimate theater setting where every seat offers good views of the stage. There is a children's theater series; call or check the Web site for a schedule.

UNUSUAL AND GREAT FOR A RAINY DAY

Westchester County Center. 198 Central Avenue, White Plains 10606; 914-995-1050; www.countycenter.biz. (Take exit 5 off I-287. If eastbound, follow NY 119 for 0.5 mile to County Center on the left. If westbound, turn left at the end of the ramp and follow to the intersection with NY 119.) There are several terrific shows all year at this multipurpose facility with forty thousand square feet of space. Make sure to check out the annual **Toy and Train Show** in February. Call for a schedule or check the Web site.

ROCKLAND COUNTY

▼▲▼▲▼▲▼

The incomparable beauty and charm of Rockland County offers pastoral countryside sprinkled with quaint villages, historic sites, and one of the world's most scenic river valleys chock-full of parks with fine recreational activities. One of the most popular family destinations in the county is **Bear Mountain State Park,** part of the Palisades Interstate Park System. This four-season outdoor wonderland offers visitors a multitude of outdoor recreation opportunities. There is also a wonderful zoo in the park, as well as a carousel housed in a stone-and-timber, Adirondack-style building. **Rockland Lake State Park,** another jewel in the crown of the Palisades Interstate Parks System, is a popular recreation area located at the base of Hook Mountain. In addition to hiking on lovely trails, families may enjoy swimming, fishing, and boating in the park—as well as special events throughout the summer season at the Nature Center. Don't miss **Stony Point Battlefield,** the mountaintop meadow where American troops defeated the British redcoats; it's still very much as it was more than two hundred years ago. Kids will enjoy seeing the **Stony Point Lighthouse** and special events—including dramatic military encampments held in the warm-weather months.

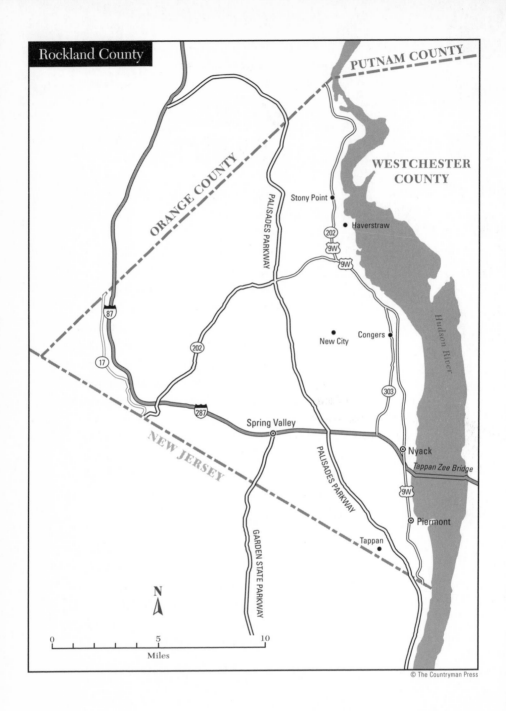

Rockland County

PUTNAM COUNTY

WESTCHESTER COUNTY

ORANGE COUNTY

PALISADES PARKWAY

Stony Point

Haverstraw

202

9W

9W

New City

Congers

303

Hudson River

87

17

202

287

Spring Valley

PALISADES PARKWAY

Nyack

Tappan Zee Bridge

9W

NEW JERSEY

GARDEN STATE PARKWAY

Tappan

Piermont

N

0   5   10
Miles

© The Countryman Press

Try to make time for a relaxing stop at **Dr. Davies Farm,** founded in 1881 by Dr. Lucy Meriweather Davies, a general practitioner who in her time delivered a significant part of Rockland's population, over 1,000 babies. She was also a farmer with acreage in Congers and her descendants operate the farm there today. This family orchard is a wonderful place to pick apples in season or enjoy a picnic.

While touring Rockland, you will hear again and again the names of those who made history here and are still remembered in ceremonies and festivals throughout the county: George Washington, Benedict Arnold, John Andre, and even Captain Kidd! Make sure to take in a couple of the special events unique to the county. Some of my favorites are the **Nyack Spring Fest,** an April weekend when the town becomes a huge street fair filled with fun family activities; October brings the **Halloween Parade** to Nyack; and in December families will enjoy a visit to Piermont for its festive holiday open house, with tasty treats for the kids offered at the town's shops. The third weekend in January, the **Knickerbocker Ice Festival** in Rockland Lake State Park, features ice sculpture competitions, a children's ice park, artwork, and many more activities.

For further information, contact **Rockland County Tourism,** 18 New Hempstead Road, New City 10956; 845-708-7300; 1-800-295-5723; www.rockland.org.

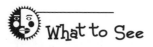 What to See

MUSEUMS AND HISTORIC SITES

Haverstraw Brick Museum. 12 Main Street, Haverstraw 10927; 845-947-3505; www.haverstrawbrickmuseum.org. Admission. The exhibits in this museum explain the century-old history of brick making in Haverstraw, once known as the brick making capital of the world. Children who are interested in local history will particularly enjoy a stop here after exploring the town and waterfront.

Historical Society of Rockland County and Annual Dollhouse Show. 20 Zukor Road, New City 10956; 845-634-9629; www.rocklandhistory.org. Open year-round. Admission.

Here you will discover a modern museum featuring changing exhibits and children's programs throughout the year. The annual doll-house miniatures and art show will delight children who have an interest in that area; call ahead or check the Web site to find out dates. There is an Old Fashioned Summer Day Camp with activities including candle dipping, crating historic toys, playing Native American games, and other diversions that entertained children in the early-19th century. The Blau-velt House and Barn, built in 1832, are located on the museum grounds. Both structures have been restored and include period furnishings.

Stony Point Battlefield. 44 Battlefield Road (Park Road off US 9W), Stony Point 10980; 845-786-2521; www.nysparks.state.ny.us. Admission. There are charges for some special events, and advance reservations are often required. Group tours are available with site staff, but call ahead to make reservations.

General Anthony Wayne led his troops on a midnight raid here in 1779, and their victory over the British forces ended up being one of the turning points of the American Revolution. A walking tour of this beautiful but wild park allows visitors to see the remnants of the battlefield and its fortifications. If you don't take a guided tour, available by advance reservation, there are many trail and battlefield markers explaining the movements of the troops during that fateful night. Costumed guides and staff members are often on hand to demonstrate blacksmithing, cooking, camp life, and artillery skills. A cannon is fired on the hour as well. At the orientation center a series of exhibits describe the history of the site. Popular with children is the Stony Point Lighthouse, the oldest lighthouse on the Hudson River (it's not open to the public, however). I recommend this site for older children who are fascinated by the American Revolution, although younger ones will enjoy the military dis-

ORANGE COUNTY TOURISM

plays and musters offered on weekends and holidays throughout the summer and fall. One treat is the series of evening battlefield walks—an interpretive tour of an actual battle, where children amble along while hearing the sounds of battle and seeing soldiers in period costume.

Facilities: Restrooms, picnic areas. Pets are not allowed. Strollers may be taken onto the battlefield.

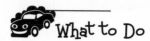 What to Do

BICYCLING

Both **Bear Mountain State Park** and **Harriman State Park** offer a number of excellent biking routes. However, both of these areas can become very congested on weekends. You will be better off at **Rockland Lake** or **Tallman State Park,** which both have paved bike paths. Another option is **Nyack Beach State Park,** located off US 9W with access from Broadway in Upper Nyack. This park runs along the river, and the paths are flat with fine views of the Hudson River. **Hook Mountain State Park** also has biking paths with scenic views of the Hudson. To get there, go east on North Broadway in Nyack; the park is located at the end of the road.

BOAT CRUISES

Hudson Highland Cruises. Haverstraw Marina, Haverstraw 10927; 845-534-7245; www.commanderboat.com. Hudson River excursions take place aboard the *Commander.* Call or check the Web site for a schedule—or wander down to the marina.

ICE SKATING

Sport-o-Rama Ice Rinks. 18 College Road, Monsey 10952; 845-356-3919; www.sportorama.com. There are two indoor ice rinks here that have scheduled public sessions as well as full hockey and recreational figure skating programs year-round. Check the Web site or call for a schedule.

Palisades Center. 4900 Palisades Center Drive (NY 59), West Nyack 10994; 845-353-4855; www.palice.com. Located on the fourth floor of the Palisades Center, the ice rink here will delight the kids year-round. There are both figure skating and hockey sessions, summer camps, clinics, and instructional programs. The public sessions on weekend afternoons are a particularly "cool" spot to take the kids on a hot summer day. Check the Web site for a complete schedule. (After skating, most kids will enjoy a stop at **Dave and Buster's** arcade/restaurant which has entertainment for children of all ages, including the latest in video and virtual reality games. It is also located on the fourth floor of the Palisades Center.)

INDOOR ACTIVITIES

Krazy City. 4900 Palisades Center Drive (NY 59), West Nyack 10994; 845-353-5700; www.krazycity.com. This indoor theme park, on the third floor of the Palisades Center, offers thrilling rides and a variety of games all in one place. There is miniature golf as well as a haunted roller coaster, to name a couple of attractions. There is a restaurant on the premises as well.

Lower Hudson Valley Challenger Learning Center. 225 NY 59, Airmont 10901; 845-357-3416; www.lhvcc.com. (Located less than a five-minute drive from the New York State Thruway exit 14B.)

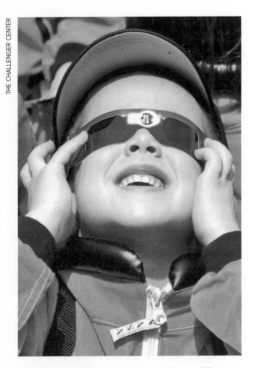

The Challenger Learning Center offers lots of hands-on activities that are both fun and educational.

The Challenger Center for Space Science Education is a global nonprofit education organization created in 1986 by the families of the astronauts lost during the tragic last flight of the Challenger Space Shuttle. The center is dedicated to the educational spirit of that mission and seeks to engage young people in science and math education. The programs offered here are designed for students in grades five through eight and feature hands-on experience. There is an interactive computerized simulator with a Mission Control room patterned after the NASA Space Center and an orbiting space station. Students can transform themselves into astronauts, engineers, and scientists. Missions for the general public are scheduled every month and are approximately three hours in duration. Missions to the moon, to Mars, and to a comet are offered on a rotational basis. There are camp programs during the summer and school breaks, for children between the ages of 9 and 14. This site will be particularly appealing to young people with a passion for space exploration.

Lucky Strikes. 4662 Palisades Center Drive (NY 59), West Nyack 10994; 845-358-1602; www.bowlluckystrike.com. Located on the fourth floor of the Palisades Center, this is not your typical bowling alley. There are 12 state-of-the-art lanes with automatic scoring, quality food, pleasant atmosphere, an upscale game room, private lounge, and sophisticated audiovisual system showing various videos and sports programs.

PARKS

For a complete list of hiking spots contact the New York–New Jersey Trail Conference; 201-512-9348; www.nynjtc.org.

Bear Mountain State Park. US 9W, off the Palisades Interstate Parkway, Bear Mountain 10911; 845-786-2701. Open year-round; call ahead for swimming schedules. There is a charge for both parking and swimming. Group tours accommodated by special reservation.

This huge park contains enough activities to fill a week of vacation time. Lovers of the outdoors will enjoy the hiking trails and views that are found around almost every turn. There are bike trails of varying lengths suitable for all ages, a swimming pool, and lakes—paddleboats and rowboats may be rented during the summer. Even the youngest children will love the zoo here, the beaver lodge, and the reptile house. Colorful birds and fuzzy mammals—in the forms of bears, foxes, coyotes, and raccoons—cavort in their zoo homes; outside, the beavers busily chip away at trees and gambol in the waters near their winter lodge/log home. In the reptile house, face-to-face encounters with snakes and lizards will thrill adventurers of all ages. Note, however, that there is a lot of walking involved and it may take up to an hour to see the entire zoo complex; it's a good idea to bring a stroller for very young children. At the **Trailside Museum,** special exhibits explain the natural and human history of the park and surrounding areas. A pavilion constructed of stone and timber houses a carousel featuring 38 carved renditions of native animals and hand-painted scenes of the Hudson Valley.

*Facilities: Restrooms, picnic areas, gift shop. Strollers and wheelchairs can be used on the paved paths throughout the zoo and museum complex. Pets are allowed, if leashed, in all areas except the zoo. At press time, **The Bear Mountain Inn** was undergoing extensive renovations; the restaurant served lunch and dinner.*

Hook Mountain State Park and Nyack Beach State Park. 698 North Broadway, Upper Nyack 10960; 845-268-3020. (To reach Hook Mountain State Park, take North Broadway in Nyack east to the end and follow the signs. To reach Nyack Beach Park, take US 9W from Broadway.) Open year-round. Free.

Hook Mountain was once referred to by the Dutch as Verdrietige ("Tedious") Hook because the winds could change rapidly and leave a boat adrift in the river. The area was also a favorite campground of Native Americans because of its wealth of oysters. For visitors today, the park provides a place to picnic, hike, bike, and enjoy scenic views of the Hudson. A hawk watch is held every spring and fall. Legend says that the park is haunted by the ghost of the Guardian of the Mountain, a Native American medicine man who appears during the full moon each September and chants at the ancient harvest festival. Nyack Beach is open for swimming, hiking, fishing, and cross-country skiing in the winter; the views of the river are outstanding.

Facilities: Restrooms, picnic areas.

Rockland Lake State Park. 87 Lake Road, Congers 10920; 845-268-3020. Open year-round.

A park packed with lots of activities and open spaces, this is a great place to stop no matter what time of year it is. In the spring and summer, fishing, boating, and swimming are popular—and a picnic is always suitable. The paved 3.2-mile loop along the lakeshore is great for walking, in-line skating, or biking. For fall and winter, pull on your hiking boots or grab your sled and head for the trails and hills. When the green flag is flying at parking field number six you can ice fish or ice skate (no equipment rentals or bait available in the winter). The nature center offers many displays—including two videos, "The Wild and Wonderful at Rockland Lake" and a film on the ice industry at Rockland Lake with actual ice-industry artifacts. Special nature-oriented events and guided tours begin here (call ahead for tour topics and hours: 845-786-2701

x. 293); during the warmer weather all the nature trails are easy to walk, even for young adventurers.

Facilities: Restrooms, picnic areas, snack bar, swimming pools (adult and child), boat rentals, bait shop.

PICK-YOUR-OWN FARMS

Dr. Davies Farm. 306 NY 304, Congers 10920; 845-268-7020; www.dr daviesfarm.com. One of the oldest pick-your-own farms in the county; you can gather berries in the spring or apples and pumpkins in the fall, and select from a wide variety of produce and other goodies at the farm stand. This is a special place, not to be missed. A family business, the owners are often on the premises, and will be happy to answer questions about how their farm has survived for several generations; only two family farms are still operating in the county. Check the Web site or call to see what crops are ready for harvesting.

The Orchards at Concklin. 2 South Mountain Road, Pomona 10970; 845-354-0369; www.theorchardsofconcklin.com. School groups by advance reservation only. This farm has been in business since 1712. You can harvest your own fruits on autumn weekends and pick a pumpkin for Halloween. This is one of only two family farms that remain in Rockland County and it's worth a visit in the fall.

THEATER

Helen Hayes Performing Arts Center. 117 Main Street, Nyack 10960; 845-358-6333, 845-358-2847. The Children's Theater here is first-rate, so it's worth calling for a schedule of events. There are 600 seats in the theater, which hosts a variety of productions including Broadway musicals, dramas, children's events, and films.

Palisades Center IMAX Theater. 4270 Palisades Center Drive (NY 59), West Nyack 10994; 845-358-4629; www.imax.com/palisades. A great place to go for indoor activities on a rainy day (or a beastly hot summer afternoon) is this mall theater with its larger-than-life escape that puts you in the heart of the action. Located on the fourth floor of the Palisades Center, offerings continually change and you will find excellent family entertainment year-round. Check the schedule on the Web site.

PUTNAM COUNTY

▼▲▼▲▼▲▼

F rom the magnificent views of the Hudson River in the west to the rolling hills of the east, Putnam County is a recreational wonderland. The county may be a small one, but boasts two excellent state parks—Fahnestock and Hudson Highlands—as well as a ski area, Thunder Ridge. There are acres of wetlands, lakes, forests, and meadows here, a virtual paradise for families who love the outdoors. And after exploring the natural wonders of the region, a visit to the charming village of Cold Spring is a must. Kids will enjoy watching the trains go by at the depot in town, while enjoying an ice cream cone or chocolate chip cookie from one of the many eateries on Main Street.

A highlight of any trip to the county includes a stop at **Boscobel,** a Federal-style mansion in Garrison dating back to 1805, which has been restored to its former elegance. A spring walk through the gardens showcases thousands of flowers in full bloom, permeating the air with their lovely scent. Overlooking the Hudson River, this is a wonderful place to enjoy an outdoor concert, summer theater production, or a nature program.

In the town of Cold Spring, **Fahnestock State Park,** with nearly 12,000 acres, has a lovely sandy beach area, boat rentals, and camping in the summer. There are

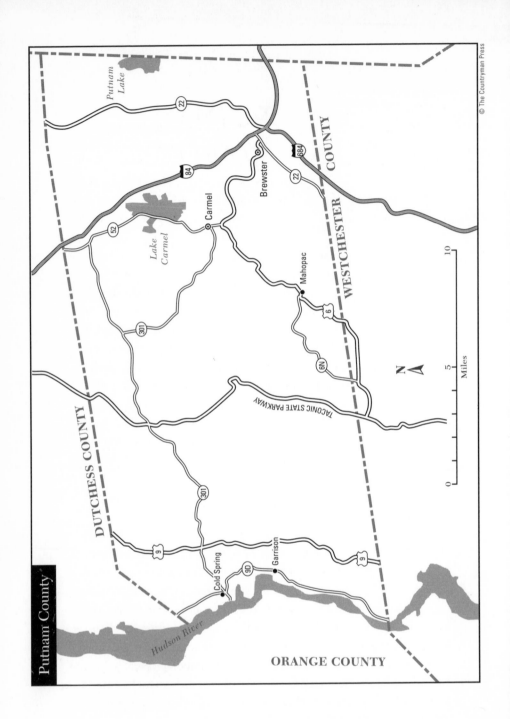

Putnam County

Putnam Lake

Lake Carmel

Carmel

Brewster

Mahopac

Cold Spring

Garrison

Hudson River

DUTCHESS COUNTY

WESTCHESTER COUNTY

ORANGE COUNTY

TACONIC STATE PARKWAY

N

0   5   10
Miles

22

84

52

301

301

9

9

90

6

6N

22

684

© The Countryman Press

wonderful places to picnic in the park, and special programs for children are offered throughout the year. This is an excellent destination for a day trip; the park offers a variety of activities that are sure to keep everyone in the family happy.

Try to coordinate a visit to Putnam with one of the county's outstanding annual events. In June kids will love the **Circle of 1,000 Drums Festival** at **Veterans Memorial Park** in Carmel; this multicultural event is geared to youngsters with drum making, games, music, and live entertainment. Also in Carmel is the county **4-H Fair** with animals, exhibits, and lots of activities for children, held every July. The **"Tri N' Du Putnam"** is a triathlon/duathlon held at Veterans Memorial Park in Kent during the month of July. In August visitors will enjoy the **Tour de Putnam Cycling Festival,** a biking event that offers several routes throughout the county of various lengths followed by a picnic lunch at Veterans Memorial Park in Kent. And the month of October ushers in spectacular fall foliage and a storytelling festival at Fahnestock State Park.

For further information, contact the **Putnam County Visitors Bureau,** 110 US 6, Building 3, Carmel 10512; 845-225-0381, 1-800-470-4854; www.visitputnam.org.

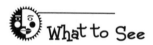 What to See

MUSEUMS, HISTORIC SITES, AND OTHER PLACES OF INTEREST

Boscobel House and Gardens. 1601 NY 9D, Garrison-on-Hudson 10524; 845-265-3638; www.boscobel.org. Admission. Group rates and school tours are available by advance reservation.

This magnificent New York Federal-style mansion on a bluff high above the Hudson River was once sold for $35 to a demolition contractor, but local interest saved the house and restored it to its new magnificence, complete with Federal-style furniture and decoration. There are also breathtaking flower gardens. Older children who enjoy seeing "mansions" will appreciate the sweeping staircases and elegant interior, but I don't recommend the house tour for the younger set. Outside, however,

BOSCOBEL HOUSE AND GARDENS

A horse and buggy on the grounds of Boscobel House and Gardens.

everyone will want to walk through the rose and tulip plantings, watch the boats on the Hudson, and visit the Orangerie (really a greenhouse) and the Gate House—a smaller, less pretentious 19th-century servants' home. There are seasonal programs and exhibitions of interest to both adults and children, including concerts, nature and gardening programs, and Christmas holiday candlelight tours. In June, children will enjoy the Annual Snapping Turtle Walk; the Hudson Valley Shakespeare Festival is in residence during July and August each year, with regular performances. Discounts ranging from 10 to 25 percent are offered for groups of 10 or more (anyone can form a group). Make sure to check the Web site for a complete schedule of events or call the Shakespeare Festival office for more information at 845-265-7858.

And after Boscobel, you may want to stop in the tiny village of **Garrison Landing** and walk down to the bandstand on the Hudson River, where children's events are held throughout the summer. Children like seeing the river up close, and you can tell them that the bandstand was once a movie location: It was used in *Hello Dolly!*

Facilities: Restrooms, picnic areas, gift shop.

Manitoga/The Russel Wright Design Center. 22 Old Manitou Road, Garrison 10524; 845-424-3812; www.russelwrightcenter.org. Open year-round. Admission.

The name Manitoga is taken from the Algonquian word for "place of the spirit," and the philosophy of Manitoga lives up to its name. Here people and nature are meant to interact and visitors are encouraged to experience the harmony of their environment. Russel Wright, who designed the center, created a 5-mile system of trails that focus on specific aspects of nature. The Morning Trail is especially beautiful early in the day; the Spring Trail introduces walkers to wildflowers; and the Blue Trail wanders over a brook and through a dramatic evergreen forest. (The trail system even hooks up with the Appalachian Trail.) This is a great stop for kids who like to walk and explore. You will find a full-sized reproduction of a Native American wigwam, which was constructed with traditional methods and tools. There are a variety of programs at the environmental learning center, so call before you go. Workshops are offered in art, photography, and botany—along with guided nature walks and music and dance concerts. Everyone will enjoy visiting Dragon Rock, the glass-walled cliff house built by Wright. Manitoga is a place where design and nature reflect and enhance each other, and it's a good place to demonstrate this to children.

Facilities: Restrooms, gift shop.

Southeast Museum. 67 Main Street, Brewster 10509; 845-279-7500; www.southeastmuseum.org. Suggested donation.

This Victorian-style building houses a small museum with an eclectic local collection. There are permanent exhibits on the Borden Dairy Condensory (condensed milk was developed by a Putnam County resident), the construction of the Croton Water System (a project remarkable for its engineering innovations), the American circus, Harlem Line Railroad, and a large collection of minerals from area mines. The focus of this museum is local history, and kids who have a curiosity about their surroundings will enjoy the exhibits.

Facilities: Restrooms.

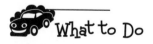 What to Do

KAYAKING AND HIKING

Hudson Valley Outfitters. 63 Main Street, Cold Spring 10516; 845-265-0221; www.hudsonvalleyoutfitters.com. Open year-round. Complete packages are available to families for both kayaking and hiking. There are guided tours with certified guides, from beginner to advanced levels, with daily rentals of all equipment for both sports. This is an excellent place to go if you are thinking about organizing an active family outing but are unsure exactly where to go or if you have the necessary equipment.

PARKS

Clarence Fahnestock Memorial State Park. 1498 NY 301, Carmel 10512; 845-225-7207; www.nysparks.state.ny.us. Located off the Taconic State Parkway at the NY 301 West exit. This park is open year-round and offers seasonal camping, swimming, boating, fishing, hiking, cross-country skiing, snowshoeing, and sledding. There is a concentration of activities here, making the park a great locale for a family outing. Several public programs are offered each year. Winter Fest, in January, celebrates winter sports such as snowshoeing, tubing, and ice fishing—and also offers bird walks and demonstrations of outdoor survival skills. Sap to Syrup in March is completely dedicated to maple sugaring and includes a pancake breakfast, demonstrations of methods used to make syrup and sugar, a blacksmith, and a naturalist. A small donation is suggested to defray the cost of the programs, and food is available for purchase at all events.

Facilities: Restrooms, swimming area, boat rentals, hiking trails.

Taconic Outdoor Education Center (TOEC). Clarence Fahnestock Memorial State Park, 75 Mountain Laurel Lane, Cold Spring 10516; 845-265-3773. The center is open year-round and is a place where schools, clubs, retreats, and scout groups immerse themselves in the outdoors. Day or residential trips are available by reservation, but TOEC is not open for drop-in activities, except for certain public programs. TOEC offers programs for groups of all ages.

The center is located on a large pond with varied terrain and habitats including mixed deciduous forest and wetlands. Wildlife is plentiful, and program participants may see or hear deer, owls, coyotes, small mammals, wild turkeys, many species of birds, and even bobcats. A wide range of environmental programs is available, including aquatic ecology (study of streams and wetlands), forest ecology (relationships between components of a forest), map and compass skills, mammal- and bird-watching, and outdoor skills. Night programs include stargazing and night walks in the woods.

Facilities: Cabins, lodge, lake trails, Project Adventure course.

PICK-YOUR-OWN FARMS

Ryder Farm. Starr Ridge Road, Brewster 10509; 845-279-3984. This farm has 125 acres of organically grown raspberries on its pick-your-own farm, in operation for over two hundred years. Betsey Ryder, the manager, is always glad to talk to visitors about the history of her family farm. Call for hours since the season is weather dependent.

BELLEAYRE MOUNTAIN

SKIING AND SNOWBOARDING

Thunder Ridge. 137 Birch Hill Road (off NY 22), Patterson 12563; 845-878-4100; www.thunderridgeski.com.

This ski center is so close to the metropolitan area that those heading north won't hear the kids ask, "Are we there yet?" Located in the rolling hills of eastern Putnam County, the owners pride themselves on running a family-oriented mountain. Skiing at all levels and ages is welcome, from beginner to expert. There are 30 trails, three chair-lifts, and one T-bar—and several slow, gentle slopes to meet the needs of the newest skiers and snowboarders. However, there are also advanced trails for the more adventurous. The ski school is dedicated to teaching the fundamentals; daily group lessons or six-week programs are offered for all levels of ability. Ski packages are available that include lessons, rentals, and lift tickets. There is snowmaking capability throughout the entire mountain system, which makes for good conditions throughout the winter season.

Facilities: Restrooms, cafeteria, nursery, babysitting.

ORANGE
COUNTY

▼▲▼▲▼▲▼

W hen Henry Hudson sailed his ship *Half Moon* up the Hudson River and into Cornwall Bay in 1609, he was the first explorer to arrive in Orange County, a place with a rich and interesting history. Today, museums, restorations, and educational exhibits are everywhere, from Native American displays in the Goshen Courthouse to the collection of military equipment at West Point. Moreover, children can watch a costumed group of interpreters reenact a battle that turned the tide of the revolution at the **New Windsor Cantonment.**

The county is rich in family attractions and the following are a few highlights. The **Hudson Highlands Nature Museum** is a must for children who love wildlife. The indoor minizoo houses small animals and plants native to the Hudson Valley. **Museum Village** has been restored in the style of a typical mid-19th-century village with over 35 buildings populated with costumed guides. Kids will enjoy watching the blacksmith hammer hot metal into a door latch, a weaver at her loom, housewives churning butter, and a potter making mugs at the wheel. The paved walkway to the Hudson River at **Newburgh Landing Waterfront** offers spectacular views of Bannerman Island, Storm King Mountain, Mount Beacon, and

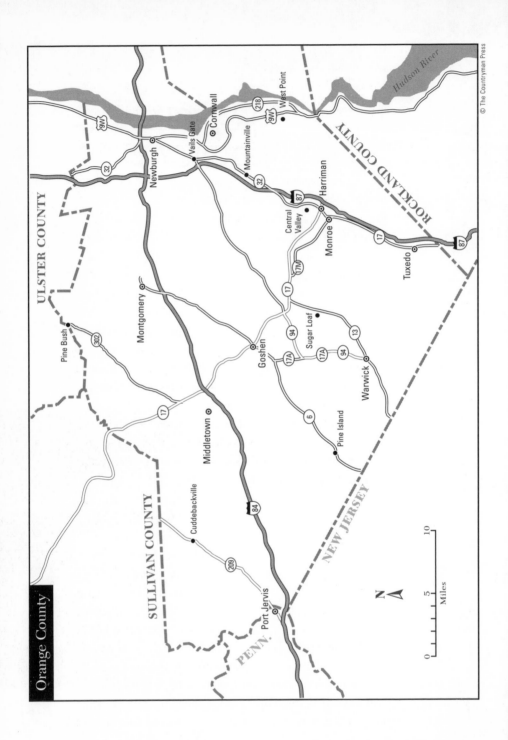

Orange County

© The Countryman Press

Newburgh Bay. There are several shops and places to enjoy a snack al fresco in the warm-weather months.

Orange County is also a place where the agricultural heritage of New York State is still strong, where farming is a way of life for families and has been for generations. Make sure to visit one of the many farmers and take home some fresh fruit and vegetables. Half the onions grown in the state come from the "black dirt" area in the southern part of the county. A drive through this unique farming district in early summer will show the kids what a bountiful harvest is all about.

When you plan a visit to Orange County make sure to take in a couple of special events. The annual **Riverfest in Cornwall-on-Hudson** is held in June and features live entertainment, crafts, and children's activities. The **Harness Racing Museum** in Goshen sponsors a series of children's programs on Saturday mornings offering a hands-on approach to learning about horses. A popular annual tradition at **Sterling Forest** in Tuxedo Park on weekends in August and early September is the **Renaissance Faire.** Experience 16th-century England—brought to life with hundreds of costumed characters, strolling minstrels, and storytellers in a Tudor-style marketplace with a living chessboard and horseback jousting. Relax and watch the Renaissance world pass by, or walk through the site; it's filled with beautiful gardens and ponds.

For further information, contact **Orange County Tourism,** 30 Matthews Street, Suite 111, Goshen 10924; 845-786-5003; www .orangetourism.org.

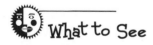 What to See

MUSEUMS AND HISTORIC SITES

Fort Montgomery State Historic Site. 690 US 9W (between United States Military Academy and Bear Mountain Bridge), Fort Montgomery 10922; 845-786-2701; www.nysparks.state.ny.us. Open year-round. Free.

At Fort Montgomery
PHOTO COURTESY OF ORANGE COUNTY TOURISM

This spot offers magnificent views of the Hudson River, interpretive signs describing the turning-point battle that occurred here centuries ago, and a pedestrian suspension bridge permitting access to nearby Fort Clinton and the Bear Mountain Zoo. It's a nice place to stop for an interesting walk that will appeal to the kids and yet also weave in some history.

Harness Racing Museum and Hall of Fame. 240 Main Street, Goshen 10924; 845-294-6330, 845-294-7542; www.harnessmuseum.com. Open year-round. Admission. Group tours by advance reservation.

Messenger and Hambletonian, pacers, trotters, and standard-breds—all call to mind the speed and grace to be found on a trotting track, and the history and color of the sport can be discovered at this unique museum established in 1951. Trotters and pacers (trotters move

their right front and left rear legs at the same time, pacers move both legs on one side at the same time) have long been a part of American history. George Washington, Abraham Lincoln, and Ulysses S. Grant spent time breeding and racing these swift horses. At the museum, the history of the sport can be traced through a world of interactive exhibits. Your kids can call and judge their own race. Three theaters also take you behind the scenes of this great sport. There are

Kids can pretend they've got the reins in a race at the Harness Racing Museum in Goshen. ORANGE COUNTY TOURISM

also several dioramas, prints, exhibits, and statues displayed throughout the former Good Time Stables building. Galleries include permanent displays of Currier and Ives prints, famous racing silks, and the amazing Hall of the Immortals—where dozens of small lifelike statues recall the greatest participants (both human and four-legged) in the sport. There are films and shows in the auditorium, changing gallery exhibits, and the world's only three-dimensional harness-racing simulator that makes you feel as if you are the driver in a race—and the kids will enjoy feeling the wind blow through their hair! Before you go, make sure to check the

Web site for a schedule of special children's programs held on Saturday mornings.

The Historic Track. Located directly behind the Harness Racing Museum and Hall of Fame (see above); 845-294-5333. This is the only sports facility in the country that is a National Historic Landmark; it has been hosting meets since the 1830s. Although the Grand Circuit races visit here only the first three Saturdays in June and over Independence Day weekend, the track is used as a training facility—so you may be able to see pacers, trotters, and a local blacksmith at work, no matter when you visit. The track is such a local institution that some of the private boxes have been passed down in families for generations.

Facilities: Restrooms, picnic areas, gift shop. The gift shop is particularly worthwhile, especially for those who love horse memorabilia and souvenirs. The museum is completely wheelchair accessible.

Interactive Children's Museum. 23 Center Street, Middletown 10940; 845-344-3131; www.theinteractivemuseum.com. Open year-round. Free. Permanent and changing interactive exhibits here focus on math, science, technology, and the arts. There are special programs with professionals who conduct workshops. Call or check the Web site for a schedule.

Karpeles Manuscript Library Museum. 94 Broadway, Newburgh 12550; 845-569-4997. Open year-round. Free. School groups from elementary to university level are welcome with advance notice.

What were the first thoughts of our forefathers as they decided what freedoms and rights should be guaranteed in the Constitution? How many people are aware of the existence of a final Indian peace treaty signed by every tribe in the country and the president? An unusual museum, Karpeles Manuscript Library Museum contains original handwritten drafts, letters, and documents of historical significance in many fields. These works enable visitors to learn about historical events and people through primary sources. Manuscripts are classified according to subject and exhibits travel between nine other Karpeles Manuscript Museums in the United States. Exhibits relate to subjects like atomic energy, children's literature, the history of flight, early baseball history, and a millennium retrospective featuring a collection of notable events over the last thousand years.

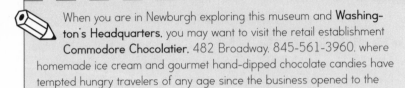
When you are in Newburgh exploring this museum and **Washington's Headquarters**, you may want to visit the retail establishment **Commodore Chocolatier**. 482 Broadway. 845-561-3960, where homemade ice cream and gourmet hand-dipped chocolate candies have tempted hungry travelers of any age since the business opened to the public in 1935.

In addition to historical documents, there is a sizable display area that features an array of rotating art exhibits. Make sure to call about the schedule of children's workshops, which offer first-hand experience in the development and creation of historic manuscripts.

Facilities: Restrooms. Stroller and handicapped accessible.

Hudson Highlands Nature Museum. Wildlife Education Center, 25 Boulevard, Cornwall-on-Hudson 12520; 845-534-7781; also Outdoor Discovery Center, 100 Muser Drive (across from 174 Angola Road), Cornwall 12518; 845-534-5506; www.hhnature museum.org. There are two locations with children's programs at both sites: The Wildlife Education Center is open year-round. Admission.

The Wildlife Education Center is an excellent site to visit with children who love animals and want to learn more about their lives and habitats. The changing exhibits in the center are geared to children's interests. The Hall of Animals has an indoor minizoo that houses small animals native to the Hudson Valley. Several amphibians, reptiles, small mammals, and birds crawl, creep, and (in the case of Edgar Allen Crow) talk. Outside the site, there are well-marked easy trails to follow.

At the Outdoor Discovery Center,

Pack binoculars for your walk at the Hudson Highlands Nature Museum. Seasonal programs here include tapping trees and making syrup.

ORANGE COUNTY TOURISM

families will enjoy hiking trails with a Quest guidebook. Through riddles, hands-on activities, illustrations, and field notes, visitors will learn about nature in an interactive way that includes "hidden messages." There are four Quest trails that cover woodlands, meadows, and wetlands with ponds and streams. Admission is free, although the guidebook is $5 (but it may be shared).

The museum is also known for summer nature camp, nature-based preschool, and weekend programs for families. Teachers will appreciate the environmental education classes offered to school groups.

Facilities: Restrooms, picnic areas, gift shop. Strollers can navigate the Wildlife Education Center and some of the trails at the Outdoor Discovery Center.

Museum Village of Orange County. 1010 NY 17M, Monroe 10950; 845-782-8247; www.museumvillage.org. (Exit 129, NY 17 west; watch for signs.) Admission. There are special rates available for groups of 20 or more (advance reservations required).

Though we sometimes forget, America was once a rural nation, without electricity and modern conveniences. At the Museum Village, children can visit a re-creation of a typical crossroads village of the mid-19th century. Many of the buildings were rescued from other parts of Orange County and moved to the village, where they now serve as working shops and houses. Children often enjoy visiting the wagon maker, the blacksmith (with a working forge), the schoolhouse, a log cabin homestead, and even the barbershop. The Natural History Museum houses a mastodon skeleton, and you can buy penny candy at the general store. Craftspeople are at work throughout the site, and children are welcome to watch the costumed weaver, printer, and broom maker go about their businesses. Some are entranced by the demonstration of open-hearth cooking. This is a wonderful place to spend a day with kids, and teachers should note that the village has an extensive variety of special workshops.

Costumed guides at Museum Village make a bygone era come alive.

Facilities: Restrooms, picnic areas, gift shop, snack bar. The site is stroller friendly.

New Windsor Cantonment State Historic Site. 374 Temple Hill Road (NY 300), Vails Gate 12584; 845-561-1765. (From New York State Thruway exit 17, or I-84 exit 7S, take NY 300 south 1.5 miles to Temple Hill Road; turn left, proceed approximately 2 miles.) Admission (a combination ticket provides admission to Knox's Headquarters in Vails Gate and Washington's Headquarters in the city of Newburgh.) Groups welcome by advance reservation only.

This site portrays the everyday life of the soldiers in George Washington's army. The northern Continental Army spent the last days of the American Revolution at the Cantonment, where log huts housed the soldiers, officers, tradesmen, and camp followers. The tour starts at the visitors center, where there are exhibits on the life of the 18th-century soldier and the use of cannons during the Revolutionary War. (There is also a fascinating exhibit, for adults, of the history of the Purple Heart, which Washington established as the Badge of Military Merit.) Then it's down a wooden walkway to the site itself, where buildings have been reconstructed from old military plans. In fact, one of the buildings might be the only surviving structure from a Revolutionary War encampment. On any given day, costumed interpreters may be drilling on the parade ground, cooking food over an open fire, forging army equipment in the blacksmith shop, or playing a fife. Special events are held throughout the season, including concerts, a Kids Day with period games, a candlelight evening, and the annual encampment of the Brigade of the American Revolution.

Facilities: Restrooms, picnic areas. Paths have gravel and are appropriate for strollers. An upper parking lot provides easier access for visitors in wheelchairs.

Storm King Art Center. Old Pleasant Hill Road (just off NY 32 north; watch for signs), Mountainville 10953; 845-534-3115; www.stormking .org. Admission (free self-guided tram tours). Group tours available by advance reservation.

Situated in a 500-acre expanse, Storm King is an outdoor sculpture park. Within the small indoor museum and the outdoor area, more than 90 artists are represented, including David Smith, Alexander Calder,

Louise Nevelson, Mark di Suvero, Andy Goldsworthy, Richard Serra, and Isamu Noguchi. Over 120 outdoor sculptures are situated along field and woodland walks. Older children will appreciate viewing modern art up close since there are few places where large sculptures are displayed in a natural environment. Unlike more conventional museums, Storm King's open landscape is liberating and provides a good way to introduce children of all ages to

Storm King Art Center is one of those rare outdoor museums where large sculptures complement the landscape.
ORANGE COUNTY TOURISM

modern art. The views are magnificent, and kids enjoy exploring the grounds. There are some special family events and guided tours throughout the season; check the Web site for a complete schedule.

Facilities: Restrooms, picnic areas. This is a comfortable place for wheelchairs and strollers. If it's a nice day, plan to bring a lunch along and spend an afternoon at this site.

Washington's Headquarters State Historic Site. 84 Liberty Street, Newburgh 12550; 845-562-1195. Call to make arrangements for group tours.

The end of the American Revolution was announced on the grounds of Jonathan Hasbrouck's stone mansion, set on a bluff overlooking the Hudson River. Construction began in 1750 but was not finished until 1782, when Washington's troops added a gunpowder laboratory, a barracks, a privy, and a larger kitchen. Washington remained here for nearly a year and a half, waiting for the British to leave New York under the terms of surrender. Acquired by the federal government in 1848, Washington's Headquarters became America's first National Historic Site on July 4, 1850, when it opened to the public.

In the adjacent museum, opened in 1910, is an exhibit called "First in the Nation," which highlights the site's history (over 160 years). The galleries here recall the events of 1882–83, including the establishment of the Badge of Military Merit, forerunner of the Purple Heart. A section of the chain and boom that was stretched across the Hudson at West

Point, a life-size portrait of George Washington, and even a lock of his hair are just a few of the many fascinating items on display that will intrigue visitors of all ages.

The story of the Revolution comes alive inside Hasbrouck House, where visitors are guided through eight rooms in which Washington and his staff lived and worked. The dining room where George and Martha ate their meals still contains the original Dutch fireplace, open on three sides. The plain bedrooms and offices are sparsely furnished, and a field bed with its tentlike covering speaks clearly of the winter cold—showing that not everyone was fortunate enough to have a room. The grounds are well kept and offer wide views up and down the Hudson. Special events are held throughout the year and include kite-flying days, Martha Washington's birthday celebration, and (of course) George Washington's birthday festivities.

Facilities: Restrooms, picnic areas. Strollers can be used around the grounds, but you will have to carry them upstairs in the museum—and you may have problems with them in the Hasbrouck House. For vision-impaired and blind visitors, a Braille tour is available.

West Point (United States Military Academy). Visitors Center, Pershing Center, West Point 10996; 845-938-2638; www.usma.edu. (Take US 9W and follow the signs.) Free. Access to the grounds is by guided tour only, except for special events. Photographic identification is required for every visitor over the age of 16. Daily tours are organized on a first-come, first-served basis. Call the visitors center for tour times. Group tours may be provided by West Point Tours, 845-446-4724. During certain times, such as graduation week and home football games, tours are unavailable.

While most people know a little of West Point's history, a tour of this historic military site is unlike any other you will take. West Point has been a continuously operating military post since 1778 and a military academy since 1802. The tour of West Point, which overlooks the Hudson River, will take you past historic buildings, athletic facilities, monuments, and chapels. As you step on a bus at the visitors center, a knowledgeable tour guide will meet you. Your first stop is the Cadet Chapel, a Gothic cathedral consecrated in 1910, with impressive stained-glass windows and the largest church organ in the United States. Depending on the tour you take, you will then either visit the West Point

Kids will enjoy watching the cadets march in formation at West Point.

Cemetery—the final resting place of over 5,000 men and women who have served their country and the home of the Old Cadet Chapel, built in 1837—or go directly to the historic Trophy Point and Plain areas. Trophy Point is home to Battle Monument, which commemorates the Union Army's Civil War dead and is ringed by large cannons. Also in the area are links of the chain that was stretched across the river in order to stop the British from bringing their warships up the Hudson. You can enjoy the famous "million-dollar view" looking north up the river. Crossing the street, from your seats alongside the historic Plain, the drilling field of the Long Gray Line, you will learn about cadet life, see the superintendent's and dean's quarters, and view monuments commemorating Washington, Eisenhower, MacArthur, and Sylvanus Thayer, father of the military academy.

Another must-see is the **West Point Museum,** open year-round. The museum is organized by wars (Revolutionary, Civil, Vietnam, etc.) and displays thousands of items that appeal to younger visitors. Of particular interest are the colorful uniforms, guns, cannons, tanks, and the display of an atomic bomb. The museum covers all of America's military history and it's a relatively painless way for children to learn about part of their heritage.

In the fall, you may wish to purchase tickets for a football game at Michie Stadium, 1-877-TIX-ARMY. Preceding the game, hundreds of cadets parade on the Plain in their dress uniforms, with music and military panoply. There is time for a tailgate picnic in the parking lot, and a view of Fort Putnam, a partially restored Revolutionary War fortress. This one of the best series of football games in the Northeast, and it's colorful with lots of excitement.

Facilities: Restrooms, gift shop. A restaurant in the Thayer Hotel on the grounds serves a particularly wonderful Sunday brunch. Strollers are usable on the site, but you may have to deal with some hilly areas and graveled walkways. All buildings are wheelchair accessible.

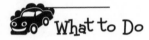 What to Do

BICYCLING

Heritage Trail. www.orangecountyparks.com. This 12-mile paved bike trail over the abandoned Erie Railroad tracks winds through woods, meadows, and villages, passing historic landmarks and a bird sanctuary. There is trail access in Monroe, Chester, and Goshen. This Orange County Rail Trail goes from Monroe to Goshen and there is a short trail from Walden to Wallkill.

Orange County Bike Club. 845-457-6027; www.ocbicycleclub.org. This club offers weekend rides (road biking with some mountain biking) year-round, as well as warm-weather weekday rides. The trips will appeal to all levels of riders and all ages. (Children under the age of 16, however, must be accompanied by a parent or adult.) This is an excellent resource to check out before going on a family bike excursion in the county.

BOAT CRUISES

Hudson Highlands Cruises. 6 Columbus Avenue, Cornwall-on-Hudson 12520; 845-534-SAIL; www.commanderboat.com. Departing from West Point, a cruise on the *Commander* (on the National Register of Historic Places) with its narrated tour offers a relaxing way to introduce youngsters to the scenic beauty of the river. There are floating classroom programs for schools by advance reservation.

Facilities: Restrooms, snack bar.

Hudson River Adventures. Newburgh Landing, Newburgh 12550; 845-220-2120, 845-782-0685; www.prideofthehudson.com. Daily two-hour narrated cruises operate (call or check the Web site for a schedule) aboard the *Pride of the Hudson.* You can also explore Bannerman's Island, which opened to the public in 2004. Customized cruises for school groups and camps can be made by advance reservation.

Facilities: Restrooms, snack bar.

River Rose Tours and Cruises. Newburgh Landing, Newburgh 12550; 845-562-1067; www.riverrosecruises.com. Cruises aboard a New Orleans paddleboat with upper and lower decks.

Facilities: Restrooms, snack bar.

HIKING

Hudson Highlands Nature Museum. Outdoor Discovery Center, 100 Muser Drive, Cornwall 12518; 845-534-5506; www.hhnaturemuseum.org. These guides provide an interactive way for children to learn about the environment. Each hike has a "hidden message," a mystery that intrigues children to explore their surroundings. The pond, field, and woodland Quest hikes take from 30–45 minutes; there is also one that lasts for two hours and would appeal to older children.

Schunnemunk Mountain. NY 32, Mountainville 10953 (Take County Route 79 off Route 32 to Taylor Road). There are six marked trails here ranging from 1.6 to 8 miles in length, and just about every trail affords spectacu-lar views. This area is recommended for older children.

ICE SKATING

Bear Mountain. US 9W, Bear Mountain 10911; 845-786-2701. Admission (there is no charge for children under the age of five). This outdoor rink is an excellent place for beginner and novice skaters. Rentals are available.

Fancher-Davidge Park. 130 Lake Avenue, Middletown 10940; 845-346-4180. Open to the public, weather permitting. Free. This large lake with lots of room for hockey and family skating is located at the end of Lake Avenue. Call in advance to check conditions.

Ice Time Sports Complex. 21 Lakeside Road, Newburgh 12550; 845-567-0005; www.icetimesports.com. Open year-round, but call or check the Web site for a schedule of public sessions. The two Olympic-sized indoor ice rinks here offer a great place for family fun. Lessons, rentals, and skating camp in the summer are all options. There are lockers, a snack bar, a pro shop, and a spacious seating area for spectators.

Mill Pond. NY 17M, Monroe 10950; 845-782-8341. Open to the public, weather permitting. Free. This small pond offers skating when a green flag is visible on the ice. When a red flag is up, the ice is unsafe. You can call in advance to check. This is a nice place to skate for those who prefer an outdoor venue.

PARKS

Algonquin Park. Powder Mill Road and NY 52, Newburgh 12550; 845-561-1880. The 27 acres of parkland include three ponds, a stream, picnic areas, and a children's playground. During the 1800s, this was the site of the only black gunpowder manufacturing facility in the region, and there are many stone structures remaining from that time that may intrigue older children.

Kowawese Unique Area at Plum Point. US 9W (across from Anthony's Pier 9), New Windsor 12551; 845-457-4900. This 102-acre park runs along the Hudson River and offers magnificent vistas and 2,000 feet of sandy beachfront.

Newburgh Landing. Front Street, Newburgh 12550; 845-569-7300. Open year-round. This city park abuts the Hudson River and is the site of an array of annual festivals and events. It's a lovely place to hang out with the kids; and there are several restaurants along the waterfront offering a variety of fare. The landing area is completely paved, which makes it easy for strollers to negotiate. Scenic boat cruises leave from this area in the warm-weather months if you care to take an excursion on the Hudson.

Orange County Park. 211 NY 416, Montgomery 12549; 845-457-4949. This park offers tennis; pedal boat and rowboat rentals on the lake; picnicking, fishing, playing fields, and even an arboretum with lovely paths to stroll through. There is snow tubing and cross-country skiing in the winter months. This is a wonderful stop for a family picnic any time of year.

PICK-YOUR-OWN AND OTHER FARMS

Applewood Orchards. 82 Four Corners Road, Warwick 10990; 845-986-1684; www.applewoodorchards.com. Open for a combination of pick-your-own apples and pumpkins. There are also free wagon rides, puppet shows, an animal petting area, and a short nature walk.

Bellvale Farms. 385 NY 17A, Warwick 10990; 845-988-1818; www.bell valefarms.com. Public milking demonstrations at the dairy barn as well as fresh ice cream, hayrides, and picking a pumpkin for Halloween.

ORANGE COUNTY TOURISM

Blooming Hill Organic Farm. 1251 NY 208, Blooming Grove 10914; 845-782-7310; www.blooming hillfarm.com. This is a wonderful place located along the banks of the Wallkill River. They are open for pick-your-own raspberries in season, but there is lots going on here. There are dozens of organically grown fruits and vegetables for sale as well as a small café serving breakfast and lunch items. The bakery on the premises serves tasty treats as well. Occasionally, there is live music.

Hodgson's Farm. 2290 Albany Post Road, Walden 12586; 845-778-1432; www.hodgsonfarm.com. Children will enjoy picking a variety of seasonal crops as well as exploring the petting zoo. There are farm and greenhouse tours available. In the autumn there are hayrides and a haunted house.

Jones Farm and Country Store. 190 Angola Road, Cornwall 12518; 845-534-4445; www.jonesfarminc.com. This fabulous family-owned and operated farm has been thriving since 1914. There are rabbits, miniature horses, chickens, ducks—and Miss Polly, the farm's 1,000-pound resident pig. Kids will enjoy a hayride here in the fall as well as the apple cider donuts, pies, and tarts from Grandma Phoebe's Bakery, also on the premises. My favorite is the double chocolate cookies—not to be missed by chocoholics! Everyone in the family will enjoy a stop here; parents can browse in the lovely gift shop.

Pine View Farm. 575 Jackson Avenue, New Windsor 12553; 845-564-4111; www.pineviewfarmny.com. Here you can cut your own balsam, Canaan, or Fraser fir; there are also blue, white, and Norway spruce trees. Candy canes, coloring books, and live animals will delight the kids.

Rogowski Farm. 327 Glenwood Road, Pine Island 10969; 845-258-4574; www.rogowskifarm.com. In season, there are dozens of varieties of crops (several pick-your-own), as well as a wonderful gift shop/farm store chock-full of tempting treats and fantastic produce. There are lots of special events and classes offered here and the farm is a wonderful stop for families, with something to intrigue children of all ages.

SKIING AND SNOWBOARDING

Mount Peter. 40 Ski Lane (NY 17A and Old Mount Peter Road), Warwick 10990; 845-986-4940; wwwrr .mtpeter.com. This mountain has a vertical drop of 400 feet, two double chairlifts, and eight downhill slopes for skiing and snowboarding. A good portion of the mountain is geared toward the beginner and novice skier so it's a good place for families to enjoy the sport.

ORANGE COUNTY TOURISM

Facilities: Restrooms, cafeteria, ski school.

Tuxedo Ridge Ski Center. 581 NY 17A West, Tuxedo 10987; 845-351-1122. Tuxedo Ridge is located in the scenic Sterling Forest and specializes in hosting beginners and families. However, they also offer lots of challenging terrain and programs for the seasoned skier and snowboarder. There is a vertical drop of 400 feet, with seven main trails and four double chair lifts. Additionally, a good-sized snow tubing area has its own lift. The Snow Playground is a fun place for families to enjoy after several hours on the slopes.

Facilities: Restrooms, snack bar, ski school, rentals.

SNOW TUBING

Thomas Bull Memorial Park. 211 NY 416, Montgomery 12549; 845-457-4949. This is a wonderful spot if you want to try snow tubing. There are five groomed lanes with a rope tow. You can rent the specially designed tubes and there are stadium lights for the evening period. It's a beautiful spot as well, with an adjacent area for cross-country skiing, sledding, and ice skating and scenic views of the Shawangunk Mountains. There is also a playground here designed with wide, low equipment, making it a great place for the smallest children.

Facilities: Restrooms, lodge, restaurant, bar, stone fireplace. Adjacent area for cross-country skiing, sledding, and ice skating.

SWIMMING

Bear Mountain Pool and Harriman Beaches. US 9W, Bear Mountain 10911; 845-786-2701; www.nysparks.state.ny.us. Admission. These swimming areas are ideal for those traveling with young children. A family-friendly atmosphere prevails, and all the services parents might need are at their fingertips. (Bear Mountain is located in both Rockland and Orange counties.)

Facilities: Restrooms, restaurant, snack bar, lockers.

Redwood Tennis and Swim Club. 620 Van Burenville Road, Middletown 10940; 845-343-9478. Admission. The pool here is huge and it is located in a 9-acre recreation area with picnic tables as well as outdoor and indoor clay tennis courts.

Facilities: Restrooms, picnic areas, snack bar, lockers, showers.

THEATER

Eisenhower Hall Theater. 655 Ruger Road, United States Military Academy, West Point 10996; 845-938-4159; www.ikehall.com. There is an array of programs featured here including drama, dance, Broadway musicals, comedy, and children's theater. Call for a schedule of events if you will be in the area.

Paramount Theater. 17 South Street, Middletown 10940; 845-346-4195; www.middletownparamount.com. The theater offers several programs throughout the year in dance, drama, comedy, and children's productions. Call for a schedule of events.

Orange County Community College. 115 South Street, Middletown 10940; 845-344-6222; www.sunyorange.edu/lyceum. There are music and dance performances, films, and plays that would be of interest to young people at the Lyceum Theater here year-round. Call or check the Web site for a schedule of events.

ADDITIONAL ATTRACTIONS

Jumpin' Jakes. 360 NY 211, Middletown 10940; 845-704-1100; www .jumpinjakes.net. Open year-round . This is a great stop to let kids blow off steam after spending time in the car traveling. The inflatable play structures here give children the chance to climb walls, crawl through obstacles, bounce, and zoom down enormous slides. There are toddler zones, video games, music, and a light floor.

Facilities: Restrooms, snack bar.

Monster Mini Golf. 88 Dunning Farms Plaza, Middletown 10940; 845-342-4653; www.monsterminigolf.com. This glow-in-the-dark indoor 18-hole miniature golf course is a fun stop year-round. There are also dozens of arcade games, air hockey, and skee ball with talking fluorescent monsters.

New York Renaissance Faire. 600 NY 17A, Sterling Forest, Tuxedo Park 10987; 845-351-5171; www.renfair.com. Admission.

Knights and ladies, sorcerers and their apprentices, fools and varlets, bumpkins and wantons all gather on the glorious grounds of Sterling Forest to re-create the lusty days of a merry Olde English fair. The festival runs for eight consecutive weekends and presents a colorful, noisy look at a distant period of time somewhere between King Arthur and Shakespeare. Falconers show off the skills of their birds, opera and Shakespeare are presented at the Globe Theater, Maid Marian flirts with

The action never stops at the New York Renaissance Faire in Sterling Forest.

ORANGE COUNTY TOURISM

Robin Hood, ladies dance beneath a maypole, and the extensive rose gardens are open for strolling. Craftspeople display and sell their wares (many belong to the Society for Anachronisms and stock things like chain mail shirts), and the aromas of "steak on a stake," mead, and cheese pie flavor the air. There are jugglers, knife throwers, mud fights, and a living chess game in which the "pieces" wander the gardens to their squares. The actors play their roles throughout the entire festival, so authenticity combines with the personal touch. Kids adore the noise and action and there is much to see and do for everyone.

Sugar Loaf Village. Sugar Loaf 10981; 845-469-9181; www.sugarloafnewyork.com. (The village is reached from NY 17 west, exit 127—follow the signs.) Open year-round. Free.

Named for the local mountain that is shaped the way sugar was during Colonial times, Sugar Loaf has been the subject of unusual speculation. Originally the mountain was a Native American burial ground, and over the years various relics and bones have been uncovered there. Over 30 years ago, Sugar Loaf established itself as a leading craft village, and it now offers many shops and demonstrations by craftspeople and artists at work. This is really a site for parents who want to shop but who would also like their children to be amused. Most of the stores offer something for children. Throughout the year, special events include concerts in the Lycian Center, a fall festival, and a Christmas caroling and candle lighting service (held the weekend before Christmas)—when Santa visits and the village glows with an old-fashioned, small-town atmosphere. This is a fun holiday stop!

Facilities: Restrooms (Barnsider Tavern, wheelchair accessible). Parents with strollers should keep in mind that this is a small village with sidewalks that may be crowded on weekends, and you will have to fold and carry strollers in and out of many shops. Parking is at either end of the village in well-marked lots.

SULLIVAN COUNTY

▼▲▼▲▼▲▼

The unspoiled beauty and mystique of the Catskill Mountains of Sullivan County has made this area a popular family vacation destination for decades. Bordered on the west by the Delaware River, one of the best places in the state to canoe or kayak, the county is also chock-full of hundreds of pristine lakes and ponds for swimming. The rugged, untamed countryside here is home to the largest population of bald eagles in the eastern United States. Renowned for excellent trout fishing by anglers throughout the world, the county is truly a thousand square miles of outdoor recreational opportunities.

There are a few musts of families traveling through Sullivan County. At the top of the list should be **Apple Pond Farming and Renewable Energy Center** in Callicoon. Kids will see horse-powered machinery, the county of organic farming, and a variety of renewable energy sources—including windmills. Another fun-filled, educational stop is the **Eagle Institute** in Barryville. On weekends from mid-December through March, when eagles migrate to Sullivan County from Canada, they can usually be found perching near and flying to and from the ice and tree line surrounding the lake here. Kids have an easy time spotting them, so don't forget the binoculars!

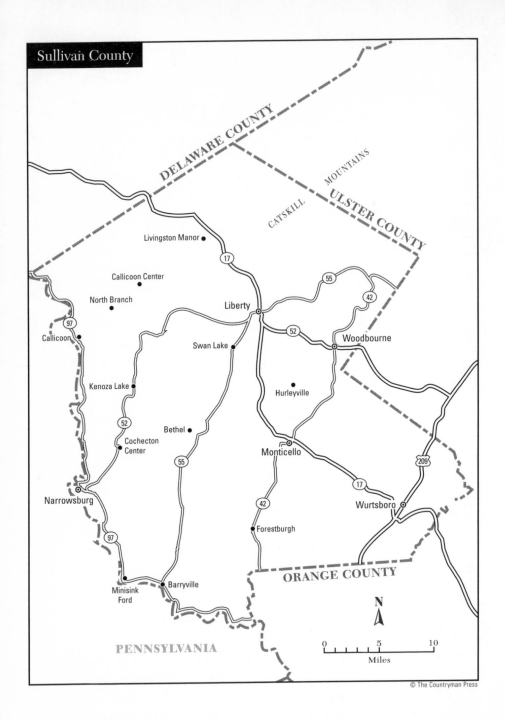

Sullivan County

DELAWARE COUNTY

CATSKILL MOUNTAINS

ULSTER COUNTY

Livingston Manor

17

Callicoon Center

55

North Branch

42

97

Liberty

Callicoon

52

Woodbourne

Swan Lake

Kenoza Lake

Hurleyville

52

Bethel

55

Cochecton
Center

Monticello

209

Narrowsburg

17

42

Wurtsboro

97

Forestburgh

ORANGE COUNTY

Minisink
Ford

Barryville

N

PENNSYLVANIA

0   5   10
Miles

© The Countryman Press

Fort Delaware in Narrowsburg offers children a fascinating journey through the early American history of the upper Delaware River and the lives of the pioneers from the French and Indian War through the Revolution.

After sightseeing, Sullivan County's combination of outdoor activities and special events will delight everyone in the family. Kids will love taking a canoe trip on the Delaware River or a chance to try their hand at fishing. The Willowemoc and Beaverkill rivers teem with trout, bass, shad, perch, and pickerel. The traditional opening of trout season is on April 1 at Junction Pool, Roscoe—Trout Town U.S.A. Every June in Livingston Manor, **The Trout Parade** celebrates the fish that means so much to the county. Floats, dancers, live music, and children's activities are all part of the festivities. In July Liberty stages a **Civil War Weekend** where hundreds of re-enactors transform the city's Walnut Mountain Park into Union and Confederate battlefields. Children will be delighted to take a step back in time and talk to the soldiers as they demonstrate their cooking, weapon drills, and camp activities—as well as participate in a full-scale battle each afternoon. In August the **Riverfest in Narrowsburg,** a celebration of music and art, features crafts, live music, and a flotilla challenge. Kids will enjoy the excellent children's theater productions at the **Forestburgh Playhouse** in Forestburgh. And any time of year, everyone in the family will enjoy a stop at the **Woodstock Museum** in Bethel Woods, home of the original 1969 music festival.

For further information, contact the **Sullivan County Visitors Association,** 100 Sullivan Avenue, Suite 2, Ferndale 12734; 845-747-4449, 1-800-882-CATS, www.scva.net.

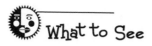 What to See

MUSEUMS AND HISTORIC SITES

Bethel Woods Center for the Arts/Woodstock Museum. 200 Hurd Road, Bethel 12720; 1-866-781-2922; www.bethelwoodscenter.org. Check the Web site for performance schedule.

The actual Woodstock Festival Site, now part of Bethel Woods

Center for the Arts, is on Hurd Road in Bethel—not in Woodstock (Ulster County), more than 50 miles away. This is where 400,000 people gathered in August 1969 for three days of peace, mud, and rock 'n' roll. There is now a state-of-the-art performance venue including an interpretive center and museum (opened in 2006) featuring jazz, classical, and country music as well as pop and rock. There are 4,800 seats under a pavilion and lawn space for up to 12,000; the 6,348-square-foot stage is twice the size of Radio City Music Hall. Bethel and the surrounding countryside is beautiful, a good place to take a leisurely drive, a walk, or a picnic. The self-guided tour of the museum is a must-see for parents and grandparents who lived through the 1960s, as well as older children who are interested in the decade and its music. The museum is beautifully designed for wandering and is filled with displays and videos, as well as a 21-minute film, *Woodstock: The Music.* The high definition images and surround sound in this captivating film capture the highlights of the 1969 festival. Additionally, the performing artists of the 1969 concert reflect on their inspiring and emotional experiences four decades ago. (I spent close to two hours in the museum and there are enough "audiovisual experiences" to keep most children over the age of six interested!)

Facilities: Restrooms, picnic areas, gift shop (the shop offers some terrific souvenirs to delight children of the 1960s, as well as everyone else!). Strollers can maneuver easily along the paved paths here. When concerts are scheduled, there are food vendors on the premises.

Catskill Fly-Fishing Center and Museum.
1031 Old NY 17 (Main Street), Livingston Manor 12758; 845-439-4810; www.cffcm.org. (The museum and center are located on the Willowemoc Creek, between Roscoe (exit 94 off NY 17) and Livingston Manor (exit 96 off NY 17)). Admission. Call in advance to make arrangements for special group tours. The center offers demonstrations on weekends in the summer.

This special site for fishermen of all ages is set in a beautiful spot on the world-famous Willowemoc Creek. This is the birthplace of fly-fishing in the United States, and it attracts sportspeople from all over the world to its pristine waters. The center was founded in 1978 as an educational resource. Today it carries on the tradition, offering environmental education classes as well as instruction in fly-tying and fly-fishing during July for 8- to 16-year-olds. Some of these workshops include overnight camping programs on the center's grounds, so parents can fish while the kids learn about ecology and biology through hands-on experiments and classes. The museum contains continually changing exhibits about the lore and history of fly-fishing, and has entertained many famous anglers—including Jimmy and Rosalynn Carter. There are plenty of tackle shops in Roscoe and Livingston Manor, so you can outfit yourself and the kids for a day of fishing on the Willowemoc.

Facilities: Restrooms. Strollers are easy to maneuver here, and the site is readily accessible to the disabled.

Fort Delaware Museum of Colonial History. 6615 NY 97, Narrowsburg 12764; 845-252-6660; www.co.sullivan.ny.us. Admission. Group rates available by advance reservation.

Relive a part of New York's pioneer history at this re-creation of the first stockade settlement in the upper Delaware Valley. Visitors to the fort will see life as it was during the mid-18th century. This site reconstructs the everyday life of the average settler; no fancy houses, just log dwellings, an armory, blacksmith shop, animal pens, weaver's shed, and fort. Costumed site interpreters around each area will explain the crafts and skills needed to survive in the wilderness. Demonstrations are offered throughout the season, so children may see candle dipping, shingle making, spinning, and musket and cannon firing. This site is particularly appealing to young children, who have a chance to pretend they are living in a wilderness fort in the days before Davy Crockett and Daniel Boone. This rugged historic site is not the polished, fancy restoration you see in places like Williamsburg, Virginia, but this makes it even more appealing to the kids. Special events held on weekends throughout the summer include a military encampment, which is staffed by members of the Fifth Connecticut Regiment of Continental Life, a group that re-creates the daily life of soldiers and their families.

Facilities: Restrooms, picnic areas, gift shop, snack bar. Strollers can manage here, but you should call ahead if wheelchair accessibility is a concern.

Minisink Battleground Park. CR 168, Minisink Ford 12792; 845-794-3000 x. 3066. (Located 1 mile northeast of NY 97 (designated as a scenic byway), at Minisink Ford in the town of Highland on CR 168.) Free.

This 57-acre park is listed on the National Register and is dedicated to the brave men who fought and died at the Battle of Minisink, the

Just across the street from the battleground entrance is **Roebling's Suspension Bridge**, a National Historic Landmark built in 1848. This is the oldest suspension bridge in America. The wire cables were spun by hand on-site, and the bridge was one of the few to ever carry a canal aqueduct above a river. The bridge has been restored and is open to visitors. The kids will enjoy being able to walk (or drive) into Pennsylvania!

upper Delaware's only major Revolutionary War skirmish in 1779. The park features three self-guided trails of less than 2 miles: the Battleground Trail, Woodland Trail, and the Old Quarry Trail, which are mapped out in brochures available at the information center.

This is an excellent place to combine history, nature study, and hiking in a few hours of outdoor fun. Kids will be fascinated to learn that this area was once so wild and inaccessible that the bones of the dead were not collected for burial until nearly 50 years after the battle. The interpretive center contains displays that tell the story of the park and the trails, which wander through wetlands, fern gardens, berry patches, and rock shelters. The trails are great to walk with young children over the age of five, since they are fairly flat and there are lots of interesting rocks and formations along the way.

Facilities: Restrooms, picnic areas. Strollers and wheelchairs cannot maneuver through these trails.

O & W Railway Museum. 7 Railroad Avenue, Roscoe 12776; 607-498-5500; www.nyow.org. Admission.

If you are stopping in Roscoe and your kids are train enthusiasts, this is a must. The O & W (Oswego and Weehauken) train line once ran from New Jersey northwest to Oswego on the shores of Lake Ontario. The museum complex contains a caboose at the site of the old Roscoe railroad station as well as a station building. The caboose contains changing displays of railroad memorabilia, and the kids will have a chance to walk around a real red railroad caboose. The station building has a self-operated model railroad for kids to operate on their own, as well as a theater that features an array of videos and slide shows describing the impact of the railroad on local history. On Independence Day weekend there is always a parade and street fair in town as well as a colorful, fun-filled railroad festival.

Facilities: Restrooms, gift shop.

Sullivan County Museum. 265 Main Street (CR 104), Hurleyville 12747; 845-434-8044; www.sullivancountyhistory.org. Free, although donations are appreciated.

The Sullivan County Historical Society is housed in this building, with exhibits focusing on county history. The renowned hotels, tanning industries, and D&H Canal are showcased along with a timeline room that traces from the days of the Leni-Lenape Indians up to the Woodstock experience. The second floor will be of most interest to young children—with a 1900 meat wagon, Grandma's Kitchen (circa 1930), Sullivan County Wall of Fame, and corresponding Wall of Shame! There is a room devoted to Frederick Cook (the great polar explorer who was born in Sullivan County) and a gallery centering on Stephen Crane (who wrote *The Red Badge of Courage* and spent much of his short life in Forestburgh). This is a stop for children interested in history; there's no glitz here!

EDUCATIONAL ATTRACTIONS

Apple Pond Farming and Renewable Energy Education Center. 80 Hahn Road, Callicoon Center 12724; 845-482-4764; www.applepondfarm.com. (Take New York State Thruway to exit 16; pick up NY 17 west to exit 101, heading toward Ferndale. Make a right onto Ferndale-Loomis Road and go 4 miles; make a left onto NY 52 west for 6 miles. In Youngsville, turn right onto Shandalee Road. Make a left onto Stump Pond Road and another left onto Hahn Road. The farm is 1 mile up the road on the left. Watch for signs.) Admission. Groups can be accommodated by advance reservation. Open year-round.

This is a very special farm and a great deal of the work here is done by horsepower: All crops are grown organically, and most of the energy needs of the farm are provided by renewable energy sources—including a wind turbine, solar thermal tubes, and photovoltaic panels. The tour begins with an explanation about how the farm operates in harmony with the natural environment. The walking tour introduces children to the sheep, goats, and horses that are pastured next to the parking lot. The wind turbine, on a 120-foot tower, is always within view; as the tour progresses, the electric and solar thermal panels on the roof come into view. There is information on alternative energy sources available as the children visit the control area for renewable energy. Next comes a visit to the organic gardens where children will learn to identify different kinds of foods and discover organic methods of growing crops. A visit to the barn presents an opportunity for kids to see the dairy goats and watch the horses being harnessed for the horse-drawn wagon ride. During the ride, children are treated to magnificent views of the countryside. Sheep graze in the high meadows and some of the horse-drawn farming equipment is visible. The final part of the tour is a visit to the wool room, where children try their hand at spinning wool. Note that tours take a minimum of one hour. There are educational programs offered with an array of hands-on activities; a full schedule is available on the Web site.

For families that want to spend more time at this farming center, there is a three-bedroom guesthouse that sleeps five and is fully furnished. Those that stay overnight can prepare meals with produce from the organic garden, collect free-range eggs, and enjoy hiking and swimming in the lake nearby. Children will enjoy feeding the animals; well-behaved dogs are welcome too.

Facilities: Restrooms, picnic areas, gift shop (with farm-made items such as wool hats and gloves), guesthouse for rent.

The Eagle Institute. 3364 NY 97, Barryville 12719; 845-557-6162; www .eagleinstitute.org.

Sullivan County attracts more bald eagles than anywhere else on the East Coast, drawing them in with open waters and virgin forests. Every winter more than one hundred eagles migrate here from Canada, and in the spring they return north. The county now has an information clearinghouse for eagle migratory and breeding data, and it is open to the public. On-site interpretive programs are offered on weekends during the winter months, when the eagles come south. The birds are sure to intrigue just about everyone, but children who have learned about eagles in school will particularly enjoy this stop. There are workshops, slide presentations, and guided eagle watches to habitat areas. Call ahead for schedule information or check the Web site. This is one of the few county attractions where winter is high season and it's a nice education destination as well.

Facilities: Restrooms.

Covered Bridges

Sullivan County is well known for the surviving covered bridges that still span waterways throughout the county. Resembling small houses, the bridges are thought to have been covered with roofs for two reasons: to protect the timbers and to allow the horses and oxen that pulled the wagons to cross over the water without getting frightened. Some of the bridges are still in use, and children will enjoy seeing these remnants of old-time travel. At the Beaverkill State Campground, the **Beaverkill Bridge**, a lattice-type construction, spans the river. Beaverkill State Campground is 7 miles northwest of Livingston Manor on Johnston Hill Road. **Chestnut Creek Bridge** (from NY 55 north to Claryville Road) is a 128-foot-long lattice bridge built in 1912 over the Neversink River. The **Livingston Manor Covered Bridge**, on CR 179 north of Livingston Manor, is the county's only existing example of a Queen Truss bridge; it was built in 1860 and spans 103 feet over Willowemoc Creek. Also in the area is the **Willowemoc Bridge**, on TR 18, 2 miles west of Willowemoc, which hangs over the creek and was built by the same man who constructed the Livingston Manor Covered Bridge. In 1913, this bridge, originally located at another site, was cut in half and moved to its present location.

Peaceful Breeze Alpaca Farm. 3301 NY 42, Monticello 12701; 845-794-1111; www.peacefulbreeze.com. This family-owned and -operated alpaca farm is open year-round. There are about 20 alpacas born each year, beginning in the spring. There is an "Alpacas Get Naked Day" in May when the animals are sheared. "National Alpaca Day" is in September and "Farm Day" falls in October, with pony rides and magic tricks to entertain all. Children will learn about the transition from raw fiber to beautiful finished items. The farm also allows children to explore an organic garden, see the chickens that provide fresh eggs daily, and walk a nature trail. Group tours should make advance reservations.

Facilities: Restrooms, picnic areas, gift shop (with yarn and clothing), hiking trails.

Wurtsboro Airport. 50 Barone Road (off US 209), Wurtsboro 12790; 845-888-2791; www.wurtsboroairport.com. (Take NY 17 west to exit 113,

After visiting the airport, you may want to stop at the **Canal Towne Emporium**, 107 Sullivan Street, in the village of Wurtsboro, a country store in a historic brick building that dates back to 1845. Open year-round, the store was originally a dry-goods establishment near the Delaware & Hudson Canal. Now restored to its turn-of-the-century charm, the fixtures, furnishings, and equipment are all antiques—which include the first electric coffee mill ever used in the store, advertising prints, tins, and jars. Today the emporium sells furniture, handcrafted items, decorative accessories, and books. The kids will enjoy the wonderful array of chocolates and penny candy. At holiday time, the rooms devoted to Christmas decorations and children's toys are phenomenal and especially worth visiting.

then US 209 north 3.5 miles.) Free for observers; there is a charge for sailplane rides. Open year-round.

Founded in 1927, this is the oldest place to go soaring in the United States. Visitors can take a ride in a sailplane, which is carried aloft by a Cessna tow plane, then released to soar quietly back to earth. For both adults and children who have flown before, the silence of sailplanes is relaxing and the closest you can get to flying like a bird. You can stay on the ground and watch the planes take off and land or sign up for a demonstration flight. Scenic rides over the Catskill Mountains are conducted by experienced FAA-rated commercial pilots and take about 15–20 minutes. The views are magnificent any time of year, but particularly in autumn.

Facilities: Restrooms (not wheelchair accessible). Snacks and drinks are available from vending machines on the premises.

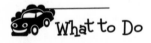 **What to Do**

BICYCLING

Bicycle Club of Sullivan County. 845-856-6899; www.sullivanstriders.org. Organized over 30 years ago, this club sponsors rides every weekend (usually on Saturday) from April through October. Many of the rides begin and end in Fallsburg, Liberty, and Neversink. Be aware that the county is rather hilly and that club excursions are advised only for older children who are enthusiastic bicyclists.

Lander's Mountain Biking Excursions. 5666 NY 97, Narrowsburg 12764; 1-800-252-3925; www.landersrivertrips.com. If you are interested in taking a mountain biking trip along the Delaware River for a day, three days, or a week, this outfitter can make it happen and provide everything you will need—from bicycles to tents. Such an outing is recommended for older children who have had biking experience.

CANOEING, KAYAKING, AND RAFTING

The Delaware River is the perfect place to canoe or kayak. It is wide and not too fast (it flows at about 3 miles an hour); the scenery is magnificent; and you can adjust the length of the trip since there are many entry and exit points along the river. The Delaware is navigable from Hancock, New York, to Dingmans Ferry, Pennsylvania; the river is managed by the National Park Service; call 845-252-3947 for information.

Sullivan County offers many places to rent canoes. As part of the standard retail package, you receive life jackets, a map, and pickup service along the river. The outfitters are accommodating, and there are many places where you can stop and rest or picnic. Anyone who takes a canoe trip must be able to swim. I recommend this kind of excursion for children over the age of 10, unless a younger child is very experienced on the water. Remember that the river has rapids and rocks and presents a more adventurous experience than a lake would. The best seasons are summer and early fall when the river is high enough without being flooded (the Delaware ranges in depth from 2–5 feet). Essentials for the river include a picnic lunch, liquids, and snacks—all packed in waterproof bags and containers. You should wear sneakers; in cooler weather, wear

MATT BUCK. HTTP.//COMMONS.WIKIMEDIA.ORG

lightweight water resistant clothing and always bring a change of clothing. Hats, sunscreen, and sunglasses will make you more comfortable. Don't let warnings scare you off: If you are new to river trips, tell the outfitter and they will suggest an appropriate journey, as well as show you how to maneuver your craft. If you are experienced at paddling your own canoe or kayak, call the Upper Delaware River Conditions Information Line at 845-252-7100 for the latest river report before you set out. The Delaware River can be dangerous during spring flood season. (I made the 35-mile trip from Narrowsburg, New York, to Matamoras, Pennsylvania, on a sunny July weekend—spending the night mid-way at a campground along the river. There were four in our party and the excursion was terrific fun, a memorable experience.)

Lander's Delaware River Trips. 5666 NY 97, Narrowsburg 12764; 1-800-252-3925; www.landersrivertrips.com. This is one of the largest outfitters on the river. They offer rentals, overnight camping packages at four campgrounds, and shuttle service from 12 riverfront locations. They can arrange motel accommodations along the river for those who don't want to camp but who do want to paddle. Discounts are available for group outings. This company also offers rafting for adults and children over the age of five. With the rise in popularity of kayaking, they have also started offering tandem kayaks, a nice option for families to consider.

Kittatinny Canoes. 102 Kittatinny Court, Dingmans Ferry, PA 18328; 1-800-FLOAT-KC; www.kittatinny.com. They have 70 years of experience in providing quality service and equipment on the Delaware River. Their seven bases are strategically located along the 135-mile river to ensure diverse trips and riverfront camping. There are day trips and calm-water trips for beginners, or overnights and white-water excursions for more advanced paddlers. Kittatinny has its own campgrounds along the river. Since much of the riverfront land is privately owned, it is sometimes difficult to find camping areas. They offer custom trips, group discounts, and classes in canoeing and kayaking.

Cedar Rapid Kayak and Canoe Outfitters. 3799 NY 97, Barryville 12719; 845-557-6158. This small outfitter at the Cedar Mountain Inn rents double and single kayaks, canoes, rafts, and tubes. There is also a lovely riverside restaurant at the inn where you can enjoy refreshments al fresco and watch the fun from shore.

FISHING

Sullivan County is an angler's paradise and this part of the Catskills offers a broad selection of lakes, ponds, and streams to fish. The famed Willowemoc and Beaverkill streams produce prize-winning trout each year, augmenting the reputation of a county already known as the cradle of American fly-fishing.

All streams on state land are open to the public; others streams often have public fishing rights through state easements, which are clearly indicated by signs. New York State requires fishing licenses for anyone over the age of 16; these waters are patrolled quite well, and the fines for violations can be substantial. Licenses can be purchased at most tackle shops and town halls. You will receive a guide to fishing areas and a book of rules when you purchase the license.

April 1 marks the opening day of fishing season—but in the Catskills the weather can range from mild to snowy on that date, so dress accordingly. Sullivan County stocks three lakes: Mongaup Falls Reservoir (in Forestburgh, watch for signs), Lake Huntington (on NY 52 in Lake Huntington village), and White Lake (at the junction of NY 17B and NY 55). If you want a real pioneer treat, try some shad fishing on the Delaware River—a good access point is NY 97, from Long Eddy to Barryville—in May and June; the run has been fished for over 200 years.

Stream and river fishing present a challenge, and kids love casting from the willow-shaded bank; try the Willowemoc (Roscoe) and the Basha Kill Marsh (US 209 near Wurtsboro). If you've never fished before, you may want to spend the day in Roscoe, also known as Trout Town U.S.A., which has everything you need—including tackle, licenses, information, and local fishing advice. One way to almost guarantee a catch is to try your cast at **Eldred Preserve** (NY 55, Eldred 12732; 845-557-8316), a private resort that opens its stocked ponds to the public. You pay both an admission fee and a per-pound price for the fish you catch, but because this is private property, a fishing license is not required. If you don't catch anything, schedule a stop at the **Catskill State Fish Hatchery** (located at exit 96 off NY 17, Mongaup Road, DeBruce 12758; 845-439-4328). Open year-round. More than 750,000 trout are raised here for stocking rivers and lakes throughout New York State, and a series of hatching ponds hold the fish. Tours are available for groups with advance notice. Be aware that there are no public restrooms here.

PARKS

Lake Superior State Park. Dr. Duggan Road, Bethel 12720; 845-794-3000 x. 3066; www.co.sullivan.ny.us/parks. There is an admission fee at the beach area only.

This beautiful 1,409-acre park is part of the Palisades Interstate Park System. Families will discover a lovely stop in the summer if they choose to spend time here. The sandy beach fronts the lake where there are boat rentals and abundant areas to picnic.

Facilities: Restrooms, picnic areas (some with fee), food concessions, bathhouse, boat launch (electric trolling motors only).

Mongaup Pond Public Campground and Day Use Area. 231 Mongaup Pond/Fish Hatchery Road, Livingston Manor 12758; 845-439-4233, 1-800-456-CAMP; www.dec.ny.gov. (Take exit 96 off NY 17 west, go 7 miles northeast to DeBruce, then 3 miles north of DeBruce in the State Forest Preserve, and follow signs to the site.) Admission. Groups accommodated; campsites available by reservation.

Located in the State Forest Preserve, this 275-acre facility is one of the nicest, most scenic recreation areas in the county for children. A small sandy beach lines Mongaup Pond, a 120-acre site where you can rent a rowboat, fish, swim, or build sand castles. Shady areas make this a comfortable beach, and when you are tired of water activities, you can hike and camp. The hiking trails are well marked and range in length from under a mile to several miles. This is a fine place to take young children for the day and keep them busy with outdoor activities. There are picnic areas with barbecue pits for day use and complete campsites with hook-ups for overnight use.

Facilities: Restrooms, picnic areas, campsites (by reservation only). There are snowmobile trails for use in the winter months.

Stone Arch Bridge Historical Park. NY 52, Kenoza Lake 12750. Open year-round. Free.

This three-arched stone bridge, spanning Callicoon Creek outside Jeffersonville, is the only remaining one of its kind in America. Built in 1872 by two German stonemasons, it was made of local stone and is supported without an outer structure. The bridge replaced wooden one that collapsed from the weight of continual use by heavy wagons. The Stone Arch Bridge became renowned for its unusual construction as well as for a murder that occurred near it in 1892. A local farmer, believing his brother-in-law had put a curse on him, convinced his son to kill him. The son committed the murder and dumped the body into the river near the bridge. Today you can fish from the banks of the creek, picnic on the grass, or stroll through the 9-acre landscaped park. Children will enjoy the small play area and nature trails.

Facilities: Portable toilets, picnic areas.

SKIING AND SNOWBOARDING

KALLERNA, HTTP://COMMONS.WIKIMEDIA.ORG

Holiday Mountain. 99 Holiday Mountain Road, Monticello 12701; 845-796-3161; www.holidaymtn.com. (Exit 107 off NY 17 west at Bridgeville.)

There are 15 slopes at this small ski center with limited facilities. The vertical drop is 400 feet, with 100 percent of the runs covered by snowmaking capability, and the longest run is 3,500 feet. (There is also a cross-country ski area and snow tubing park.) I would suggest this area only to beginner skiers and snowboarders. Note that there is no nursery for the youngest children.

Facilities: Restrooms, cafeteria, ski school, ski shop, lounge, rentals.

Hanofee Park. Located off NY 52 east, Liberty 12754; 845-292-7690. This park has 110 acres of cross-country trails and offers rentals and lessons for all ages and abilities. This is a terrific spot to introduce the youngest children to cross-country skiing.

Town of Thompson Park. Old Liberty Road, Monticello 12701; 845-796-3161 Open year-round. This park is 4 miles past the Monticello post office and has trails through 160 acres of parkland. There are no facilities and you must bring all your own equipment if you want to ski here.

THEATER

Forestburgh Playhouse. 39 Forestburgh Road, Forestburgh 12777; 845-794-1194; www.fbplayhouse.com. This summer-stock theater housed in a 130-year-old barn offers drama, comedies, musicals, and children's productions. Call for schedule in season or check the Web site.

Catskill Art Society. 263 Main Street, Hurleyville 12747; 845-436-4227; www.catskill artsociety.org. Open year-round. This group sponsors theater, music, dance, art exhibits, and a variety of arts activities throughout the county. Some are specifically geared to young people. Call or check the Web site for locations and schedules of events.

ADDITIONAL ATTRACTIONS

Amapro Family Fun Center. 2807 NY 52 west, Liberty 12754; 845-292-2386. There are six paintball fields, a paintball target range, inflatable bounce house village, 18-hole championship miniature golf course, 300-yard driving range, carnival games with prizes, and sand art and crafts. Children will enjoy a stop here no matter what they choose to do. Fee charged for various activities.

VILLA ROMA RESORT

Breezeway Farm Petting Zoo. 161 Anawana Lake Road, Monticello 12701; 845-794-4543; www.breezewayfarmpettingzoo.com. Admission. Children will love petting and feeding the friendly farm animals here in a delightful environment. The farm has cows, chickens, donkeys, ducks, geese, goats, horses, pigs, sheep, rabbits, turkeys, and llamas. There are pony rides as well.

Butterfly Botanicals. 363 Petticoat Lane, Bloomingburg 12721; 845-733-7713; www.nybutterflies.com. Admission. Children will love the live butterfly exhibit, flight house, and hands-on atmosphere here. There is also a greenhouse with perennials, annuals, and herbs for sale.

Holiday Mountain Family Fun Park. 99 Holiday Mountain Road, Monticello 12701; 845-796-3161; www.holidaymtn.com. This park features go-carts, bumper cars and boats, a rock wall, paintball, miniature golf, potato sack slide, arcade, mechanical bull, and batting cages—to name just some of the fun attractions. The miniature golf course is the largest in the Hudson Valley. Fee charged for activities.

Samba and Little Duck House. 4893 Main Street, Jeffersonville 12748; 845-482-5900; www.littleduckhouseandsamba.com. It is rare to find a bookstore, juice bar, coffeehouse, and gift shop under one roof in charming village of Jeffersonville. Andrea and Tim Corcoran make visitors feel right at home; a Latin-American brunch is served on weekends in spring, summer, and fall. If you decide to stay overnight, ask about the recently renovated **Little Duck Guest House** tucked away on the Callicoon Creek, just behind Samba—a perfect getaway for families and exceedingly reasonable pricewise.

FAMILY RESORTS

There are dozens of resorts throughout Sullivan County offering a range of accommodations to suit every taste. The two included here offer very different experiences and have been operating in the county for many years.

Eldred Preserve. 1040 NY 55, Eldred 12732; 845-557-8316; www.eldred preserve.com. Open year-round. This fishing resort is set on nearly 3,000 acres of unspoiled forest, with three stream-fed trout ponds and two bass lakes. It makes a great escape for families who want a low-key getaway with fishing and hiking at their doorstep. The ponds are stocked with rainbow, brown, brook, and golden trout. The cozy log-cabin-style buildings with 25 motel rooms are simply furnished and the restaurant is informal. There are tennis courts, an outdoor pool, and boat rentals. Guests at the resort do not need a fishing license for trout fishing, although one is required for bass fishing.

Villa Roma Resort. 356 Villa Roma Road, Callicoon 12723; 845-887-4880, 1-800-533-6767; www.villaroma.com. Open year-round. This is a 150-room, full-service resort with all the amenities—18-hole championship golf course, indoor and outdoor tennis courts, five pools, racquetball, fitness center, restaurant, and even an eight-lane bowling alley. There is cross-country skiing during the winter months. The hotel was completely rebuilt and redesigned in 2008 after being destroyed by fire. The children's program is excellent, and offers several activities for kids from tots to age 17. There are scavenger hunts, volleyball games, face painting, a rock climbing wall, and much more to keep all ages happy. Special family packages and theme weekends are offered throughout the year; check the Web site for details.

ULSTER COUNTY

▼▲▼▲▼▲▼

The magnificent Catskill Mountains tower above the scenic Hudson River, making Ulster County a strikingly beautiful place to visit, a year-round family vacation destination alive with entertainment, outdoor activities, culture, and history. In the warm-weather months, take a boat ride on the majestic Hudson or plan a trip to go bicycling, hiking, or camping in the Shawangunks or Catskills. You can also visit the oldest street in America (New Paltz) or the first capital of New York State (Kingston).

The following attractions make for some of the best family outings in the county. A must-see is the **Hudson River Maritime Museum,** the only museum in New York State dedicated to preserving the maritime heritage of the Hudson River. For almost 200 years the Hudson has been a major water highway between New York City and Albany, and kids will enjoy the ever-changing display of river vessels here. One of the most enjoyable ways for families to experience Ulster County is on the **Catskill Mountain Railroad,** a scenic 6-mile rail ride along the Esopus Creek, which begins in Mt. Pleasant. It's a wonderfully relaxing way to take in the countryside, and kids love trains. Don't miss **Forsyth Park Nature Center** in Kingston, one of the city's gems. There are llamas, deer,

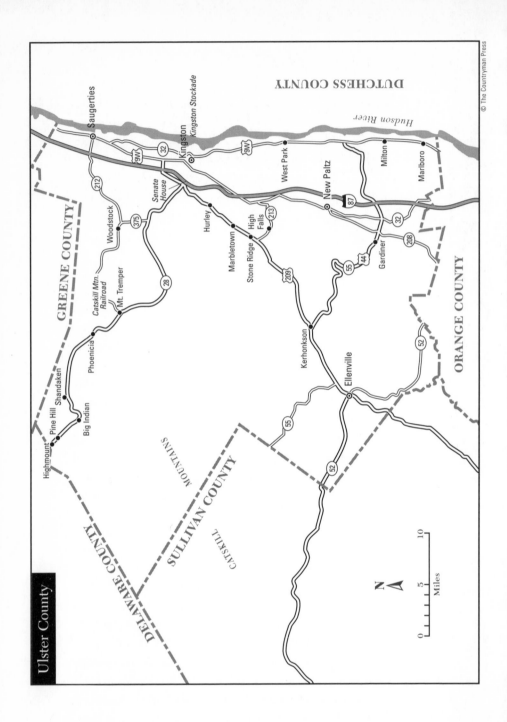

Ulster County

© The Countryman Press

bulls, pygmy goats, and sheep along with an aviary. The adjoining playground makes this a wonderful outing.

Ulster is a region with a vast array of family-friendly events year-round. The **Woodstock/New Paltz Art and Craft Fair** is a tradition at the county fairgrounds on both Memorial Day and Labor Day weekends. The **Hurley Corn Festival** at the Hurley Reformed Church—with craft demonstrations, a cooking contest, and lots of children's activities—is held on a Saturday in August, rain or shine. The **Soapbox Derby** in August will delight everyone in the family with unique handmade vehicles that are as original as their creators, who drive them down Broadway in Kingston. The **Ulster County Fair** is held in early August in New Paltz, and one-price admission includes all entertainment, rides, and shows. The **Headless Horseman Hayride and Haunted House** in Esopus in September and October has become an autumn family tradition in the county. Named the best Halloween haunted hayride in the country, this 35-minute experience is followed up with a 4-acre scary corn maze and visit to a haunted house. The last Saturday in October is the **Ashokan Fall Festival,** with hands-on activities including apple cider making, black-smithing, and broom making; there is live music all day and a square dance in the evening. In late November, the Sunday before Thanksgiving, the village of Rosendale hosts the **Annual Pickle Festival** at their Community Center with dozens of varieties of pickles for tasting and purchase.

For further information, contact **Ulster County Tourism**, 10 Westbrook Lane, Kingston 12401; 845-340-3566, 1-800-342-5826; www.ulster tourism.info.

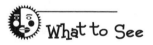 **What to See**

MUSEUMS AND HISTORIC SITES

Delaware & Hudson Canal Museum. 23 Mohonk Road, High Falls 12440; 845-687-9311; www.canalmuseum.org. (Take NY 213 to High Falls, and turn right onto Mohonk Road—the museum is located on the left side of the road.) Admission.

This museum is dedicated to the history and lore of the great Delaware & Hudson Canal. Built in the early 19th century, the canal was used to ship coal from the mines in Pennsylvania to the factories of New York; later, cement was transported for the construction of bridges and skyscrapers. The canal's designer was also responsible for the Erie Canal, and the locks, basins, and dams were engineering wonders of their era. In the museum, kids can discover a miniature setup of the canal and its operations. After leaving the museum, take the self-guided tour of the canal locks across the road, where you will see examples of stonework, locks, and loading slips.

Facilities: Restrooms, gift shop.

Empire State Railway Museum. Station Road, Phoenicia 12464; 845-688-7501; www.esrm.com. Suggested donation.

This museum brings to life the history of the Ulster & Delaware Railroad, its people, and the towns they served. Built in 1899, this historic structure is the center of restoration of these antique railway cars, and houses photos, films, and artifacts. Kids will enjoy seeing the old cars in the process of restoration. These same railway cars took city residents to boardinghouses in the mountains and returned to New York City with lumber, bluestone, and agricultural products.

Facilities: Restrooms. Wheelchair and stroller accessible.

Gomez Mill House. 11 Mill House Road, Marlboro 12542; 845-236-3126; www.gomez.org. Admission (you must take a scheduled tour to see the house).

Gomez Mill House is the oldest homestead in Ulster County, and is listed on the National Register of Historic Places. It is also the oldest surviving Jewish homestead in North America. This is truly an educational site, with a dam, wheel, bridge, and museum. A variety of programs are offered throughout the summer for young people. Check the Web site or call for a schedule of events. School groups are welcome by advance reservation.

Facilities: Portable toilets, picnic areas.

Hudson River Maritime Museum and Rondout Lighthouse. 50 Rondout Landing, at the foot of Broadway, Kingston 12401; 845-338-0071; www.hrmm.org. Admission.

The Rondout Lighthouse

This museum preserves the maritime heritage of the Hudson River. For almost 200 years, the Hudson has been a major water highway linking Manhattan to Albany. One of the ports of call along the way was the Rondout Landing, once a bustling area of boatyards and rigging lofts that echoed with steam whistles and brass ships' bells. But when shipping on the Hudson fell into decline, so did the fortunes of the Rondout. In 1980, the museum was opened and has since restored several riverside buildings and historic vessels; kids will enjoy seeing a working part of the Hudson's legacy here. An exhibit hall features shows on maritime history. Outside there is a changing display of river vessels, including the 1899 steam tug *Mathilda* and the cruise boat *Indy 7*. Visitors to the landing have included the presidential yacht *Sequoia* and the sailing ships *Clearwater* and *Woody Guthrie*. Special weekend festivals are a great time to visit and they are usually held during the summer. The season opens in early May and there is usually a Harvest Festival in October, with lots of local color and fun activities for children. Check the Web site for a complete schedule.

Facilities: Restrooms, gift shop.

Tours of the Rondout Lighthouse, a satellite museum, are offered at certain times by special arrangement for groups of 25–42. Make sure to call in advance for details.

The brick Rondout Lighthouse, located on a spit of land in Kingston's Rondout Creek, dates back to 1915 and replaced a wooden structure that dated back to 1837 and a second constructed in 1867. The tour gives visitors a glimpse into the former lives of Hudson River lighthouse keepers and their families.

Kingston Heritage Area Visitors Center. 20 Broadway and 308 Clinton Avenue, Kingston 12401; 845-331-7517, 1-800-331-1518. There are two locations in different parts of the city; both are open year-round. Free.

New York State has designated Urban Cultural Parks where there are urban settings of particular historic interest. Kingston is known for its importance in the history of transportation. The Clinton Avenue center is located in the Stockade area—once surrounded by walls of tree trunks 13 feet high—and offers orientation displays that cover the city from its 17th-century Dutch settlement to the present. Directions for self-guided walking tours are available. While in the uptown area, you may want to stop by two nearby places of interest. (The Broadway location, on the Rondout, offers permanent exhibits on Kingston history and architecture, and is a clearinghouse for travelers filled with brochures, maps, and calendars of events.)

John R. Kirk Planetarium. Coykendall Science Building, SUNY New Paltz campus, New Paltz 12561; 845-257-2121 x. 3818; www.newpaltz.edu/planetarium. (Located just off the ground-floor foyer. Take NY 32 south to Mohonk Avenue and watch for campus signs.) Open year-round; check the Web site or call for a schedule. Group shows available by advance reservation. Admission.

This stop is recommended for the child who is fascinated by space, stars, and the universe. Some of the programs assume some knowledge of astronomy, while others introduce all ages and backgrounds to the joys of stargazing and sky watching. The planetarium boasts a powerful Spitz Space Systems projector, which allows a look at the universe—past, present, and future. Shows have included exploration of an eclipse, a trip in a homemade rocket, the relationship of stars and Greek mythology, and the Christmas star in the Bible.

If your children have any interest in art, make sure to stop at the **Samuel Dorsky Museum of Art.** 75 South Manheim Boulevard, New Paltz 12561; 845-257-3844; www.newpaltz.edu/museum. Open year-round. There are changing exhibits of contemporary art in this 9,000-square-foot addition to the campus that opened in 2002. There is an emphasis on the cultural heritage of the Hudson Valley and Catskills, so stop in if your children enjoy museums. Donation.

Facilities: Restrooms. Strollers may be left in the lobby; if wheelchair accessibility is a concern, call ahead.

Opus 40 and the Quarryman's Museum. 50 Fite Road, Saugerties 12477; 845-246-3400 and 845-246-2800, x. 345; www.opus40.org. (Off NY 212, east of Woodstock, or take US 9W north of Kingston and follow signs.) Free.

This environmental bluestone sculpture, rising out of an abandoned quarry, covers more than 6 acres and was built over a 37-year period by sculptor Harvey Fite. Brendan Gill wrote in *Architectural Digest:* "This is one of the largest and most beguiling works of art on the entire continent." Visitors will be astonished by the amount of stone that was

Opus 40 is an enormous bluestone sculpture that families will enjoy exploring together. ULSTER COUNTY TOURISM

quarried, dressed, and moved into place to form the steps and monolith. Children will enjoy walking the pathways around the pools, fountains, and crannies. Stones curl around the trees, and wishing ponds abound, but it's best to wear rubber-soled shoes for walking. A stop at the Quarry-man's Museum will introduce viewers to quarrying equipment and hand-forged "folk" tools; there's also a DVD show about the history of Fite and Opus 40 itself. Special events, including an occasional concert, are scheduled; check the Web site or call in advance for details since the events make for a fun-filled family outing and picnic. At press time, Opus 40 was in the process of becoming a Town of Saugerties Cultural Park.

Facilities: Portable toilets, picnic areas (bring a blanket). Strollers can be used along the surrounding grounds but are not permitted on the sculpture itself. Wheelchair access is extremely limited. No dogs allowed.

Saugerties Lighthouse. 168 Lighthouse Drive, Saugerties 12477; 845-247-0656; www.saugertieslighthouse.com. (From the center of town, follow Main Street to the end, heading north; make a right turn onto Mynderse Street, which becomes Lighthouse Drive, although there are no signs.

Keep bearing to the left; the site is also accessible by boat from the US 9W boat launch area.) Donation.

The kids will enjoy walking through the Ruth Glunt Nature Preserve and, at low tide, being able to walk out to the historic lighthouse (a short stroll), which has a museum with artifacts from the commercial heyday of the Saugerties waterfront. There is a live-in lighthouse keeper residing on the premises who will be glad to answer questions about days gone by.

Facilities: Portable toilets. *Wheelchair and stroller access are difficult here.*

Senate House State Historic Site. 296
Fair Street, Kingston 12401; 845-338-2786; www.nysparks.org. Group tours available by appointment year-round. Admission. (Make sure to call before going since hours may be curtailed due to New York State budget constraints.)

This site will appeal to older children who are studying New York State

It's a short hike to the Saugerties Lighthouse, but only at low tide. Don't even think about taking the stroller! ULSTER COUNTY TOURISM

history in school. There are two buildings here: a modern museum and a 17th-century Dutch house where the first New York State Senate met. At the museum, a colorful display explains the American Revolution in New York State, and there are changing exhibits that tell the story of Kingston. At the Senate House, visitors will experience what a state senator would have seen during a stay in the 18th century and see several rooms, including the kitchen with its huge fireplace. New York State's first constitution was adopted in Kingston, and the building, along with many others in the city, was burned by the British troops in October 1777. Outside the building the Colonial gardens are delightful, especially in the month of June when the roses are in full bloom.

Facilities: Restrooms, picnic areas.

Trolley Museum. 89 East Strand, Kingston 12401; 845-331-3399; www.tmny.org. (Follow Broadway south to where it ends, turn left, and watch for signs.) Admission.

Housed in an old trolley shed along the Rondout, this is a pleasant stop for anyone who remembers the ring of a trolley bell. The kids will love the ride along the Hudson River in a restored trolley car, from which you can see the Rondout Lighthouse. The museum offers displays that evoke lots of nostalgia.

Facilities: Restrooms. The museum is stroller-accessible.

ADDITIONAL ATTRACTIONS

Catskill Animal Sanctuary. 316 Old Stage Road, Saugerties 12477; 845-336-8447; www.casanctuary.org.

This haven for abused horses and farm animals is home to over 250 cows, goats, sheep, rabbits, turkeys, and more. Since 2001 it has provided refuge for over 1,700 such animals and serves as an educational resource for schools and youth organizations. This is a wonderful place to bring children where they can get up close to an array of animals. There are special events throughout the season, so check the Web site for a schedule.

Catskill Mountain Railroad. NY 28, Mt. Pleasant 12457; 845-688-7400; www.catskillmtnrail road.com. Admission (children under the age of four ride free). Bus and group tours available by advance reservation.

Travel along the beautiful Esopus Creek by train and take a 12-mile round-trip along the scenic Esopus Creek through the heart of the Catskill Mountains. The trains operate on the tracks of the historic Ulster & Delaware Railroad. At Phoenicia, passengers can detrain and experience life in the Catskills both past and present by visiting the village merchants and the historic 1900 railroad station, home of the Empire State Railway Museum. Special events include a September Teddy Bear Train Ride, and October

A relaxing ride on the Catskill Mountain Railroad is a great way to take in the fall foliage.

ULSTER COUNTY TOURISM

brings a Haunted Halloween Ride. During the summer months, you can tube the Esopus and take the train back upriver (**see Tubing, 127**). The train stops at the Empire State Railway Museum on High Street in Phoenicia (**see pg. 102**), where riders can enjoy a guided tour. This is a wonderfully relaxing way to take in the countryside if you are traveling with children: Just about everyone loves train rides!

Facilities: Restrooms, picnic areas, snack bar, gift shop, parking area.

Catskill Mountain Railroad.
ULSTER COUNTY TOURISM

Forsyth Nature Center.
125 Lucas Avenue, on the right just beyond Millers Lane (which is on the left), Kingston 12401; 845-339-3053; www.forsythnaturecenter.org. Free.

There are nine species of mammals in this small zoo, including llamas, deer, bulls, pygmy goats, and sheep. An aviary on the premises is filled with a variety of birds. There is a large playground in the park, and the combination of activities and animals makes a terrific outing for those with young children. This has been a favorite spot of local residents since 1936 when it opened and was known as Forsyth Park Zoo.

Facilities: Restrooms.

The Forsyth Nature Center is a small zoo in the city of Kingston.
ULSTER COUNTY TOURISM

Headless Horseman Hayride and Haunted House.
778 Broadway (US 9W), Ulster Park 12487; 845-339-2666; www.headlesshorseman.com.

One of the best haunted hayrides you will find anywhere, this 35-minute traveling tale of terror will amuse and frighten the kids. There is also a 4-acre Murder Corn Maze, which you can try to find your way through. There are three haunted houses on the premises as well. A

Ulster Park's Headless Horseman is one of the scariest haunted hayrides to be found anywhere.

special children's weekend, known as A Tiny Taste of Terror, is held on the third weekend in October, and makes a particularly fun time to visit.

Facilities: Gift shop, food concessions, live entertainment.

HITS-on-the-Hudson Horse Shows.

454 Washington Avenue Extension, Saugerties 12477; 845-246-8833; www.hitsshows.com. Admission on weekends only.

Located on nearly 300 acres, horse-loving kids will enjoy seeing a horse show here. There are 10 permanent all-weather hunter, jumper, and equitation rings, two amphitheaters, and hundreds of stalls on the show grounds. A fairly new addition to the horse show circuit (opened in 2004), HITS (Horse Shows in the Sun), is a fun place to visit for the entire family, especially during one of their special Saturday events like the Chili Cook-Off in July or Kids Day in August. Check the Web site for a complete schedule of the shows.

Facilities: Portable toilets, gift shop, food concessions.

Youngsters compete at HITS-on-the-Hudson Horse Shows, where there is always lots of action.

ULSTER COUNTY TOURISM

Across the street is **Sports Connection**, Washington Avenue, Saugerties 12477, 845-246-4501. Admission.

This is an activity-filled fun place for kids who love go-carts; the track is a figure eight with some extra turns tossed in for good measure.

After a ride, try the batting cages with adjustable speeds (softball and baseball), or play a round on the 18-hole miniature golf course complete with waterfalls and fountains—a good way for the kids to expend extra summer energy!

Facilities: Restrooms, retail shop, food concessions.

Homegrown Mini-Golf at Kelder's Farm. 5755 US 209, Kerhonkson 12446; 845-626-7137; www.homegrownminigolf.com. Admission.

The unusual miniature golf course here is landscaped with real fruits, vegetables, and grains, and all the plantings are edible. There are also fun and challenging hazards made of vintage farm tools. An enormous gnome, Chomsky, greets visitors. According to the Guinness Book of World Records, he is the world's largest garden gnome standing tall at 13 feet 6 inches (and makes a terrific photo op!). After golf, check out the pick-your-own farm and see what's ready for harvesting (**see Pick-Your-Own, pg. 120**).

Facilities: Restrooms, farm store.

Kaleidoworld at Emerson Resort and Spa. 5340 NY 28, Mt. Tremper 12457; 845-688-5800; www.emersonplace.com. Admission (only for Kaleidoworld).

The Emerson Resort and Spa is housed in a restored 19th-century building and has become known by travelers in the county for fine dining, accommodations, shopping, and family entertainment. Kaleidoworld is where kids will enjoy seeing the world's largest kaleidoscope, at 60 feet in height. They will actually enter the scope, lean back on supports, and view the changing colors and patterns overhead while music plays in the background. The result is an indescribable sound and light show that kids will find impressive. After seeing the show, visit the variety of shops in the complex—one of them with an enormous collection of kaleidoscopes ranging in price from a few dollars to thousands of dollars. There is a café in the hotel with a deck where you can

The Emerson Resort is home to the world's largest kaleidoscope. Don't miss the multi-media Kaleidoshow!

enjoy a snack alfresco as well as a full-service restaurant. Another café is located in the excellent bookstore that features a wonderful selection of regional books and maps. For those interested in overnight accommodations, the Emerson Lodge's log-built exterior has 27 rooms (including many multiroom suites) and offers a family-friendly atmosphere. Additionally, from the lodge it's just a short walk to the Emerson Country Store and restaurants.

Facilities: Restrooms, gift shop, restaurant, café, parking area. Wheelchair and stroller accessible. Full service resort, lodge, and spa.

A display of old ships at the Hudson River Maritime Museum recalls a time when the Rondout was a bustling port. ULSTER COUNTY TOURISM

Rondout Waterfront and Gazebo. At the end of Broadway, Kingston 12401. Open year-round.

At the on-site Hudson River Maritime Museum (**see pg. 102**), children interested in ships will enjoy the changing exhibits—which have featured tugboats, fishing, and sailing craft. Outside on the waterfront, both old and new ships tie up in port and in the summer visitors have a chance to view some historically important vessels. At the gazebo on weekends there is often live music and the ambiance is festive and colorful. Strollers will have an easy time maneuvering through the streets and waterfront area. This is a great place to enjoy refreshments and ice cream on a hot weekend afternoon. This area was one of the leading maritime centers of upstate New York during the 19th century, and today the restored buildings, museum, and ships make this a bustling port once more.

Water Street Market. 10 Main Street, New Paltz 12561; 845-255-1403; www.waterstreetmarket.com. Open year-round. This quaint open-air market is chock-full of action. There are 20 lovely stores (many featuring locally made items), a coffee bar, a café (serving excellent organic soups, sandwiches, and other creations that may be enjoyed al fresco in the warm weather), sculpture garden, antiques center, and more. Do check the Web site for special events; there's live music on many weekends.

Facilities: Restrooms, gift shop, restaurant, parking area. Easily navigated by strollers and wheelchairs on paved paths. Access to the Wallkill Valley Rail Trail is across the street and is a nice place to take a walk in the woods after a visit to the shops.

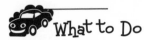 What to Do

ARCHERY

Robin Hood Archery. 707 Fischer Lane, Accord 12404; 845-626-0983. Open year-round. There are both indoor and outdoor ranges and shooting areas here. It's a great place to introduce children to the sport of archery, and an excellent activity for a rainy day.

BICYCLING

Ashokan Reservoir. Take NY 28 west to Shokan and make a left onto Winchell Road. Bear left at the fork in the road onto NY 28A and follow signs. Open year-round. Free. This is a wonderful place to bicycle, walk, run, or in-line skate. A 1.25-mile stretch of pavement along part of the reservoir, it offers magnificent views of the surrounding Catskill peaks. The area is also renowned for its eagles' nests; if you are lucky, you may see one fly by or get a glimpse of an eagle perched in a tree. The area is closed to vehicular traffic and dogs are not permitted. The sign on NY 28A that reads "Public Parking" is the entrance to this special spot.

Hudson Valley Rail Trail. 12 Church Street, Highland 12528; 845-483-0428, 845-691-8666; www.hudsonvalleyrailtrail.net. Open year-round. This 4.2-mile nature trail extends from the Mid-Hudson Bridge through the town of Lloyd. There is a 2-mile paved portion of the trail. A great spot for family bicycle outings, this trail is part of a network of over 1,000 rail trails that cover 10,000 miles across America. Turnoffs along the way run to overlooks and down to the banks of the Hudson, and these are great places to get off your bicycle for a picnic.

Shawangunk Rail Trail. 14 Central Avenue, Wallkill 12589; 845-895-2611; www.traillink.com. Open year-round. This 3-mile section of unpaved rail trail with views of the Shawangunk Mountains provides easy access to the Wallkill River and village of Wallkill. It is also a nice ride for mountain bikers.

Wallkill Valley Rail Trail. www.gorail.org. Open year-round. This 12-mile trail is where a railroad line ran during the late 19th century. The easiest access is near the entrance to Water Street Market in the village of New Paltz, just before the bridge over the Wallkill River. Once a busy link to New York City, used by both commuters to get to work and by farmers to ship their goods to market, it is now a popular recreational park. The rail trail, located between the New Paltz–Rosendale and Gardiner-Shawangunk town lines, officially opened to the public in 1993. Visitors of all ages are encouraged to walk, jog, or ride bicycles here. It provides an excellent place for children to learn to bike or roller-skate. Motorized vehicles used by the disabled are permitted. Check the Web site for information on flora and fauna along the route as well as any special events.

BOAT CRUISES

Hudson River Cruises. Rondout Landing, Kingston 12401; 845-340-4700, 1-800-843-7472; www.hudsonriver cruises.com.

The offering here is a two-hour cruise going south from Kingston for one hour toward the Hyde Park area, passing both the Kingston and Esopus Meadows lighthouses. Enjoy the roomy ship *Rip Van Winkle,* which

A sightseeing cruise on the Rip Van Winkle includes a close-up view of the Esopus Meadows Lighthouse.

features plenty of seating, a snack bar, and restrooms for the comfort of passengers. The river tends to be less choppy than the ocean and the ride is smooth and pleasant. Some trips feature themes and live music; check the Web site for a schedule of events.

North River Charters. Rondout Landing, Kingston 12401; 845-750-6025; www.theteal.com. The *Minsis,* a 40-foot express motor yacht, holds up to six people and is fully safety equipped as well as air-conditioned for your comfort. John Cutten, an experienced captain, will tailor a river trip to suit your interests and budget. **North River Cruises** (a sister company)

PHOTO COURTESY OF ULSTER COUNTY TOURISM

operates the *Teal,* a medium-sized boat fitted with rich wood and brass; the atmosphere aboard takes one back to a time of genteel river travel. Still, there are all the modern amenities, including restrooms and a snack bar.

CANOEING AND KAYAKING

Atlantic Kayak Tours. 320 West Saugerties Road, Saugerties 12477; 845-246-2187; www.atlantickayaktours.com. For kayak trips on the Hudson River, Esopus, and other local waterways, this outfitter will make an excursion fun for paddlers of all ages; this a particularly good way to go for first-timers.

City of Kingston Kayak Tours. 467 Broadway, Kingston 12401; 845-331-1682 x.132; www.forsythnaturecenter.org. Guided nature-oriented kayak tours on the Hudson River and Rondout Creek are given here. Sightings include bald eagles, osprey, turtles, and more. This is perfect for children who are particularly interested in wildlife. Check the Web site for a full schedule of tours.

FISHING

Ulster County is a good place to take your children fishing for the first time since it's easy to get to many fishing areas that are well marked— and well stocked (so chances are good the kids will catch something and enjoy the outing!). The waters here offer a variety of fish—trout, bass, and pickerel, to name just a few. Remember that New York State licenses are required for anyone over the age of 16, and you must have a permit to fish in the **Ashokan Reservoir** (NY 28A, west of Kingston) and the **Kingston City Reservoir** (off Zena Road between Kingston and Woodstock). Call the **Department of Environmental Conservation Department of Fisheries,** 845-256-3161, in New Paltz for information. There are few fishing guide services in the region due to the fact that the Esopus and other streams are so accessible.

Some of the better-known streams in the county include the following: The renowned **Esopus Creek** is easily accessed along NY 28 west of Kingston. The **Rondout Creek** has a number of access points along US 209 south of Kingston. **Plattekill Creek** is easy to get to from NY 32 in Saugerties, and **Sawkill Creek** is close to NY 212 in Woodstock.

Many access points for fishing in the county are indicated by brown-and-yellow state signs, and some have parking areas.

HIKING

Black Creek Forest Preserve. US 9W and Winding Brook Acres Road, Esopus 12429; 845-473-4440.

A 130-acre gem that lies along a major Hudson River tributary, Black Creek Forest Preserve is a wonderful choice for young hikers. Walkers will cross a suspension footbridge over Black Creek and pass through forest woodlands with vernal pools on the three hiking trails (a total of 2.5 miles) that have direct access to the Hudson River. This is a great place for a short hike; keep in mind that it always seems somewhat cooler here since much of the trail area is shaded and close to the river.

Esopus Meadows Point Preserve. About 1 mile from the intersection of US 9W and River Road, Port Ewen 12466; 845-454-7673.

This 100-acre site offers great views of the Esopus Meadows Lighthouse, three trails, and an environmental center. The trails are easy to walk, with gently sloping terrain, and they follow the Hudson River in many places.

Frost Valley YMCA. 2000 Frost Valley Road, Claryville 12410; CR 47 off NY 28, near Big Indian; 845-985-2291; www.frostvalley.org. Open year-round.

This YMCA has over 5,000 acres to explore and is a wonderful place for school groups and families to spend an overnight visit. Some of the activities in addition to hiking include ropes courses, astronomy, archery, and summer special events including workshops in the arts. There is an emphasis on projects that involve the entire family. In the winter this is a great place to go cross-country skiing or participate in an array of activities like snowshoeing, a bowl-a-thon, or a maple-sugarhouse hike. The lodge is built in the elegant style of the older Catskill camps, and the cafeteria even has an exhibit that focuses on nature writer John Burroughs. The programs are all reasonably priced.

Minnewaska State Park. US 44/NY 55, New Paltz 12561; 845-255-0752; www.nysparks.state.ny.us. Open year-round. Admission.

The Shawangunk trails here are beautiful and offer magnificent views, although the park can get quite crowded on summer weekends. Some of the longer hikes are best for older children but the walk to Awosting Lake may be a good choice for those with younger kids. (Make sure to call before heading out to Minnewaska since hours of operation here may be curtailed due to New York State budget constraints.)

Mohonk Mountain House and Skytop Observation Tower. 1000 Mountain Rest Road, New Paltz 12561; 845-255-1000; www.mohonk.com. Open year-round. Admission. This Victorian-style resort surrounding a beauti-

A sweeping view of the Shawangunk Ridge from the Skytop Observation Tower at Mohonk. ULSTER COUNTY TOURISM

ful lake is world-famous and has been owned and operated by the same family for generations. The spirit of the resort revolves around preservation of the 2,200 acres located in the heart of the Shawangunk Mountains. You can visit Mohonk for a meal, a day, or overnight—although restrictions apply to day-use passes. It's a nice place to visit for a day hike; the trail around the lake is fairly flat and is easy for even the youngest children. Considering its old-fashioned ambience, Mohonk caters surprisingly well to families. Supervised children's programs are available on weekends year-round and daily in the summer season—for overnight guests only. Mohonk specializes in theme weekends and some are particularly suitable for children. If you need to get away with the kids during the winter, try a stay here during President's Day weekend—with snow tubing, cross-country skiing, ice skating, snow sculpture contests, and more.

Onteora Lake. NY 28, Kingston 12401. Located approximately 4 miles west of the New York State Thruway exit 19, on the right; the parking lot is next to Catskill Mountain Coffee Roasters. There are approximately 12 miles of marked trails here that traverse relatively flat terrain. There is also a small lake, and for those who have their own kayak or canoe, it's a nice place to paddle and enjoy a picnic!

Overlook Mountain. Meads Mountain Road, Woodstock 12498. This trail is a moderate walk up a graded roadbed. From Tinker Street at the village green, take Rock City Road to Meads Mountain Road. The trailhead begins across from the Tibetan monastery on the right side of the road. The summit takes about an hour to reach, walking at a leisurely pace. You pass the ruins of the Overlook Mountain House on the way up; a lookout tower and picnic tables await you at the top of the moun-

From the top of Overlook Mountain you can see the Ashokan Reservoir as well as the Hudson River. ULSTER COUNTY TOURISM

tain, where the views are spectacular. On a clear day you can see the Rhinecliff Bridge, the Ashokan Reservoir, and the Hudson River.

Wilson State Park. 859 Wittenberg Road, Mt. Tremper 12457; 845-256-3099. (Take NY 28 west from Kingston 13 miles to NY 212, and make a right. Wittenberg Road is the first right turn; follow to the park entrance on the right.) Open year-round; limited winter hours. Admission (charged during the summer).

This is a small state park where you can enjoy canoeing on a small lake as well as walking on several marked trails. The park is surrounded by mountains and is close to the village of Woodstock. This is a wonderful place to stop with small children. There are picnic areas with tables. The hiking trails are transformed into cross-country ski trails during the winter. Keep in mind there are no services here, however. Groups are accommodated and campsites for overnight stays may be reserved by advance reservation.

When you are finished at Wilson Park, head into **Woodstock;** follow Wittenberg Road east (make a right out of the park) and then make a left at the fork. Continue to the junction with NY 212; make a right and follow the road into the village. This is the town of the Aquarian Age, and there are often an array of colorful characters on the village green— including musicians and tarot card readers. There are a number of interesting shops to be seen while wandering along Tinker Street, the main thoroughfare. The kids will enjoy an ice cream, and on a summer day the village green is usually packed with young people. At **Woodstock Wonderworks** (NY 375, in back of the elementary school; 845-679-2316; open daily year-round; free), kids will see a Robert Leathers-and-children-designed playground. The multilevel wooden structure includes a castle maze, space tunnel, dragon slide, Viking ship, haunted house, and more—all designed to stimulate a child's imagination. This stop is a good one for those with active children. Facilities include wheelchair accessible areas, but no restrooms.

HORSEBACK RIDING

Mohonk Mountain House. 1000 Mountain Rest Road, New Paltz 12561; 845-255-1000; www.mohonk.com. Open year-round.

Enjoy the trails and carriage rides through 2,200 historic acres by advance reservation only. Those who are not guests of the hotel must purchase a day pass in addition to the charge for horseback riding.

Pine Grove Ranch. 30 Cherrytown Road, Kerhonkson 12446; 1-800-346-4626, 845-626-7345; www.pinegroveranch.com. Open year-round.

For over 35 years, this family-owned and -operated resort has provided an informal, inexpensive getaway for people of all ages. The 600-acre property offers a host of activities. In addition to horseback riding, there is an indoor pool, an outdoor pool with a double-flume water slide, archery, handball, table tennis, a rock wall, a fitness center, volleyball, paddleboating, lake fishing, and a daily activity schedule offering guests a range of choices. Children from the ages of 3–11 can enjoy Li'l Maverick Day Camp, which runs from 9–5, while parents enjoy a game of shuffleboard, relax by the pool, or have a massage. There is a baby animal farm on the premises, as well. Inexperienced riders will feel comfortable going on a leisurely beginner ride through the woods. More experienced riders may go on a cattle drive and enjoy the flavor of the Old West. With nightly entertainment, there is a lot to amuse the entire family. A down-home atmosphere prevails, and all-inclusive rates include three meals, snacks, and activities. All rooms have private baths, TV, and air-conditioning. A great getaway if the kids are horse lovers.

Rocking Horse Ranch. 600 US 44/NY 55, Highland 12528; 845-691-2927, 1-800-64-RANCH; www.rockinghorseranch.com. Open year-round.

For decades, this family-owned and -operated ranch resort has offered a variety of vacation packages. The all-inclusive room rate incorporates sumptuous meals and horseback riding on acres of trails. During the summer months, there is waterskiing and boating on the lovely lake here, as well as tennis, miniature golf, and volleyball. The ranch also has heated indoor and outdoor pools, saunas, a gym, a petting zoo, and organized activities for the kids. There is entertainment in the lounge nightly. All rooms have private baths, TV, and air-conditioning.

ICE SKATING

Kiwanis Ice Arena. Cantine Memorial Complex, Washington Avenue, Saugerties 12477; 845-246-2590; www.kiwanisicearena.com. Admission.

Sessions are 1.5 hours long and there are rentals, restrooms, a snack bar, and bleachers at this enclosed (not indoor) rink. It can be quite cold on frigid winter days so dress the kids accordingly. I skate here regularly and most weekdays the rink has very few skaters. Weekends are always busy. Admission and rental charges are very reasonable.

Mohonk Mountain House. 1000 Mountain Rest Road, New Paltz 12561; 845-255-1000; www.mohonk.com. Admission. (Skating here can be an expensive family outing; a day pass must be purchased along with skating fees for each person.)

This beautiful outdoor rink, in a Victorian open-air pavilion constructed of stone and wood, is a lovely place to ice skate. The rink is fairly small and can get quite crowded on winter weekends. However, the setting is picturesque—with a huge outdoor fireplace adjacent to the rink so skaters can warm up if they feel chilled. This is a terrific place for the youngest skaters and for novices. (The ice here is always like glass . . . in excellent condition!)

PICK-YOUR-OWN FARMS AND MAPLE SYRUP HOUSES

Ulster County has the largest number of on-farm retail markets of any county in New York State and this is just a sampling of some of the wonderful places to add to your itinerary when you are driving through the county. March is usually the time to stop at one of the maple syrup houses. And during autumn apples and pumpkins are ready for picking and fresh cider is being pressed; this is my favorite time to visit!

Arrowhead Farm. 5941 US 209, Kerhonkson 12446; 845-626-7293. The time for maple syrup tasting and tours is mid-February to mid-April, depending on the weather. The owners of Arrowhead Farm will be glad to show you around and sell you their delicious syrup, maple cream, and honey. It's a good idea, however, to call before you go, since erratic weather affects the sap season.

The area has a couple of other maple syrup producers open to the public. **Lyonsville Sugarhouse,** 591 CR 2, Accord 12404 (845-687-2518), offers tours in season. **Oliverea School House Maple Syrup,** 609 Oliverea Road, Oliverea 12410 (845-254-5296), is open year-round for tours with 3,000 taps in the Catskills. Syrup is also available for sale throughout the year. **Sugar Brook Maple Farm,** 351 Samsonville Road, Kerhonkson 12446 (845-626-3466), has wonderful tours and is open year-round for sales.

Jenkins-Leuken Orchards. NY 299 West (4 miles west of village of New Paltz), Gardiner 12525; 845-255-0999; www.jlorchards.com. You can pick your own apples and pumpkins here in season. They have a large variety of apples, including those marvelous Macouns. Pears, peaches, tomatoes, and vegetables are also available in season. Honey and cider are produced on the farm as well. Check the Web site or call to see what crops are ready for harvesting.

Kelder's Farm. 5575 US 209, Kerhonkson 12446; 845-626-7137; www .kelderfarm.com. Open year-round. This family-owned and -operated farm has been in business since 1836 offering an array of crops, including berries of all kinds and pumpkins too—all for picking. There is a lot to do and see here for the youngest children, who will enjoy the petting zoo and milking a cow. A miniature golf course will delight children as well (**see Additional Attractions, pg. 110**). There are excellent farm tours too, making this an ideal place for school groups. Arrangements must be made in advance for group visits. Check the Web site for special events.

Liberty View Farm. 340 Crescent Avenue, Highland 12528; 845-883-7004; www.libertyviewfarm.biz. This delightful farm, with spectacular views of the Shawangunks, is one of the best places in the Hudson Valley to pick apples, and one of the few places where apples are grown organically. Absolutely no chemical pesticides are used on the crops, and their Cortlands are among the best I've ever tasted. The free-range heirloom-breed chickens and goats will delight the children. Make sure to visit the chicken coop and speak with owner Billiam van Roestenberg who organizes several festivals at the farm. Children can also participate in the Lease-an-Apple Tree and Charter-a-Chicken program: Farmer Billiam will be happy to explain how they work. The Web site lists a full schedule of special events at the farm.

Billiam van Roestenberg of Liberty View Farm is one of the few farmers who grows apples using only organic methods. JOANNE MICHAELS

Saunderskill Farm. 5100 US 209, Accord 12404; 845-626-2676; www.saunderskill.com. This beautiful family-owned and -operated farm, named for the tributary of the Rondout Creek that flows through the farm, is one of my favorite places to pick strawberries, blueberries, and pumpkins in season. There is a wonderful market and greenhouse on the premises offering an array of fruits, vegetables and homemade baked goods. (Try their wonderful cider doughnuts!) During the autumn months, children will enjoy a horse-drawn hayride. Special events throughout the season include an antique tractor pull and corn festival. There are 800 acres here and it is the second oldest farm in the country . . . and still run by the Schoonmaker family.

Stone Ridge Orchard. 3012 NY 213, Stone Ridge 12484; 845-687-0447; www.stoneridgeorchard.com. Open in season for pick-your-own apples, pumpkins, and raspberries. They have over a dozen varieties of apples here, and the orchard is surrounded by hundreds of acres of forest and farmland. There are hayrides for the kids, picnic benches, and fresh cider. The shop on the premises offers maple syrup, home-baked pies, and other treats. This spot is easy to find, right off US 209 on NY 213, and it's a beautiful place to stop for a couple of hours on an autumn afternoon.

Tantillo Farm. 730 NY 208, Gardiner 12525; 845-255-6196; www.tantillos farm.com. You can pick cherries, apples, pears, peaches, tomatoes, and pumpkins (depending on the season) at this 130-acre property south of

New Paltz. The Tantillo family farm is a diverse operation—so when you tire of picking, stop into the ice cream bar or bakery for one of their homemade treats. There is also a farm stand and farmer's market on the premises.

Wilklow Orchards. 341 Pancake Hollow Road, Highland 12528; 845-691-2339; www.wilkloworchards.com. (From New York State Thruway exit 18, turn right on NY 299 and go 2.3 miles. Turn right on New Paltz Road, go for 1 mile, and make a right on Pancake Hollow Road. The orchard is 1 mile up the road.) One of the oldest family-run pick-your-own farms, Wilklow has been in business for more than 100 years. They are open for apple picking (10 varieties are offered) and pumpkins. The farm stand on the premises sells homegrown vegetables, fruits, and cider. Children will enjoy seeing the farm animals here as well.

ROLLER-SKATING

Skate Time 209. 5164 US 209, Accord 12404; 845-626-7971; www.skate time209.com. Open year-round. Check Web site for schedule. Note that some sessions are appropriate for beginners and young children while others are not. This completely indoor roller-skating rink, skateboard park, and arcade center is a great place for kids to be on a rainy day or when it's exceedingly hot and humid. The owners run a first-class operation and safety comes first here.
Facilities: Restrooms, snack bar, skateboard and apparel shop.

Wood 'N Wheel Family Entertainment Center. 365 Broadway, Ulster Park 12487; 845-331-9680; www.woodnwheel.com. Open year-round. Check Web site for schedule of sessions. Both roller-skating and in-line skating are featured on the 10,000-square-foot rink here. Other activities are laser tag, bumper cars, a space ball ride, rock climbing, and an arcade—lots to keep most children amused for at least an afternoon.
Facilities: Restrooms, snack bar, skateboard shop.

SKIING AND SNOWBOARDING

Belleayre Mountain. 181 Galli Curci Road (off NY 28), Highmount 12441; 845-254-5600, 1-800-942-6904; www.belleayre.com.
Belleayre is the largest downhill ski area in Ulster County and it has

Schussing along one of the many hills at Belleayre Mountain. ULSTER COUNTY TOURISM

the longest ski trail in the Catskills (the Deer Trail, at 12,024 feet). Owned by New York State, the top elevation is 3,429 feet, the highest peak in any Catskill ski area. It is also the only ski area in the state with a natural division: The upper mountain is for intermediate and expert skiers, the lower mountain is for beginners and novices—which makes it ideal for the youngest skiers. There is plenty of free parking, and a courtesy shuttle runs throughout the parking area all day. The upper mountain has nearly 40 trails and all are serviced by snowmaking equipment. There are eight lifts: a quad as well as double and triple chairlifts. New equipment makes the wait shorter and gets skiers up the slopes quickly. Runs range from novice and intermediate to extreme expert. There is also a racing program for both adults and children as well as Kidscamp, Snow Explorers, and other youth-related events. (Make sure to check out Belleayre for various activities during the warm-weather months too!)

The ski school at Belleayre is outstanding, with capable patient instructors who can teach the youngest beginner or help advanced experts polish their skills. According to *Skiing* magazine, Belleayre is the best place in the East to learn, with some of the best-trained instructors available for both private and group lessons. The Snow Explorers program is for ages three to five and offers children a gentle introduction to the sport with a half-day of on-snow instruction. A morning session (9–12) or afternoon session (1–4) may be booked and the cost includes skis, poles, helmets (required), and goggles. Lunch is also provided at a small additional cost. The basics are all covered—from putting on equipment properly and walking in ski boots, to sliding on snow. The next level is the Kidscamp that offers a full day of instruction for children aged 4–12 for skiing and 7–12 for snowboarding. The program includes four hours of lessons, rentals (if needed), lunch, and supervision for the day. Groups are formed according to level of ability as well as age. Participants may advance to a higher level as abilities progress throughout the day. Registration runs from 8–9 in the morning and a full day of activities continues until 3:30. There is a break for lunch from 12–1. There is a program just for children ages five to seven between 11–1 with parental participation required, as well as group clinics throughout the day for those age eight and older. Private lessons run hourly from 9–3. There is also a program for young people who are physically challenged with highly trained staff. (Snowboards are popular here—with rentals, sales, and instruction available—and there is a terrain park and half-pipe).

The Overlook Lodge (upper lodge) is a huge, welcoming log building with a fieldstone fireplace, bar, ski shop, cafeteria, lounge area, and outside deck. The Discovery Lodge (lower lodge) has a cafeteria and ski shop. Both offer rental equipment, restrooms, and lockers.

There are music festivals and children's programs in summer and fall and Belleayre is very family and service oriented. The Belleayre Beach at Pine Hill (**see Swimming, pg. 125**) provides swimming, picnicking, horseshoe pits, volleyball, basketball, rowboats, pedal boats, kayak rentals, and fishing. There is an Aqua School with swimming lessons for children. The Eco-Adventures are a place for children and adults to explore together during the summer with hikes, hands-on nature crafts, projects on solar power, ecosystems, and local legend and lore—all the programs are free of charge.

The old-fashioned feeling about the ski center reminds me of the place I learned to ski in the Hudson Valley in the early 1960s. It's a favorite of many local residents, offering good value for the money and a variety of discount days (check the Web site) and package deals for families (including a kids ski free/stay free program for those under the age of 17). I shouldn't neglect to mention you get to ski free on your birthday!

Facilities: *Restrooms, cafeteria, snack bar, lodge, ski shop, lockers, rentals.*

Sawkill Family Ski Center. 167 Hill Road, Kingston 12401; 845-336-6977; www.sawkillski.com. (Located off Sawkill and Jockey Hill Roads.)

This is the smallest ski area in the East, with one rope tow and a snow tube run with its own lift. There are three ski trails and a nice terrain park for snowboarding; they make lots of snow here and keep the area in great condition. This is an ideal place for young children to learn to ski and the lift tickets are relatively inexpensive. Rentals of skis and snowboard equipment are available.

Facilities: *Restrooms, snack bar, ski shop (both new and used equipment and clothing for sale), full equipment rental.*

SWIMMING

Kingston Point Beach. 53 Delaware Avenue, Kingston 12401; 845-338-0670. (Take Broadway to the end, turn left, and follow East Strand [becomes North Street] 1 mile to the park.) Open year-round. Free.

This small beach on the Hudson River is run by the city. There are no services, and it isn't advisable to swim in the Hudson River even now that it is much cleaner than it once was, but it is still a beautiful spot to sunbathe and enjoy the river views. Kids will love the sandy beach and small playground; they will also enjoy watching the boats pass by on the river. There are no facilities here.

Minnewaska State Park. US 44/NY 55, New Paltz 12561; 845-255-0752. Admission. Open for swimming in Lake Awosting and in the park at designated beach areas only where there are lifeguards on duty. (It is recommended that you call ahead to make sure the swimming areas are operating and lifeguards are on-site.)

This is a great place to be since there is also excellent hiking in the park when you want to move on to another activity. Keep in mind that being high up in the Shawangunks, the weather is always a few degrees cooler than at lower elevations in the valley below; bring sweatshirts and a change of clothes for the late afternoon. The scenery here is phenomenal and Minnewaska is one of the most scenic places in the region. There are restrooms and picnic areas but this is not a place for strollers or wheelchairs.

Pine Hill Day Use Area. NY 28, Highmount 12441; 845-254-5600, 845-254-5202. Admission. This lovely lake offers swimming, boating, and fishing, with a beach area, picnic pavilions, and a snack bar. Bring your own canoe or rent a kayak, paddleboat, or rowboat at reasonable prices. The area is run by the State of New York and admission is charged per car. The beach is roped off into different sections with a diving area and special place for toddlers, which makes this area a good choice for those with very young children.

Ulster Landing Park. Ulster Landing Road (off NY 32), Kingston 12401; 845-336-8484, 845-340-3300. This county-owned and -run park offers a small, quiet, sandy beach area just north of the Rhinecliff Bridge, with swimming in the Hudson River—although, as with Kingston Point Beach, swimming in the Hudson is still not advisable. Restrooms and a picnic pavilion make it an inviting spot for families, along with the fact that it is somewhat off the beaten track and less crowded than other swimming areas.

THEATER

Bird-On-a-Cliff Theatre Company. 45 Comeau Drive, Woodstock 12498; 845-247-4007; www.birdonacliff.org. This theater company has been producing the plays of Shakespeare for over a decade at the Comeau property (where the town offices are located). This is a wonderful pastoral place to enjoy a picnic dinner and take in some theater at the right price ($5 suggested donation per person). It is also a fine way to expose young children to classical theater in a venue where they can run around if they get restless (the property is extensive and there are places away from the stage area to move around with the children). They also offer dramatic productions at the Woodstock Playhouse during the summer months; check the Web site for a current schedule.

Shadowland Theatre. 157 Canal Street, Ellenville 12428; 845-647-5511; www.shadowlandtheatre.org. This is the county's only professional non-profit theater company featuring a five-play main-stage season in a 90-year-old building, once an art deco movie and vaudeville house. Now there are 148 seats and all of them are within 25 feet of the stage. Most of the offerings would only be appropriate for older children, but check the Web site for the season schedule since there are comedies and new plays that often appeal to all ages.

Shandaken Theatrical Society. 10 Church Street, Phoenicia 12464; 845-688-2279; www.stsplayhouse.com. This community theater organization produces a musical like *Godspell* or *Hair* every spring, a drama or comedy in the fall, and a summer production. The choices are often classics that will appeal to the entire family. There are also films and children's events during the summer. Prices are extremely reasonable. Check the Web site for dates and times of the various productions.

Unison Arts and Learning Center. 68 Mountain Rest Road, New Paltz 12561; 845-255-1559; www.unisonarts.org. Open year-round. This multi-arts center hosts performances of jazz, folk, dance, and children's theater, and has some excellent programs at reasonable prices. Check the Web site or join their mailing list for schedule updates. The center itself has a lovely outdoor sculpture garden.

UPAC. 601 Broadway, Kingston 12401; 845-331-1613; www.bardavon.org. Listed on the National Register of Historic Places, this renovated theater is the latest arts showcase in the county, offering a variety of theater and musical performances. Call or go to the Web site for a complete schedule.

Woodstock Playhouse. 103 Mill Hill Road, Woodstock 12498; 845-339-4340; www.woodstockplayhouse.org. This summer performing arts venue features a variety of events in music and theater, including children's performances. Check the Web site; it lists the complete schedule. (At press time, plans were underway to enclose the open-air structure and make other improvements so that the Woodstock Playhouse can be used year-round.)

TUBING

Town Tinker Tube Rental. 10 Bridge Street, Phoenicia 12464; 845-688-5553; www.towntinker.com.

If you want to try tubing, head to Phoenicia and spend the day floating on the whitewater of the Esopus Creek. This makes an adventurous, fun outing for older children (at least 12), who will enjoy bouncing along on a large inner tube. Although this is a popular activity, there are some caveats: The water is usually not more than 60 degrees, so pick a very hot day or rent a wet suit to ensure that the trip is comfortable. Life vests, helmets, and sneakers (for protection against the rocks) are required for those under the age of 14. Kids should never tube alone. July and August are the top months for this activity, and there are both novice and advanced river courses. On weekends, you can take the Catskill Mountain Railroad (**see pg. 107**) back upriver to where you started your journey.

Facilities: Portable toilets, changing areas, picnic areas, parking area.

DUTCHESS COUNTY

▼▲▼▲▼▲▼

An area of 800 square miles with 30 miles of Hudson River shoreline, Dutchess County has something to please everyone in the family. Get back to simpler times on the farm; visit exotic animals at a zoo; or marvel at aerobatic demonstrations at a museum of antique airplanes. You can also experience nature's marvels at an environmental education center or attend a hot-air balloon festival. These are just some of the activities families will enjoy on a trip here.

County highlights include the **Trevor Zoo** in Millbrook has more than a hundred exotic and indigenous species in exhibits covering 4 acres on the grounds of the Millbrook School. The **Old Rhinebeck Aerodrome** showcases antique and replica planes in displays and theatrical air shows that include costumed performers and period cars. Families that yearn for the opportunity to feel connected to the natural world on vacation might visit pick-you-own farms, which allow visitors to enjoy fresh air, exercise, and plenty of delicious treats. Summer's bounty includes a variety of berries, while fall brings apples and pumpkins.

Nature and education centers are recommended for Dutchess-bound families seeking to combine fun and learning. The 756-acre **Stony Kill Environmental**

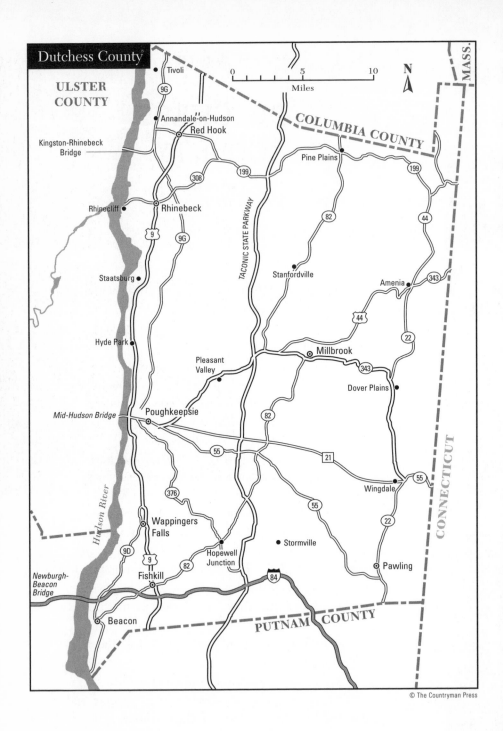

Dutchess County

ULSTER COUNTY

COLUMBIA COUNTY

MASS.

Tivoli

9G

0   5   10
Miles

N

Annandale-on-Hudson
Red Hook

Kingston-Rhinebeck
Bridge

Pine Plains

199

199

308

199

82

44

Rhinecliff

Rhinebeck

9

9G

TACONIC STATE PARKWAY

Stanfordville

Amenia

343

Staatsburg

44

22

Hyde Park

Millbrook

343

Pleasant
Valley

Dover Plains

Mid-Hudson Bridge

Poughkeepsie

82

55

21

Hudson River

55

Wingdale

55

376

22

Wappingers
Falls

55

Stormville

9D

9

82

Hopewell
Junction

Pawling

Fishkill

84

Newburgh-
Beacon
Bridge

Beacon

PUTNAM COUNTY

CONNECTICUT

© The Countryman Press

Center in Wappingers Falls provides children's programs focusing on natural history, ecology, and farming. The **Mid-Hudson Children's Museum** in Poughkeepsie gives young people a chance to learn while they explore over 50 art and science exhibits, including a computer center, interactive videos, and dinosaurs.

Whatever the season, Dutchess has a wealth of festivals and special events to celebrate the spirit of family fun. The **Mid-Hudson Balloon Festival** takes place at various sites in the county in July. And one of the biggest special annual events, the **Dutchess County Fair,** is held the third week in August in Rhinebeck—it's the second largest agricultural fair in New York State. There are competitions for the best cows, sheep, and horses—and the kids will love the rides, games, and cotton candy. It's a great way to show children where their food comes from and to expose them to the people who produce it, the county's farmers. If you visit in September, try to get to the **Celtic Day** in the park in Staatsburg, a cul-

Fun for the kids is central whether you attend the annual Dutchess County Fair in Rhinebeck in August or a Renegades game at Dutchess Stadium.

tural celebration featuring Scottish pipe bands, Irish dancing, caber tossing, and sheepdog herding. **The Kids' Expo** is also held in September in Poughkeepsie, with more than 100 hands-on projects and exhibitions. My favorite autumn event is the **Tivoli Street Painting Festival,** when kids are assigned a segment of pavement and receive free pastel chalks to decorate the street as they wish—a rare privilege!

Relatively recent major cultural additions to the landscape include the **Fisher Center for the Performing Arts** at Bard College and **Dia: Beacon Arts Museum,** which both draw thousands of visitors to the county. The future looks bright for Dutchess, one of the most prosperous counties in the state.

For further information, contact the **Dutchess County Tourism Promotion Agency,** 3 Neptune Road, Poughkeepsie 12601; 845-436-4000, 1-800-445-3131; www.dutchesstourism.com.

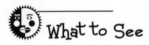 What to See

MUSEUMS AND HISTORIC SITES

Beacon Institute for Rivers and Estuaries. 199 Main Street, Beacon 12508; 845-838-1600; www.thebeaconinstitute.org. Free.

An evolving global center for research and education, this organization is dedicated to rivers, estuaries, and their connection to the world. The activities offered here will interest most children. The institute is housed in a couple of locations in the city. Building 1 (a visitors center), at Dennings Point along the waterfront, focuses on educational activities. The structure has solar panels, composting toilets, and a "green roof" filled with plants that act as natural insulation. (Make sure to take a walk here on one of the two short scenic trails. The Denning Point State Park trail offers wonderful views of the Hudson River and is an easy loop less than 2 miles in length. The Riverside Trail connects this area to the train station and is less than a 1 mile walk.) The main building will be a state-of-the-art environmental research facility with labs, conference rooms, and a center for advanced technology that will be under development in the future. There are other continually changing venues to explore as well. The Web site contains up-to-date information about the array of exciting exhibits and events taking place here, so it's a good idea to check in advance and discover what will be happening when you visit Beacon.

Facilities: Restrooms, picnic areas, bookstore (Main Street location).

Dia: Beacon. 3 Beekman Street, Beacon 12508; 845-440-0100; www .diabeacon.org. (Located off I-84 and NY 9D on Beekman Street; follow signs to the railroad station.) Admission (children under the age of 12 enter free).

This 240,000-square-foot museum, which contains works from Dia's permanent collection, is housed in a renovated printing plant originally built in 1929 by Nabisco along the shores of the Hudson River. The name "Dia," taken from the Greek word meaning "through," was chosen to suggest the Dia Art Foundation's role in enabling extraordinary artistic projects that might not be realized without financial assistance. The foundation has become internationally recognized as one of the world's most influential contemporary art institutions. Kids will enjoy the exhibits of American art of the 1960s and 1970s (including works by Andy Warhol, Agnes Martin, and Richard Serra, to name just a few) since most of it is large scale. And if they are not engaged by the artwork, they will certainly appreciate the structure—which is fascinating, with the galleries illuminated almost entirely by natural light.

Facilities: Restrooms, cafeteria, gift shop. Wheelchair and stroller accessible. Backpack and baby pack carriers are not permitted inside the museum.

A visit to Locust Grove gives children a glimpse of family life in the early 20th century.

DUTCHESS COUNTY TOURISM

Locust Grove (Samuel Morse Historic Site). 2683 South Road (US 9), Poughkeepsie 12601; 845-454-4500; www.lgny.org. Admission (children under the age of six are admitted free). Group tours by advance reservation.

This charming house, a National Historic Landmark, was the home of Samuel F. B. Morse, artist and inventor. The Italianate villa, designed by Morse and architect Alexander Jackson Davis, contains the extensive collection of furniture and decorative arts assembled by the Young family, who purchased the estate from the Morse heirs in 1901 and lived there until 1975. Children may know that Morse developed the telegraph and Morse code, but are surprised to learn that he was also a famous painter.

After the house tour, be sure to follow the short trail behind Locust Grove that leads down to the Hudson River.

In the museum galleries, several of Morse's paintings are on display along with antique telegraph equipment and interactive exhibits for youngsters to use. A tour of Locust Grove shows the life of a family in the early 20th century, complete with fine examples of artwork, furniture, and even a billiards room. The house is fascinating for children who enjoy history, but the tour is recommended for children over the age of five. The exquisite flower and kitchen gardens have been restored with flower-filled urns and lush plantings. The house is surrounded by 150 acres of lawns and trees. There are 3 miles of carriage roads and hiking trails accessible to children who like the outdoors and walking through ravines and around ponds. The area is teeming with wildlife and is easy for young children to wander. The train tracks and the Hudson River are visible from certain trails as well. There are few hills on the trails; this makes for easy walking!

Facilities: Restrooms, picnic areas, gift shop, hiking trails (self-guided tour). Wheelchairs can be accommodated in the museum and on the grounds, but not in the house.

Mid-Hudson Children's Museum. 75 North Water Street, Poughkeepsie 12601; 845-471-0589; www.mhcm.org. (At the waterfront, close to the train station.)

This hands-on museum features permanent and changing exhibits that focus on the arts and sciences. Children ages 2–12 will enjoy these educational displays, examples of which include a horizontal rock-climbing wall, a huge play structure of the heart and lungs, and "science on wheels"—which includes a bicycle gyroscope and giant bubble machine. Check the Web site or call for a schedule of activities.

Facilities: Restrooms.

Hyde Park Railroad Station. 34 River Road, Hyde Park 12538; 845-229-2338; www.hydeparkstation.com. (Located at the foot of the hill that is formed by West Market Street and River Road, off US 9.) Open year-round. Free.

This railroad station was built in 1914, based on a design shown at the Pan American World Exposition of 1898. The building was nearly demolished in 1975, when the Hudson Valley Railroad Society acquired the station and set about restoring it. Almost 30 years later, the station is on the National Register of Historic Places and houses exhibits that tell the story of the area's railroads and their history. Model trains run throughout the building, and there are always people on-board to answer questions. This is a nice stop along historic US 9, close to the Vanderbilt Mansion and Mills Norrie State Park.

Facilities: Restrooms.

Staatsburgh State Historic Site (Mills Mansion and Norrie State Park). Old Post Road, Staatsburg 12580; 845-889-8851, 845-889-4646; www.staats burgh.org. The park and mansion grounds are open year-round. Free for grounds, admission is charged for the mansion tour.

This unusual combination of state park and historic mansion is situated on over 900 acres along the Hudson River. Day-trippers will enjoy the outdoor activities of a park—there are hiking trails with lovely river views. If you want to picnic, the bluffs on the river are a great place to sit and watch the boats running up and down the Hudson. Fishing can be tried in any area of the park where there is access to the Hudson River. In the winter, cross-country ski trails snake around the park, and the mansion's hilly grounds are renowned for sledding, a sport that has been popular there for almost 300 years. The park also contains a small environmental museum with displays of local plants and animals. Special education programs are offered during the summer on birds, plants, and astronomy. Special events occur throughout the year. Everything from square dances to banjo bands, jazz ensembles, and bluegrass take place as part of the county's summer Music in the Parks program. At holiday time, plan to visit and take in the elaborate arrangements of greens and flowers, including a huge Christmas tree. Any time of year, the mansion's furnishings and decorations exemplify the wealth of the Hudson River families at the turn of the century, and while adults and older children will enjoy the house tour, younger children may prefer to stay outside in the park.

Facilities: Restrooms, picnic areas, cabins, boat launch, golf course, campsites. The clubhouse at the golf course has a restaurant open to the public. There is some wheelchair accessibility within the park. Strollers can be used on the paved walkways, but they have to be carried upstairs in the mansion.

Vanderbilt Mansion.

119 Vanderbilt Park Road, Hyde Park 12538; 845-229-7770; www.nps.org/vama. Open year-round. Admission.

While this imposing beaux-arts mansion used by Frederick Vanderbilt and his family as a spring and fall residence is a great example of Gilded Age living in the 19th century, the estate offers phenomenal views of the Hudson River along the pathways on the grounds here. The property also has some of the most amazing trees you will see anywhere in the region and most children will be delighted seeing them. The restored formal Italian gardens feature a reflecting pool, terraces, and a pergola with three levels of annuals, perennials, and roses. Older children interested in American history would enjoy the house tour, but those traveling with younger children are advised to tour the grounds on their

The majestic Vanderbilt Mansion; its formal Italian gardens are particularly beautiful in full bloom during the spring and summer months. DUTCHESS COUNTY TOURISM

own. There is an excellent gift shop on the premises open free of charge and it has a terrific selection of regional books.

The **Music in the Parks** programs held on the mansion grounds during some summer months is free and open to the public.

Facilities: Restrooms, gift shop, hiking trails. Stroller and wheelchair accessibility.

Warthin Geological Museum at Vassar College.

124 Raymond Avenue, Poughkeepsie 12603; 845-437-7000; www.earthscienceandgeography.vassar.edu. Free.

Young rockhounds will want to check out the scores of fossils, gems, and minerals that line this exhibit hall. Dioramas tell the story of the earth's formation and geologic history, and a demonstration geyser spouts every now and then. The Vassar campus is a nice place to walk after exploring the exhibits.

Facilities: Restrooms. Call ahead to be certain the museum is open on the day you plan to visit.

ADDITIONAL ATTRACTIONS

Culinary Institute of America. 1946 Campus Drive (off US 9), Hyde Park 12538; 845-452-2230, 1-800-888-7850; www.ciachef.edu. Free.

This is a terrific place to take children who enjoy cooking and baking. There are tours available by advance reservation for groups of 12 or more. Parent and Teen Days are held twice each year on Saturdays.

Founded in 1946, the school is a first-rate training institute for those who want to enter the food-service industry. The grounds provide visitors with magnificent views of the Hudson River. The courtyard has a fine display of carved pumpkins for Halloween and ice sculptures during the winter. Visitors can sample the wares at the Apple Pie Bakery Café

Visitors to the Culinary Institute can observe students hard at work in class. DUTCHESS COUNTY TOURISM

and watch confectionery experts at work. The restaurants on the premises usually require advance reservations, but you can check with the information desk if you want to dine at one and haven't planned ahead.

Facilities: Restrooms, gift shop, restaurants, café.

Dutchess County Fairgrounds. 6550 Spring Brook Avenue, (main entrance is on US 9), Rhinebeck 12572; 845-876-4000; www.dutchessfair.com. Admission.

Home of the renowned Dutchess County Fair (held annually for six days in late August) with award-winning cows, sheep, pigs, rabbits, as well as a midway with games and rides, this wonderful venue also hosts

For most kids the best part of the Dutchess County Fair is the rides!

agricultural exhibits, a flea market, and a variety of amazing shows from May through October—including a gem and mineral expo, craft fairs, car shows, and a sheep and wool family festival that shouldn't be missed if you are visiting the county in mid-October. Do check the Web site to see what's happening when you plan to be in Dutchess County.

Facilities: Restrooms, food concessions, various vendors. Wheelchair and stroller accessibility is not a problem here as there are paved paths throughout the fairgrounds.

Fisher Center for the Performing Arts at Bard College. 845-758-7900; www.fishercenter.bard.edu. (Cross the Kingston-Rhinecliff Bridge, and at the first traffic light make a left onto CR 103 or River Road; drive north for 3.5 miles.) Open year-round.

Experience music and dance performances in the East Coast's only Frank Gehry–designed performing arts center, which opened in 2003. This unique and controversial venue, an architectural wonder that enchants kids, is worth a detour for all travelers, even if just to see the

The Fisher Center, designed by Frank Gehry, is an architectural wonder that will enchant just about everyone.

exterior. The building, with a performance space consisting of two theaters, is a work of art in itself.

Facilities: Restrooms. Wheelchair accessible.

Fun Central. US 9, Wappingers Falls 12590; 845-297-1010; www.fun-central.com.

This multiactivity indoor and outdoor recreational facility with miniature golf, bumper boats, an arcade, a virtual-reality roller coaster, and laser tag is a great place to stop if you are traveling with children, especially on a rainy day. At night, teenagers hang out here in large numbers; it's best to go early in the day with young children.

Facilities: Restrooms, snack bar.

Institute of Ecosystem Studies (IES) at the Mary Flagler Cary Arboretum.

2801 Sharon Turnpike/NY 44A (off US 44), Millbrook 12545; 845-677-7600; www.ecostudies.org. Free.

Founded in 1983, the IES is dedicated to research and education relating to ecological systems. This magnificent property with an extensive internal road system may be explored on foot, bicycle, or by car. Passing the Fern Glen, you will wind through fields and lowland forests, which provide ample bird-watching opportunities. The roadway will lead to the IES greenhouse; there, learn about its integrated pest management program, follow the Economic Botany Trail, or just find a bench near a bubbling fountain and bask in the tropical splendor. The IES offers monthly ecology programs, continuing education classes, a day camp in the summer months, and a variety of other ongoing programs. This is a wonderful excursion for school groups. Through the programs here, children are offered a chance to become ecologists and immerse themselves in nature, where they can explore and discover new worlds. Check the Web site for a complete schedule.

Facilities: Restrooms.

Old Rhinebeck Aerodrome. 9 Norton Road, Rhinebeck 12572; 845-752-3200; www.oldrhinebeck.org. Admission (children under 6 admitted free, reduced admission for children ages 6–10). Group rates available for over 15 people.

This site is colorful, corny, exciting, and full of activity, especially during the air shows. Founded by the late Cole Palen, this is America's original living museum of old and restored airplanes, and it recaptures the thrill of flying that prevailed when the Red Baron and barnstorming were all the rage. The tour guides are enthusiastic experts on the finely restored planes housed in several hangars. A walking tour incorporates the Fokkers, Sopwith Snipes, and Curtiss airplanes, as well as old engines and many other vintage aircraft. Make sure you attend one

One of the vintage aircraft—and a vintage truck—at the Old Rhinebeck Aerodrome. DUTCHESS COUNTY TOURISM

of the weekend air shows in the summer—when the air hums and whines with planes, and the crowds cheer on the heroes and bad guys. Saturdays highlight the pioneer era of airplanes, with demonstration flights of old planes; on Sundays, the battles of World War I are reenacted—complete with full costumes, a parade, and the best villains in the region. The planes are either original aircraft or powered with original engines of the period, and audiences are likely to feel that each show is especially for them. Announcers describe all the overhead antics. Brave souls can schedule barnstorming rides in a 1929 open-cockpit biplane before or after the shows for an extra charge. Spectators view the air shows from an outdoor stand, so sun hats in the summer and jackets in the fall are heartily recommended. Call or check the Web site for a schedule of air shows and special events.

Facilities: Restrooms, picnic areas, parking area (free). Snacks are available, and the area is navigable by strollers and wheelchairs.

Overlook Golf and Recreation Center.
39 DeGarmo Road, Poughkeepsie 12601; 845-471-8515; www.overlookgolfcenter.com. This recreation center offers a golf driving range, an 18-hole miniature golf course, 10 lighted baseball/softball batting cages, and a go-cart track. There is plenty of activity to keep the kids occupied for an afternoon.

Facilities: Restrooms, food concessions.

Rainbow's End Butterfly Farm and Nursery.
13 Rainbow's End, Pawling 12564; 845-832-6749; www.rainbowsendfarm.biz. This wonderful 96-acre farm and breeding center for butterflies welcomes visitors to walk and picnic among the butterflies. Patricia and Cornelius du Plessis, a retired couple, own the farm with their three daughters. Make sure to visit the "flight house" where 150 monarchs, painted ladies, and black swallowtails reside. Kids may hold Gatorade "lollipops" (Q-Tips soaked in the juice) that attract the butterflies to drink right from their hands. This educational detour will delight everyone.

Facilities: Restroom, gift shop (carries caterpillar kits, jewelry, books, homemade honey, and maple syrup).

Splashdown Park/Adventure Island.
16 US 9, Fishkill 12524; 845-897-9600; www.splashdownbeach.com. Admission. Groups welcome by advance reservation.

Water parks are a wonderful break from sightseeing in the summer months, especially when younger children get hot and tired of traveling in the car. This park has five large water slides, a half-pipe, an interactive shipwreck island pool, a wave pool area, bumper boats, and an enormous arcade area. Whew! There is something that will amuse just about every child in this place, including an area for toddlers.

"The Bullet Bowl," a new attraction at the water park next to "Pirate's Plunge," offers the latest in water slide technology. Children shoot down a 200-foot tube, barreling out into a tightly shaped bowl. Centrifugal force has everyone holding on as they go whirling around the bowl before blasting out the bottom. This one is definitely for the most daring!

Facilities: Restrooms, picnic areas, snack bar, lockers. Strollers are easily maneuvered here, and the park is wheelchair accessible.

Stony Kill Farm Environmental Education Center. 79 Farmstead Lane (off NY 9D), Wappingers Falls 12590; 845-831-8780; www.dec.ny.gov/education. Free. Year-round weekend programs are offered to the public; call or check the Web site for a schedule.

Children who enjoy the outdoors or are studying the environment and nature should like this 756-acre facility, which offers a wide variety of habitats for local plants and animals. Rolling meadows, woodlands, ponds, swamps, and vernal pools attract many species of wildlife. Five trails can be used for hiking, snowshoeing, or cross-country skiing. The working 19th-century replica farm includes a barn with livestock (cows, sheep, chickens, turkeys, and pigs), and the center has an Open Barn program for visitors from spring through fall. A community garden plot program is also offered to those interested in growing their own vegetables and food. Major annual festivals include the Fall Harvest Festival (October), the Holiday Open House (December), the Horse-Drawn Sleigh Rally (February), Backyard Maple Sugaring (March), and the Earth Day Celebration (April).

Facilities: Restrooms, picnic areas, perennial and herb gardens, fishing ponds. There is stroller and wheelchair accessibility.

Trevor Zoo. 131 Millbrook School Road, Millbrook 12545; 845-677-3704; www.trevorzoo.org. (Located on the grounds of the Millbrook School, 6 miles east of the village of Millbrook off US 44.) Open year-round; groups welcome by advance reservation. Free.

This small zoo, the only one in the region, is part of the Millbrook School's curriculum, and visitors are welcome. On the 4-acre site you will see seven endangered species, including red pandas and red wolves, as well as a collection of 120 local and exotic species. The kids will also enjoy seeing hawks, snakes, deer, and badgers. The self-guided walk through the zoo is both stroller and wheelchair accessible.

Facilities: Restrooms.

Walkway Over the Hudson. 845-454-9649; www.walkway.org. The bridge spans Highland to Poughkeepsie with access at both sides. To get to the Poughkeepsie entrance, coming from the north, take NY 9G heading south to the city and make a left onto Haviland Road; parking and the entrance are a short distance ahead on the left.

The Walkway Over the Hudson is an ideal venue for strollers as well as leashed dogs. DUTCHESS COUNTY TOURISM

This fantastic walkway provides pedestrians, runners, cyclists, and hikers with access to the Hudson River. People with disabilities may also easily enjoy the walkway. The bridge itself is a 1.25 miles long (6,767 feet from end to end). The top of the bridge deck is 212 feet above water level, making for spectacular views. The site of a former railroad bridge opened in 1888, this was once the longest bridge in the world. The tracks were nearly destroyed by fire in 1974. The public pedestrian walkway, opened in October 2009, is now a New York State park and makes a delightful outing for people traveling with children. Dogs are permitted on the walkway if they are leashed.

Facilities: Portable toilets (at both ends of bridge).

With its Gothic arches, stone spires, and moat, a visit to Wing's Castle is like stepping into a fantasy world.
DUTCHESS COUNTY TOURISM

Wing's Castle. 717 Bangall Road, Millbrook 12545; 845-677-9085; www.wingscastle.com. (Located 5 miles north of Millbrook on Bangall Road, 1 mile north of CR 57.) Admission. Group tours by appointment.

This unique castle-in-progress has been under construction for the last 35 years. Visitors can see this fieldstone edifice on a tour conducted by owner and builder Peter Wing. He and his wife, Toni, have used salvaged materials from antique buildings to create this unique structure, whose style they have dubbed Recycled Americana. An antique ship has been used as a balcony in the house, and children delight in the "cauldron" bathtub—complete with terra-cotta fountain. Youngsters will view the whole house as something out of a fairy tale, as they visit the many rooms and the grounds. You may even be lucky enough to meet the giant macaw, the castle's mascot. The house is crammed full of antiques, bric-a-brac, and collectibles—with carousel horses and suits of armor vying for space with stained-glass windows and military weapons. The details will keep everyone on the tour visually entertained, and Peter Wing is only too happy to answer any and all questions about his castle.

Facilities: Strollers may be difficult to maneuver. Call ahead if wheelchair accessibility is a concern.

 What to Do

BALLOONING

Blue Sky Balloons. 909 Teller Avenue, Beacon 12509; 1-888-999-2461; www.blueskyballoons.com. The best time of year for hot-air balloon trips is April through October, but flights are available year-round, weather permitting. This company has been in business for over 35 years and organizes family-oriented outings. Flights are always within two hours after sunrise or two hours before sunset. FAA-certified pilots are in charge.

BASEBALL

Dutchess Stadium. 1500 Route 9D, Wappingers Falls 12590; 845-838-0094; http://www.minor leaguebaseball.com/index.jsp?sid=t537. The Hudson Valley Renegades, a minor league baseball team, have been playing at Dutchess Stadium since "The Dutch," as locals refer to it, was built in 1994. If your kids are aficionados of the sport, make sure to check the Web site for a schedule and take in a game. The stadium hosts a variety of special events throughout the year

Dutchess County hosts a balloon festival during the summer at several sites throughout the county.

DUTCHESS COUNTY TOURISM

BICYCLING

Harlem Valley Rail Trail. 845-297-1224, 518-789-9591; www.hvrt.org. Two paved sections of this 20-mile rail trail are open, and the Dutchess County section, about 8 miles, runs from Amenia to Millerton. There is access to the bike trail in both towns—in Millerton across the street from Railroad Plaza, in Amenia at the Mechanic Street parking lot.

There is easy access to the Hyde Park Rail Trail from the stately Franklin Delano Roosevelt Home. DUTCHESS COUNTY TOURISM

Hyde Park Rail Trail. 845-229-8086; www.traillink.com. Part of the Hudson River Greenway, open dawn to dusk, this 13-mile trail runs from Mills Mansion to Norrie Point and between the Vanderbilt Mansion, the FDR Home, and Val-Kill (Eleanor Roosevelt's home). Bicycling is permitted on the 1.5 miles between the FDR Home and Val-Kill only.

Mid-Dutchess Trailway. 845-486-2925; www.nysdot.gov. This 12-mile bike path runs from Hopewell Junction north to the city of Poughkeepsie.

Mid-Hudson Bicycle Club. 845-635-1184; www.midhudsonbicycle.org. This club has a wealth of information about both road and mountain biking in the county; they also sponsor social events and an annual group ride. Call or check the Web site for a schedule or to receive their newsletter.

Wilbur Boulevard Trailway. 845-451-4100; www.nysdot.gov. This trailway runs along Wilbur Boulevard in the city and town of Poughkeepsie. The paved length is 1.2 miles and it's a great place to go with young children.

BOAT CRUISES

Hudson Maritime Services. Beacon Municipal Dock, Beacon 12508; 845-265-7621; www.angelfire.com. Private sightseeing trips are available on the *Manitou,* a 25-foot sloop. There is an 18-foot powerboat that can also be chartered. Sightseeing trips to Bannerman Island may be arranged as well.

Hudson River Sloop Clearwater. 112 Little Market Street, Poughkeepsie 12601; 845-454-7673; www.clearwater.org. Call or check the Web site to find out dates, times, and locations of departures, as well as the public sail schedule.

River Rose Tours and Cruises. Poughkeepsie and Newburgh docks; 845-565-4210; www.riverrosecruises.com. The *River Rose* is a Mississippi-style paddle-wheeler that runs sightseeing cruises as well as charter trips. There is an open upper deck and a fully enclosed, climate-controlled main deck. This is a pleasant way to travel with the kids on a summer afternoon.

Sloop Woody Guthrie. Beacon Railroad Plaza, Beacon 12508; 845-297-7697; www.beaconsloopclub.org. Free. This wooden boat is a replica of a Hudson River ferry sloop; it goes out on weekday evenings only during the summer and fall. If you are in the area, head down to the Beacon waterfront and take a ride.

DRIVE-IN MOVIES

Only a few hundred drive-in movie theaters survive in America today, and two of them are located in Dutchess County. Take the kids and lawn chairs for an evening of fun that the family will remember for years to come. Both drive-ins listed here have snack bars and radio sound.

Hyde Park Drive-In. 4114 US 9, Hyde Park 12538; 845-229-4738; www .hydeparkdrivein.com. Check the Web site or call for a complete schedule of features and times.

Overlook Drive-In. 126 DeGarmo Road, Poughkeepsie 12601; 845-452-3445; www.driveinmovie.com. Call or check the Web site for a schedule of features and times.

HIKING

Burger Hill Park. NY 9G, Rhinebeck 12572; 845-473-4440; www.scenic hudson.org. (The park entrance is on the right, 2.5 miles south of the intersection of US 9 and NY 9G.) Open year-round. Free.

There are 76 acres of open meadows and rural scenic beauty at this spot, a popular place for picnicking, hiking, and sledding during the winter months. Rising to a 550-foot hilltop, Burger Hill boasts panoramic vistas of the Hudson River, Shawangunk Ridge, and the Catskill, Berkshire, and Taconic Mountains; it is owned and maintained by Scenic Hudson.

Harlem Valley Rail Trail. 518-789-9591; www.hvrt.org. Open year-round. There are 20 miles of scenic paved trail, linking villages and parks on the rail bed from Amenia and Millerton to Copake Falls in Columbia County. There is easy access to the trail at Railroad Plaza in Millerton, and in Amenia on Mechanic Street. Free.

Historic Hyde Park Trail. 845-229-9115; www.traillink.com. Open year-round. There are 8.5 miles of hiking trails here connecting several parks and historic sites. Bikes are not permitted, and access is behind the FDR Presidential Library Visitors Center.

Mills Norrie State Park. Old Post Road (just off US 9), Staatsburg 12580; 845-889-4646; www.nysparks.state.ny.us. Open year-round. Free. There are 1,000 acres of woodlands here with hiking trails, a marina, a boat launch, picnic areas, and a golf course; it is also near Mills Mansion.

Poet's Walk Romantic Landscape Park. River Road (CR 103), Red Hook 12571; 845-473-4440; www.scenichudson.org. (Crossing from west to east on NY 199, make a left at the first light and go approximately 1 mile; the park entrance is on the left.) (There are gates here that are locked at 6 sharp; cars still in the parking lot at that time risk being unable to leave until 9 the following day.) Free.

DUTCHESS COUNTY TOURISM

Dedicated by Pulitzer prizewinner John Ashbery in the summer of 1996, this 120-acre park is located on one of the most beautiful roads in the Hudson Valley, only a few miles from the Kingston-Rhinecliff Bridge. This is a great place for organized nature walks and excursions for school groups. It is one of the few places that allow easy access to the Hudson River. The walking paths consist of gently sloping terrain and young children will be able to walk here with ease. (Do stay on the paths since deer roam freely here and Lyme Disease is always a concern.)

ICE SKATING

McCann Ice Arena/Mid-Hudson Civic Center. 14 Civic Center Plaza, Poughkeepsie 12601; 845-454-9800 x. 212; www.midhudsonciviccenter .com. Open year-round. Admission. Group rates.

This indoor ice rink is part of the Mid-Hudson Civic Center, a recreation, entertainment, and convention center that offers a variety of figure skating and hockey programs year-round. It is one of the best places to ice skate indoors in the Hudson Valley. Kids will enjoy the large skating area, the music, and the bustling ambience. Inquire about lessons in the skating school office (x. 205).

Facilities: Restrooms, snack bar, lockers, rentals.

KAYAKING

Hudson Valley Pack and Paddle. 45 Beekman Street, Beacon 12508; 845-831-1300. This retail outlet also offers kayaking tours on the Hudson, by appointment only. Rental equipment is available.

The River Connection. 9 West Market Street, Hyde Park 12538; 845-229-0595; www.the-river-connection .com. This retail outlet (just off US 9) is an excellent place to go if you're new to kayaking and don't have equipment. They organize outings on the Hudson River and offer classes for beginners as well as more advanced students. Marshall Seddon, the owner, is devoted to kayaking and is an enthusiastic, excellent

DUTCHESS COUNTY TOURISM

guide. I went on one of their river trips and found it to be an amazing experience, particularly just before sunset—a memorable way to experience the Hudson.

PARKS

James Baird State Park. 14 Maintenance Lane, Pleasant Valley 12569; 845-452-1489; www.nysparks.state.ny.us. (Go 1 mile north of NY 55 on the Taconic State Parkway.) Open year-round. Free.

This is a complete outdoor entertainment center with basketball courts, a playground, a volleyball court, a softball field, tennis courts, hiking trails, a golf course, and a full-service restaurant. The park is a great outdoor excursion destination for families, with picnic areas and hiking trails throughout. On weekends, the nature center is open with displays of live and preserved specimens of fish and wildlife native to the park. During the winter, cross-country skiing is available, but bring your own equipment.

Facilities: Restrooms, picnic areas, restaurant (open April through November). Wheelchair and stroller accessible.

Riverfront Park. West Market Street, Hyde Park 12538; 845-229-8086. Open year-round. Free.

This small 4-acre park along the Hudson River has a children's play area, educational programs, and nature trails; it's also easily accessed from US 9. This is a nice place to take a break if you are sightseeing in the area.

Facilities: Restrooms, picnic areas.

Sylvan Lake Beach Park. 18 McDonnells Lane (off CR 9), Hopewell Junction 12533; 845-221-9889. Parking fee.

This 95-acre park boasts athletic fields, a sandy beach that's great for swimming, a children's play area, and fishing. It's a wonderful place to have a picnic, and kids who enjoy sports and the beach will love it here.

Facilities: Restrooms, picnic areas, showers.

Taconic State Park/Rudd Pond Area. 59 Rudd Drive, Millerton 12546; 518-789-3059; www.nysparks.state.ny.us. (Located east of the village of Millerton on CR 62.) Picnic area open year-round. Seasonal day-use admission charged per vehicle.

This is a great place to take the kids swimming. Rudd Pond is a 64-acre pond with a sandy beach, lifeguards, and rowboat rentals. Fishing is permitted as well but you need a New York State fishing license for anyone over the age of 16. There are over eight different types of fish in the pond. Camping season opens the first Friday in May and goes until the Sunday night of Labor Day weekend; advance reservations are strongly recommended. During winter families may enjoy cross-country skiing here, but you must bring your own equipment.

Facilities: Restrooms, picnic areas, bathhouse, campsites.

Taconic State Park/Copake Falls Area. NY 344, Copake Falls 12517; 518-329-3993; www.nysparks.state.ny.us. Open daily year-round.

In this area, there is an Ore Pit Pond for swimming (but no beach) as well as a wading pool for young children. Campsites can be rented, but reservations are suggested. There are 96 campsites, which can be reserved in advance. For day visitors, there are hiking trails, a playground, fishing, access to the Harlem Valley Rail Trail (bike path) and Bash Bish Falls. In the winter, the youngest cross-country skiers will enjoy the wild surroundings, but you must bring your own equipment.

Facilities: Restrooms, picnic areas, bathhouse, campsites.

Walkway Over the Hudson. Located between Highland, off NY 9G, and the city of Poughkeepsie; 845-454-9649; www.walkway.org. Open year-round. (Due to budget constraints, the walkway may be closed from January through March; call or check the Web site for the latest information.)

The grand opening of this new state park was in October 2009: A landmark railroad bridge was transformed into a 1.25-mile linear park and trail way. There is public access to the Hudson River's landscape for pedestrians, joggers, and bicyclists. Dogs are permitted if they are leashed. (Interestingly, the cost of removing the old railroad bridge would have been over twice the cost of preserving it in this fantastic way!) Eventually restaurants will be built on both sides of the bridge and it will connect with a network of rail trails and parks. This is a must for families; it is easy walking even for the youngest children and strollers can maneuver without difficulty. Do try to visit during weekdays, early in the morning, when the walkway is less crowded. On weekends, particularly in the warm-weather months, it can become exceedingly busy.

Facilities: Portable toilets (at both ends of bridge).

Wilcox Park. NY 199, Stanfordville 12581; 845-758-6100; www.dutchess ny.gov. Admission.

This is one of the nicest county parks to visit with young children during the summer. It has a small lake and a sandy beach area. Paddle-boats are popular to rent for older children, and when the water fun wears off, miniature golf and a special children's playground will keep the kids occupied. The hiking trails vary in length, so even the youngest in your party will enjoy taking a nature walk, on which you might come across deer and raccoons.

Facilities: Restrooms, picnic areas, snack bar, bathhouse, campsites (electric and water hook-ups available, by reservation).

PICK-YOUR-OWN AND OTHER FARMS

Barton Orchards. 63 Apple Tree Lane, off CR 7 (Beekman-Poughquag Road), Poughquag 12570; 845-227-2306; www.bartonorchards.com. Open for pick-your-own crops, including berries of all kinds, apples, pumpkins, Christmas trees, and vegetables. This is a wonderful place to visit with children, especially in autumn when there are hayrides. Special events are held throughout the season as well.

Battenfeld and Son. 856 NY 199, Red Hook 12571; 845-758-8018; www.anemones.com. This farm (a family operation for several decades) has been renowned for decades as the place to go for colorful anemones and Christmas trees in season. People line up on NY 199 to cut their own trees here in December; it has become a tradition in Dutchess County, so arrive early in the day!

Blueberry Park. 2747 CR 21, Wingdale 12594; 845-724-5776. They live up to their name, stocking only pick-your-own blueberries during the summer months. You can also get a tour of the farm by calling in advance.

Fishkill Farms. 9 Fishkill Farms Road, Hopewell Junction 12533; 845-897-4377; www.fishkillfarms.com. Open year-round. This is a fantastic place to take the kids for picking an array of fruits and vegetables. There are cherries, blueberries, raspberries, strawberries, and peaches during spring and summer; apples and pumpkins are ready for picking in the fall. The lovely market offers homemade baked goods plus freshly

One of life's pleasures is a June afternoon in the strawberry fields!

pressed cider and doughnuts in season. On autumn weekends, visitors may enjoy live entertainment and children's activities, as well as hayrides. An outdoor café (open on weekends) offers magnificent views and serves up delicious organic sandwiches, wraps, and salads. Do check the Web site for a schedule of special events at the farm.

Greig Farm. 223 Pitcher Lane, Red Hook 12571; 845-758-1234; www .greigfarm.com. (Located off NY 9G, 3 miles north of town; follow the signs.) There are acres of fields here available for pick-your-own harvesting, as well as a wonderful farm market and winery. Berries, beans, apples, pumpkins, and peaches are only some of the seasonal treats to be gathered; you will also find a greenhouse and extensive herb and cut-your-own flower gardens down the road from the market and winery. This is one of the largest and most popular stops for pick-your-own food in the county (and one of the first in the state to offer pick-your-own food), and participating in all the farm has to offer may take a couple of hours if you spend time in the fields. Don't forget hats for everyone!

Hahn Farm. 1697 Salt Point Turnpike, Salt Point 12578; 845-266-5042; www.hahnfarm.com. This is a wonderful 400-acre working family farm offering an array of activities year-round—with the highlight of the year being their Harvest Festival on weekends in October, an ideal time to visit. Kids will love the hayrides, baby farm animals, the enormous hay fort, huge corn maze, pony rides, hundreds of pumpkins and gourds, as well as fresh cider doughnuts. Excellent all-natural meats (beef, pork, and chicken) are on sale in the farm market on the premises. This autumn celebration at a working farm that has been in the

A harvest display at Hahn Farm.

same family for over two centuries should not be missed. The Maple Weekend Pancake Breakfast is held in March. A store on the premises (open on weekends only or by appointment) sells meat, chicken, eggs, and other products from the farm. An additional nice treat for the kids are the alpacas here.

Ronnybrook. 310 Prospect Hill Road, Pine Plains 12587; 518-398-6455; www.ronnybrookfarm.com. Open year-round (call in advance to arrange a tour of the farm). For over 50 years the Osofsky family has been raising dairy cows. Kids have probably seen their products in the supermarket. The milk produced here is hormone-free and the cows are treated like family, according to owner Ronny Osofksy. This is a wonderful stop to show young children where milk comes from up close! They have a store on the premises that sells their milk (the chocolate milk is some of the best you'll find!) and yogurt.

Secor Farms. 63 Robinson Lane, Wappingers Falls 12590; 845-452-6883. Open for picking strawberries (which they are famous for) as well as apples, berries, and pumpkins in autumn. The kids will enjoy going on a hayride here as well.

Sprout Creek Farm. 34 Lauer Road, LaGrangeville 12540; 845-485-8438; www.sproutcreekfarm.org. This 200-acre working farm is a nonprofit organization with a mission to connect children with nature. A visit here may include touring the barn to see sheep, goats, cows, and lambs; watching cheese being made (a cheese maker is on staff); and perhaps participating in one of the many weekend programs or events. There is also a summer camp (with two- and three-week sessions) and a market store. This is a busy place and the atmosphere is welcoming and friendly to families. It is a phenomenal farm and a great stop on any family's itinerary in Dutchess County.

Wild Hive Community Grain Project. 2411 Salt Point Turnpike, Clinton Corners 12513; 845-266-5863. Farm store and bakery/café open year-round; mill tours are seasonal and by advance appointment only.

Wild Hive began producing its critically acclaimed breads, grains, and baked goods in the mid-1980s. The project includes a farm store and bakery-café showcasing an array of foods grown with 100 percent organic local grains sourced 10 miles from the store. Originator Don Lewis appreciates promoting community through food and he has established a colorful hub in his hometown. A short distance from the store, there are two 16-inch mills and a 30-inch mill housed in a large converted barn. A modern kitchen and conference room in the structure are used for school programs. Children can observe the milling process from raw grain to fresh milled flour and finished product and better understand where their food comes from. The tour offers opportunities for young people to watch the mill and then bake and eat delicious locally grown treats. Wild Hive is a wonderful place to visit for an educational—and fun—field trip.

RAINY DAY ACTIVITIES

Hyde Park Roller Magic. 4178 Albany Post Road (US 9), Hyde Park 12538; 845-229-6666; www.hydeparkrollermagic.com. This is the place to roller-skate, in-line skate, or enjoy video games on a rainy afternoon. Open year-round.

Kids Kingdom Indoor Play Center. 36 Firemens Way (off NY 55), Poughkeepsie 12603; 845-471-7529; www.kidskingdompc.com. This center is geared for children between the ages of one and nine. There are two large bi-level play structures, a toddler play area, a sandbox, air bounce, air hockey, floor activities, two ball pits (sanitized weekly), a spiral slide, and an indoor basketball court. Socks are required. This is a good place to let the kids blow off steam after being on a long car ride!

Pawling Gamepad. 158 NY 22, Pawling 12564; 845-855-5683; www.pawlinggamepad.com. This game lounge is a place for older children and features an arcade, skee ball, roller ball, and sports games. There is also Wii, XBox 360, and PS3—and tournaments. When it's too hot, too cold, or raining, this is a good place to be with the kids!

THEATER

Bardavon 1869 Opera House Children's Theater. 35 Market Street, Poughkeepsie 12601; 845-473-5288; www.bardavon.org.

This is one of the last (and best) of the old-time opera houses that once operated as cultural centers in small towns and cities all across America. Built in 1869, Bardavon still operates as a lively theater and performing arts center, with a history of fine entertainment; past performers have included Mark Twain, Sarah Bernhardt, Ethel Barrymore, and Milton Berle. The theater was refurbished in the 1920s, and today it offers audiences a wide range of nationally known entertainers. It is a perfect place to introduce young people to musical performances and theater. In past years, life-sized puppet shows, incredible magic shows, plays, ballets, and musicals have entertained youngsters. The selection of shows appeals to many different age groups, and Bardavon notes which performance is appropriate for what age. Make sure to check the Web site for a complete schedule.

Facilities: Restrooms. The theater is wheelchair accessible, and there are designated seats for the disabled, but you should call ahead about this service. Hearing-impaired children can also be accommodated with lightweight headphones for rent. Groups should inquire about special offerings, like the theater tours and question-and-answer sessions with the performers.

Center for Performing Arts at Rhinebeck. 661 NY 308, Rhinebeck 12572; 845-876-3080; www.centerforperformingarts.org. Open year-round. This multipurpose cultural and educational center features dramatic plays, musicals, dance, concerts, lectures, staged readings, and workshops. There are several children's shows throughout the year as well. Check the Web site for a complete schedule.

Facilities: Restrooms. Wheelchair and stroller accessible.

COLUMBIA COUNTY

▼▲▼▲▼▲▼

V isit Columbia County and take a tour through American history. Rambling horse farms and stately center-hall Colonials with expansive lawns pepper the rolling countryside. Mansions of prominent early American families, the home of America's eighth president (Martin Van Buren), the Moorish villa of a major Hudson River School painter, a Shaker settlement, and a museum of fire fighting are just some of the places families can experience our American heritage. The county is also filled with pristine lakes, dense forests, mountain trails, and winding roads—making it a giant outdoor playground. Whether your family loves swimming, boating, hiking, cycling, or skiing, this is the place to enjoy it.

Many of Columbia County's highlights combine education and recreation. **Clermont,** the ancestral home of the politically and socially prominent Livingston family, is one of the county's treasures. Situated along the Hudson River, children will be entranced by the special events offered on weekends, from Revolutionary War encampments to summer brass band concerts, Independence Day celebrations, and autumn fairs. At the **Old Chatham Sheepherding Company** youngsters can watch goats being milked and see the process of cheese making step

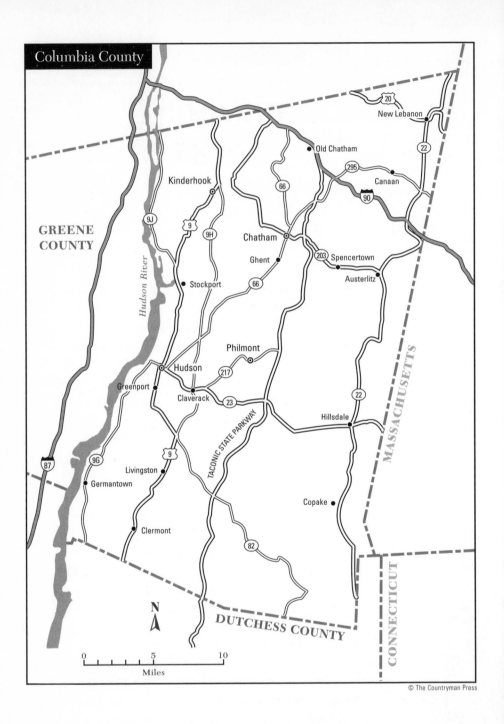

Columbia County

New Lebanon

Old Chatham

Kinderhook

Canaan

GREENE
COUNTY

Hudson River

Chatham

Ghent

Spencertown

Stockport

Austerlitz

MASSACHUSETTS

Philmont

Hudson

Greenport

Claverack

Hillsdale

TACONIC STATE PARKWAY

Livingston

Germantown

Copake

CONNECTICUT

Clermont

N

DUTCHESS COUNTY

0   5   10
Miles

© The Countryman Press

by step at the largest sheep dairy farm in the country. **Farm Day,** the last Saturday in April, is a great time to visit with the kids. **Mud Creek Environmental Learning Center** in Ghent, open year-round, has a marvelous nature trail that wends its way through wetlands with two kid-friendly loops; children who are interested in nature will love this stop. **Lake Taghkanic State Park** is located on 1,569 wooded acres adjacent to the Taconic Parkway. The 156-acre lake offers families two beaches, boat rentals, and several picnic areas—and is great for swimming. The park also has playgrounds, a ball field, volleyball courts, a camping area, and numerous hiking trails. Children of all ages will appreciate a visit to the **American Museum of Fire Fighting** in Hudson. It's packed with one of the nation's largest collections of colorful equipment and art relating to the fireman's trade.

Columbia County offers a number of wonderful family festivals throughout the year. Highlights include **special children's programs** at **Olana** on summer weekends, featuring drama, nature, games, and art projects at this beautiful state historic site just outside the city of Hudson. The **Shaker Museum** puts on a **Strawberry Shortcake Festival** in July. Last, but not least, the **Columbia County Fair** in Chatham is a Labor Day weekend tradition. The oldest continuously held fair in the country, the five-day celebration features prizewinning horses, sheep, cows, and other livestock; musical entertainment, midway games, and fabulous rides.

For further information, contact **Columbia County Tourism,** 401 State Street, Hudson 12534; 518-828-3375, 1-800-724-1846; www.columbiacountyny.com.

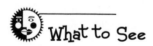 What to See

MUSEUMS AND HISTORIC SITES

American Museum of Fire Fighting. 117 Harry Howard Avenue (next to the Firemen's Home), Hudson 12534; 518-822-1875; www.fasnyfire museum.com. Call in advance for group tours. Free, but donations are welcomed.

Children of all ages will appreciate an hour in this museum, five halls packed with one of the nation's largest collections of colorful equipment and art of the fireman's trade. As you step into the large display room called the Engine Hall, you will discover more than 90 pieces of antique fire engines, pumps, and trucks—all in fine condition, and (of course) many of them painted bright red. The exhibit contains samples of equipment dating back to 1725, when fires were fought by bucket brigades. Elaborate engines include the Volunteer, which is like a Victorian fantasy. The walls of the museum are lined with old fire banners, lovely paintings that were used by the various companies in parades and at festivals. The image of the fireman (and firewoman) is immortalized in paintings, advertisements, statues, helmets, and elaborate fire horns carried during processions. A September 11 memorial display filled with photographs lists the names of all the firefighters who lost their lives that day. Each display is clearly marked, and there are often fire buffs around to answer your questions. The museum will also be of interest to older children. Throughout the museum there is lots of gleaming brass, bright-red paint, and an oddity or two—like ornate fireman's parade trumpets, hand-grenade-style fire extinguishers, and brass fire markers that indicated which fire company had the right to fight a particular fire.

Kids love to pretend they're on the way to put out a fire in one of the antique vehicles at the American Museum of Fire Fighting. COLUMBIA COUNTY TOURISM

Facilities: Restrooms, picnic areas, gift shop. *The museum is wheelchair accessible.*

Clermont State Historic Site. 1 Clermont Avenue, Germantown 12526; 518-537-4240; www.friendsofclermont.org. (Located off NY 9G, north of Tivoli; follow signs to Clermont State Historic Park.) Open year-round. Admission. Group tours available by advance reservation.

This is the ancestral home of the American branch of the Livingston family, established circa 1730 and in use by the same family until 1964. Chancellor Robert Livingston, one of the five drafters of the Declaration

of Independence, served as minister to France under Thomas Jefferson and was the partner of steamboat inventor Robert Fulton. Today, parents may wish to tour the elaborately restored house that overlooks the Hudson River and is filled with magnificent 18th- and 19th-century family heirlooms. Their children will enjoy the special events offered on many weekends throughout the year, including replica Revolutionary War encampments, music festivals, sheepshearing, and Independence Day festivities. The site offers a great place to picnic, with views upriver and downriver, and children can run around and have a good time. School tours are welcomed all year, and at Christmastime there are special tours of the elaborately decorated house. Don't miss Clermont if you are traveling with children of any age.

Facilities: *Restrooms, picnic areas, BBQ pits. Pets are allowed in most areas if leashed. There are paths and miles of walking trails, but you may have trouble with a stroller or wheelchair on them. While strollers and back carriers are not allowed in the mansion, the first floor is wheelchair accessible.*

Olana. 5720 NY 9G, Hudson 12534; 518-828-0135; www.olana.org. (Located 1 mile south of the Rip Van Winkle Bridge.) Open year-round, but the house is viewed by guided tour only, and group size is limited; call to reserve tickets before you go. Admission.

Frederic Edwin Church, a 19th-century American landscape painter, started construction on his Persian-style mansion overlooking the Hudson River in 1870. The hand-painted roof tiles and colorful turrets will intrigue most children. Inside they will have the opportunity to see Church's painting studio, set up just as it was in his day, as well as the interesting décor, which includes a pair of gilded crane lamps that look as if they stepped out of an Egyptian wall painting. Church and his wife, Isabel, traveled extensively throughout the Middle East and Europe, and the treasures collected on their journeys may be seen throughout the 37 rooms of the house. During the holiday season, Olana is decorated with elaborate greenery and Yuletide confections grace the tables. Older children will particularly enjoy the tour. There are art- and nature-oriented special programs at Olana for young people, so check the Web site or call in advance to see what is scheduled before visiting.

Facilities: Restrooms, gift shop, video (on Church's life). Stroller and wheelchair accessible. The walking trails on the property are excellent for even the youngest children to explore.

Parker O'Malley Air Museum. 435 Old Post Road (US 20), Ghent 12075; 518-392-7200; www.museumsusa.org. (The museum is located at the southwest side of Columbia County Airport.) Admission; children under the age of 12 are admitted free.

The Parker O'Malley Air Museum has military and civilian aircraft from the 1920s, 1930s, and 1940s, as well as a varied collection of wartime memorabilia. Students of the Parker O'Malley band play music of the era. The nonprofit foundation seeks to improve the academic, artistic, and social abilities of its young visitors through participation in a variety of activities and events. Call before you go for the current schedule.

Facilities: Restrooms.

Shaker Museum and Library. 88 Shaker Museum Road, Old Chatham 12136; 518-794-9100; www.shakermuseumandlibrary.org. (From Chatham, take NY 295 east to the East Chatham Post Office, and turn left; follow the road into Old Chatham Square, and bear left onto CR 13; then turn right onto Shaker Museum Road.)

This Shaker museum is not as well known as its larger Massachusetts counterpart (**see pg. 296–297**), but it offers children a unique look at the tools, farm equipment, and inventions of the Shakers, a sect that flourished in New York during the 19th century. The walk-through exhibits are well marked, and there are displays of Shaker baskets, clothing, and a large selection of woodworking tools. Children are given a guidebook that leads them through the museum on a detective search to find various artifacts; by following the clues, kids will learn about the life of Shakers. Outside they can visit the schoolhouse and walk through the herb garden. There are special events for children during summer and fall, and this museum is an enjoyable introduction to an often-neglected part of America's social history.

Facilities: Restrooms, picnic areas, gift shop, snack bar. Strollers are welcomed here and are easily maneuvered through the exhibits. Limited wheelchair accessibility.

ADDITIONAL ATTRACTIONS

Art Omi/The Fields Sculpture Park. 1405 NY 22, Ghent 12075; 518-392-2181; www.artomi.org. (From Hudson take NY 9H north; make a right onto CR 22, then go left onto Letter S Road. The second driveway on the left is the park.) Free.

Founded in 1988 as public grounds for viewing contemporary sculp-

COLUMBIA COUNTY TOURISM

ture—as part of the Art Omi International Arts Center—the park features more than 50 sculptures on view, with works by Liberman, Lipski, Highstine, Knowlton, Venet, and others. Each year about 10 new works are added to the park. It is best to stop at the visitors center first to find out what is currently on exhibit. The arts center is located on more than 150 acres, of which 90 are dedicated to the sculpture park that stretches through rolling fields, wooded knolls, and wetlands. Art Omi is a terrific place to expose children to sculpture and other works of art and it takes approximately one hour to tour the entire park. Kids will enjoy exploring freely at their own pace as they wander through the scenic rolling hills. Some of the sculptures are located on farmlands so children will see crops growing amid the artwork, giving the park an interesting connection to the landscape. Throughout the year there are workshops and programs for children. Check the Web site to see current offerings.

Old Chatham Sheepherding Company. 155 Shaker Museum Road, Old Chatham 12136; 518-794-7733, 1-888-SHEEP-60; www.blacksheep cheese.com. Open year-round, but call before going to find out what is happening at the farm. Free.

The kids will be enchanted by a visit to this working farm where they can see the cheese-making process from beginning to end. The farm produces several types of sheep-milk cheeses and yogurt—it is the largest sheep dairy farm in the country. In 1994, the operation started with 150 sheep and now there are more than 1,200 East Friesian cross-bred sheep grazing on 600 beautiful acres of rolling pasture land. European methods are used to create new American cheeses, which have won culinary awards and have been praised in gourmet food publications. Visitors take a self-guided tour here.

Facilities: Restrooms, gift shop.

Petting Zoo at Love Apple Farm. 1421 NY 9H, Ghent 12075; 518-828-5048; www.loveapplefarm.com.

This is truly a special place that kids will love. In addition to the petting zoo (and children may feed the baby animals from bottles and cups of dried food), there are dozens of varieties of apples to pick in season—along with pears, strawberries, cherries, and peaches. The doughnuts and home-baked fruit pies are first-rate and are for sale at the beautiful market on the premises. There is also a tree forest playground where children will enjoy running around freely.

Taconic Sculpture Park. Stever Hill Road, Spencertown 12165; 518-392-5757. Open year-round. Free.

Roy Kanwit, a working sculptor, has 40 of his pieces exhibited on the grounds outside his home/studio, a stone castlelike structure. The park attracts a few thousand visitors each year. Children will thoroughly enjoy this stop, where they can go inside many of these enormous sculptures. If you are in the area, it's worth stopping by.

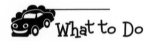 What to Do

BICYCLING

Harlem Valley Rail Trail. Undermountain Road (off NY 22), Ancram 12501; Valley View Road, Copake 12516; Taconic State Park entrance near Depot Deli, Copake Falls 12517; www.hvrt.org.

When completed, this paved bicycle/pedestrian path will stretch from Wassaic in Dutchess County to Chatham in Columbia County, and run some 46 miles. It was built on the old railroad bed that connected New York City, the Harlem Valley, and Chatham. New York State purchased 22 miles of land to build this linear park, about half of which lies in southern Columbia County. The area is ideal for hiking and bicycling. Kids will enjoy seeing many species of birds on the trail, as well as deer, coyotes, foxes, hawks, turtles, and beavers (or at least their dams!). The trail passes through the hamlets of Amenia and Millerton in Dutchess County, as well as Copake Falls in Columbia County.

CANOEING AND KAYAKING

Keep in mind that Columbia County doesn't have an array of outfitters where visitors can rent canoes or kayaks. The state parks are the best places to canoe or row on a lake. However, if you have your own equipment, the following two spots are excellent places to explore with the kids.

Rogers Island. Row or paddle out to this paradise (under the Rip Van Winkle Bridge) to watch an array of birds. There are eagles, waterfowl, and an amazing variety of birds that inhabit this intriguing island in the Hudson River between Greene and Columbia counties.

Stockport Flats. Station Road, Greenport. If you are traveling north on US 9, look for Station Road, which is on the left just after crossing the Columbiaville Bridge. These 250 acres of state land offer the perfect place to explore by canoe. The waters of these flats are easy to navigate and a good place for beginners and young canoe enthusiasts to practice paddling.

FISHING

The county is filled with deep lakes, clear streams, and stocked creeks, making it a fine destination for a fishing outing with the kids. Remember that a New York State fishing license is required for anyone over the age of 16. The following creeks are stocked by the Department of Environmental Conservation and are fairly easy to find. To get to the **Claverack Creek** turn onto Roxburgh Road, off NY 217, and look for the bridge that crosses the creek; this is a good spot to fish. There is also access on

NY 23 at Red Mills (off the south side of the bridge only), and on CR 29 halfway between Webb and Hiscox roads. A nice spot to try your luck is **Kinderhook Creek**. From NY 66 in the town of Chatham there is easy access at Bachus Road; you can also get to the creek at Malden Bridge. **Roeliff Jansen Creek** is accessed from CR 2 between Elizaville and the Taconic State Parkway; another place to fish this creek is off NY 22, 2 miles south of Hillsdale on Black Grocer Road.

HIKING

When walking through wooded and grassy areas be aware that Lyme disease is transmitted by deer ticks and is extremely prevalent in this county. Wear appropriate clothing and check yourself and the kids if you wander off marked trails for any reason. The following are some nice places with relatively short trails to comfortably hike with kids.

Borden's Pond Conservation Area. 518-392-5252; www.clctrust.org. (Take NY 203 east, just outside the village of Chatham; look for sign on the left.) Open year-round, this 52-acre preserve provides a nice change of pace after shopping in town. This is a relatively new area, with an old woodland millpond surrounded by forest and a series of gently sloping trails.

Greenport Conservation Area. 518-392-5252; www.clctrust.org. Open year-round. Heading south on US 9 to Greenport, go right onto Joslen Boulevard, across from a condominium complex; then make a right onto Daisy Hill Road. There is a parking area and information kiosk with interpretive brochures detailing the 3.5 miles of trails marked in red, blue, and green. This is a wonderful place to take kids who want to go on a short hike; the trails wend their way through meadows, woodlands, and wetlands along the Hudson River. A hand-hewn cedar gazebo overlooking the river is a great spot to rest and enjoy the view.

Mud Creek Environmental Learning Center. 1024 NY 66, Ghent 12075; 518-828-4386; www.ccswcd.org. Open year-round. Free. Groups by advance reservation. There are two short trails (one is about 1 mile and the other is 0.5 mile long) that go through forests, fields, and wetlands— and are detailed in a self-guiding pamphlet. The environmental center building has a Hudson River estuary exhibit, other educational displays, and restrooms. A full-time educator is on staff to assist visitors from schools and private groups.

Pachaquack Preserve. Elm Street (off NY 203), Valatie 12184; 518-758-9806. Open year-round. The word *pachaquack* means "cleared meadow" in the language of Native Americans who once inhabited the area. This 43-acre preserve dates back to the late 17th century and is now operated by the town of Valatie. This is a beautiful spot for a walk any time of year with 2 miles of walking trails, picnic areas, and a gazebo. The walking is extremely easy, so even the youngest travelers will feel comfortable here; three trails follow Kinderhook Creek, where there is excellent fishing.

Wilson M. Powell Wildlife Sanctuary. Hunt Club Road (off CR 13), Old Chatham 12136. Open year-round. This 130-acre sanctuary offers a variety of walks with lovely views of the mountains; some trails meander around a pond. One marked trail leads you on a 0.5-mile walk to the observation area called Dorson Rock. Kids will enjoy watching the ducks and birds at the pond.

PARKS

Lake Taghkanic State Park. 1528 NY 82 (11 miles south of Hudson, at the Taconic Parkway), Ancram 12502; 518-851-3631; www.nysparks.com. Open year-round. Seasonal vehicle use fee.

The beach at Lake Taghkanic State Park is ideal for swimming, picnicking, and boating. COLUMBIA COUNTY TOURISM

The park is a delightful getaway with its 1,568 acres of lush rolling hills and 156-acre lake. There are many recreational opportunities for the entire family to enjoy year-round. During the summer months, visitors can enjoy boating, kayaking, swimming, picnicking, fishing, and guided hikes. The nature center operates during the peak season and offers children educational programs to explore plant life and animal life. During the winter, families can enjoy cross-country skiing, ice skating, and snowshoeing. There are also cabins and campsites in the park for those who wish to camp overnight. Check the Web site for a complete schedule.

Facilities: Restrooms, picnic areas, snack bar, bathhouse, campsites, boat rentals (rowboats and paddleboats), cabins and cottages (available May to October). Pets must be kept on a leash and are restricted to special areas.

Taconic State Park. NY 344 (off NY 22), Copake Falls 12517; 518-329-3993; www.nysparks.state.ny.us. Open year-round.

A 25-mile network of hiking trails ranges from very easy to difficult in this 5,000-acre park, one of the largest in the Hudson Valley. The park spans two counties (Dutchess and Columbia) and borders Massachusetts and Connecticut, running for 16 miles along the Taconic Ridge with spectacular views in many places. This is a good stop for families; there's a small nature center with displays, camping areas are open from May through November, and cabins may be rented year-round. Older children may be interested in the historical section of the park, which includes the Copake Iron Works—a relic from 1845, when iron making was the main industry in town. For over 60 years, iron ore, limestone, and hardwood were extracted locally with waterpower from Bash Bish Creek; 2,500 tons of blast iron, much of which was used for making car wheels, was taken out of the "park." In the 1920s the owner of the foundry sold the site to the state. The cabins that once housed laborers are now rented out as overnight lodging to travelers.

Facilities: Restrooms, campsites, swimming area, hiking trails, cabins.

PICK-YOUR-OWN AND OTHER FARMS

The Berry Farm. 2309 NY 203, Chatham 12037; 518-392-4609; www .chathamberryfarm.com. The Berry Farm is a haven for berry lovers, offering everything from gooseberries and currants to boysenberries, strawberries, and even kiwi fruit. Call the farm to find out when the crops are ripe for picking since this largely depends on the weather.

Hawthorne Valley Farm. 327 CR 21C, Ghent 12075; 518-672-7500; www.hawthornevalleyfarm.org. (Take the Taconic State Parkway north and exit at Route 217/Harlemville. Make a right off the exit ramp and travel 1.5 miles; the farm is on the left.) Open year-round.

You have probably seen or purchased their excellent yogurt in the local health food store. This is a certified biodynamic farm (balancing the interrelationship among people, plants, and animals) located on 400

pastoral acres—with a herd of 60 cows, sheep, goats, and horses. A variety of fruits and vegetables are grown and sold in the beautiful market store. There is lots going on here and visitors are encouraged to take a self-guided tour of the farm that has been in operation since 1972. Some highlights include a bakery and market store, the Rudolf Steiner school and summer camp, milking barn (the cows are milked twice each day at 5:30AM and 4PM), a biodiesel "still," and pig pens. Interested young people can apply to be an apprentice, join the "farmscape" ecology program, or participate in another summer course offered at the farm. Do stop at the office and pick up a free written guide for your tour. Check the Web site for details about programs for youngsters.

Love Apple Farm. 1421 NY 9H, Ghent 12075; 518-828-5048; www.love applefarm.com. They have an amazing variety of fruit to pick here, including 10 varieties of pears, 24 types of peaches, and 30 kinds of apples. There are nectarines, cherries, and plums as well. The children will enjoy the petting zoo and playground (**see Additional Attractions, pg. 164**) after being out in the fields. It is best to check the Web site or call since the harvest schedule is weather dependent.

The Philip Orchard. 270 NY 9H, Claverack 12513; 518-851-6351. (Take the New York State Thruway to exit 21. Make a left onto NY 23 and follow the signs to the Rip Van Winkle Bridge. After crossing the bridge, continue north on NY 23 to the junction of NY 9H. Make a left onto NY 9H, go through Claverack, and the orchard is on the right.)

There are Cortlands, Macouns, Golden Delicious, Mutsu, and Macintosh as well as Jonna Golds, Spartans, Empires, and a host of heirloom apples along with five varieties of pears and raspberries on this 100-acre farm that dates back to the 17th century and is still in the same family. Julia Philip, now in her mid-80s, runs the farm and she is often around to answer questions and talk to visitors.

Spruce Ridge Alpaca Farm. 434 CR 13, Old Chatham 12136; 518-794-6294; www.spruceridgefarm.com. Located 1.5 miles south of the old Chatham Country Store, they specialize in quality, registered alpacas and have been involved with them since 1997. Open on certain days to the public but any time for tours by appointment. Every month there is a herd health day when the farm is open to visitors.

This full-service alpaca farm is a fascinating place to visit. There are only 100,000 alpacas in the United States today, and those being raised at this farm are diverse in color and bloodlines. Alpacas are the oldest livestock industry in the Americas. The owners, Jeff and Steve, have a shop on the premises that specializes in the wonderful products made from the fiber of these intriguing animals. (There are 22 natural colors and the fiber is three times warmer than sheep's wool and seven times stronger!) The owners have unusual enthusiasm for their business—and the *crias* (baby alpacas)—that is genuine, and they enjoy sharing their experience with visitors. This is a terrific stop the kids will love if you're in the Chatham area.

SKIING AND SNOWBOARDING

Catamount Ski and Snowboarding Area. NY 23, Hillsdale 12539; 518-325-3200; www.catamountski.com. Charge for lift ticket, but children under the age of six ski free when accompanied by a ticketed adult. Group rates and special weekday rates.

Catamount is one of the oldest ski areas in the state. It is privately owned and operated and the atmosphere reflects a down-home warmth that is

COLUMBIA COUNTY TOURISM

nice for young skiers and their families. When you ski here, you can see three states (New York, Massachusetts, and Connecticut) from the top of the runs. There are 32 trails along with seven lifts and snowmaking on 98 percent of the mountain. This is a full-service ski area with all the amenities. The varied terrain suits all ages and skill levels, and a full children's ski program is offered. There is a program for skiers from age 4–12, and for snowboarders from age 7–12. The nursery will care for children ages 2–6 from 8:30–4, while parents enjoy the slopes.

Facilities: *Restrooms, picnic areas, restaurant, snack bar, ski shop, retail shop, rentals, nursery.*

SWIMMING

Knickerbocker Lake. US 9, just outside the village of Valatie. This large lake, managed by the town of Kinderhook, has a nice beach, making it a popular place to swim among residents, especially those with young children. It is also open to the public for a fee of $10 per car.

THEATER

MacHaydn Theatre. 1925 NY 203, Chatham 12037; 518-392-9292; www.machaydntheatre.org. This theater specializes in summer-stock musical productions. The intimate setting is the perfect venue for all-time crowd-pleasers like *Oliver, Oklahoma, Fiddler on the Roof,* and other performances the kids will enjoy. Check the Web site for a complete schedule.

Spencertown Academy. 790 NY 203, Spencertown 12165; 518-392-3693; www.spencertownacademy.org. Built in 1847 as a private school, Spencertown is now a cultural arts center where visitors can enjoy films, dance, theater, and a variety of other cultural events. The academy has a reputation as a leading venue for great folk music and jazz. Groups of local, regional, and national renown play this intimate setting at all times of the year. There are also workshops, performances, and a variety of classes geared to children. Two galleries on the premises feature changing arts and crafts exhibits. Check the Web site or call for a schedule of events here if you will be in the area.

GREENE COUNTY

▼▲▼▲▼▲▼

G reene County offers the perfect family outdoor experience at any time of year. During the winter, families can visit the slopes at Hunter or Windham Mountain, which provide some of the best downhill skiing in the East. Spring brings an annual tour of homes, farms, and estates run by the county historical society. Summer celebrates its warmth with the pleasure of icy brooks for feet tired from hiking, as well as a flood of cultural and music festivals. Come autumn visitors wonder at the colors that transform the hills and villages into paint pots full of orange and red. The magic that enchanted Rip Van Winkle in the Catskills still impresses visitors today!

Watch your children's eyes light up as they pet and feed a baby llama at the zoological park at the **Bailiwick Ranch and Discovery Zoo,** home to several exotic and farm animals. The hands-on petting and feeding area, along with an education program, will entertain the entire family. When it's 90 degrees in the shade, splash down in the **Zoom Flume Water Park** in East Durham. The Raging River ride and Zoom Flume let the kids slosh and slide their way down beautiful Shady Glen Canyon. **Armstrong's Elk Farm** is a fascinating educational detour where you can learn how the elk antler velvet is harvested

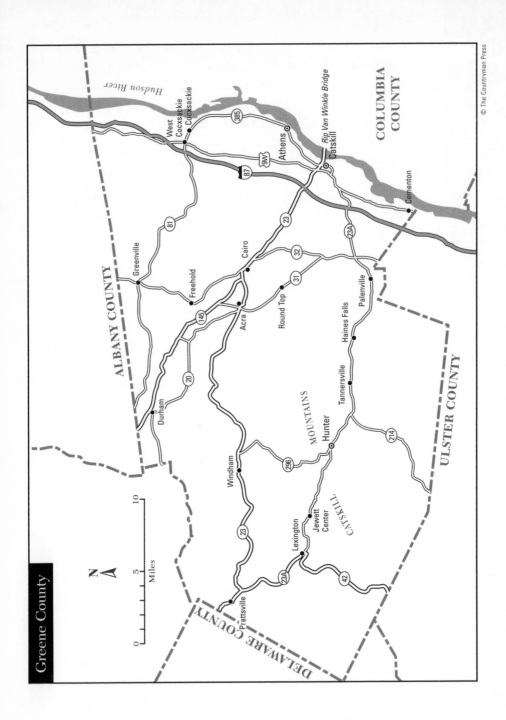

Greene County

N

0 5 10
Miles

© The Countryman Press

and used for a variety of drugs and natural remedies. The owner loves to show visitors around the farm and explain about the business of raising these gentle animals. **Bear Creek Recreational Park** in Hunter has a challenging sport-putting course, driving range, and horseback riding. In winter there is snowmobiling at this family sports complex surrounded by mountains. **North and South Lakes** provide breathtaking scenery and a multitude of activities. Kids can swim in a mountain lake with a clean sandy beach. Boat rentals and fishing are also available. A short hike away from North Lake is **Kaaterskill Falls,** one of the highest waterfalls on the East Coast and a popular subject for Hudson River School artists.

The following are just a few of the wonderful celebrations held annually in the county that may fit into your travel plans. On Memorial Day weekend, the **Annual Irish Festival** in East Durham is a great stop if you love music and dance. In July, the **Grey Fox Bluegrass Festival** at Walsh Farm in Oak Hill features a weekend of top talent. The **Greene County Fair** in Catskill, also in July, is a festive event—amusement rides, lawn mower races, and live entertainment are all part of the fun.

For further information, contact **Greene County Promotion Department**, 518-943-3223, 1-800-355-CATS; www.greenetourism .com.

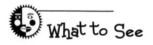 What to See

MUSEUMS AND HISTORIC SITES

Thomas Cole National Historic Site (Cedar Grove). 218 Spring Street, Catskill 12414; 518-943-7465; www.thomascole.org. Admission. Groups welcome by special appointment.

Thomas Cole, a 19th-century painter and poet, inspired the land conservation movement in America and is credited with founding the Hudson River School of landscape art. His Federal-style home and lovely gardens offer some of the most fantastic views of the Catskills. There are house tours, lectures, and events throughout the summer (usually on Sunday afternoons), but most children will enjoy a stop at the grounds and the towering 200-year-old honey locust tree Cole mentions in his writings. Those older children interested in art will enjoy the tour that includes the artist's studio as well as the house.

Facilities: Restrooms, gift shop.

Zaddock Pratt Museum and Pratt Rocks. 518-299-3395; www.pratt museum.com. Admission. Pratt Rocks Park, on NY 23 just outside of Prattsville, is open daily year-round and is free.

The museum/home of Zaddock Pratt, a 19th-century community leader who owned a thriving leather-tanning business, may be of interest to some older children. However, just about all kids will enjoy a visit to Pratt Rocks, a memorial carved by a stonemason into the wall of rock. The parklike setting is easily accessible, and the huge stone relief 500 feet above the road shows Pratt's son, his favorite horse, and Zadock Pratt himself. There is a short hiking path, great views from the summit, and a nice picnic area overlooking Schoharie Creek. Note that the hike may be too steep for very young children.

Facilities: Restrooms (museum), picnic areas (Pratt Rocks).

ADDITIONAL ATTRACTIONS

Armstrong's Elk Farm. 936 Hervey Sunside Road, Cornwallville 12418; 518-622-8452. (Take the New York State Thruway to exit 21; pick up NY 23 west for 12 miles; make a right onto Hervey Street.) Open year-round. Free.

This is a captivating educational detour for just about anyone. There are over 40 Rocky Mountain elk in their own habitat at this farm, and spring is when the baby elk are born. Learn how the antler velvet is harvested and used for a variety of drugs and natural remedies. The farm is an excellent place for birdwatchers—the kids will enjoy identifying orioles, finches, bluebirds, and many more species. Owner Les Armstrong loves to tell visitors about the farm and the business of raising elk. He is a fascinating character and makes this a special stop for families.

Facilities: Restrooms.

Bailiwick Ranch and Discovery Zoo. 118 Castle Road, Catskill 12414; 518-678-5665; www.bailiwickranch.com. Admission.

In addition to horseback riding (**see What To Do, pg. 182**), this site offers a zoological park where children get to see both exotic and

farm animals up close. There is an enclosed area for petting and feeding the baby animals, including lambs, llamas, and deer. A few times during the day there is an educational program that will appeal to the entire family as well as narrated tours of the grounds. Additionally, there is a paintball park—masks, suits, and guns are provided to participating children.

Facilities: Restrooms, gift shop, playground. Handicapped accessible.

Bear Creek Recreational Park. Located at the junction of NY 214 and NY 23A, Hunter 12442; 518-263-3839; www.bearcreekrestaurant.com. Admission fee is charged for activities. They have quite a challenging miniature golf course here with dramatic rock waterfalls, sand traps, and terrific views of the Catskills. The 400-yard, 20-station driving range is wonderful for young golf aficionados and lessons are available in season. In the winter months, families can enjoy snowmobiling on the scenic trails. Horseback riding and a paintball arena are two activities available at this site year-round. Pony rides will delight those under the age of six. The restaurant and pub on the premises is a relaxing place to enjoy a drink or lunch.

Facilities: Restrooms, restaurant.

Catskill Mountain Country Store and Looking Zoo. 5510 NY 23, Windham 12496; 518-734-3387; www.catskillmtcountrystore.com. This old-fashioned country store is a busy place with lots of activities to please children. In addition to the wonderful "looking" zoo (although the mini-horses Lovey, Raccoon, and Lily love when visitors feed them grass) including chickens, turkeys, potbelly pigs, horses, sheep, goats, and rabbits, there is a bakery on the premises turning out some of the best homemade fresh fruit pies you will find in the Catskills. (The restaurant's pancakes and French toast are renowned as well.) The fabulous doughnuts are a must and are baked fresh daily. Owners Natasha and

Drew Shuster have involved their young daughter, Sydney, in making the delicious homemade fudge sold at the store. For those who prefer candy, Jolly Ranchers, Pez, and strawberry laces are just a few of the dozens of choices. The Shusters also display jams, jellies, and relishes (from family recipes, of course) for sale; the store has an excellent selection of toys and regional books as well. Whether you're in the mood to browse or buy, this is well worth a stop if you're in the Windham area.

Facilities: Restrooms, restaurant, gift shop.

Mountaintop Arboretum. CR 23C and Maude Adams Road, Tannersville 12485; 518-589-3903; www.mtarboretum.org. Open year-round. Call about guided tours, which may be arranged in advance.

This nonprofit organization features a collection of exotic and native trees and shrubs on a lovely 21-acre site. Each season brings new sights, from the flowering height of spring to the brightly colored autumn foliage. Many of the plants have identification markers, and there are educational workshops throughout the year, some of which will appeal to children. Those kids who always want to know "What is that tree?" will enjoy this stop. The arboretum serves as a botanical research facility and a place for programs on a variety of horticultural topics.

Facilities: Restrooms.

Ice skating fun at Windham Mountain Adventure Park

WINDHAM MOUNTAIN

Windham Mountain Adventure Park. South Street (0.25 mile west of Windham Mountain), Windham 12496; 1-800-754-9463; www.windhammountain.com. Activities are charged for separately.

Most kids will love the speed and thrill of riding a snow tube down a 650-foot chute or gliding over the ice rink here, especially if they aren't interested in skiing or snowshoeing on the mountain. The indoor climbing wall is sure to beckon children who prefer indoor activities in winter. During the summer months, a bungee trampoline, paintball area, and a skateboard park will keep youngsters on the go. This fun-filled center is a great destination year-round.

Facilities: Restrooms, snack bar.

Zipline at Hunter Mountain.
NY 23, Hunter 12442; 1-800-486-8376; www.huntermtn.com. Admission.

This is the longest and highest zipline tour in North America and it opened at Hunter Mountain in 2010. Starting from the summit of Hunter, the most daring in the family can zip to seven platforms on over 10,000 feet of cable at 50 miles per hour. If this is too

There is now a zipline tour in the Catskills—at Hunter Mountain. GREENE COUNTY TOURISM

intense a recreational experience, there is an excellent alternative for the majority of families—the ecological canopy tour. Short zips, suspended walking bridges, and other wooded features to climb on and over are an exciting part of the tour that lasts over two hours. Afterward, kids can play on the 60-foot Adventure Tower filled with obstacles and fun climbs. This is definitely a unique attraction in the Catskills and will appeal to all ages.

Facilities: Restrooms, cafeteria, gift shop, snack bar.

Zoom Flume Water Park.
Shady Glen Road (just off NY 145), 2 miles north of East Durham 12423; 518-239-4559; www.zoomflume.com. Admission (good for all activities).

This lovely "aquamusement" park is set in Shady Glen Canyon, a natural formation of steep walls and running water, so the site itself is beautiful and worth a stop, even if you are going to observe rather than participate in the array of water activities. The Raging River Ride and Zoom Flume let you slosh and slide your way down the canyon; there's also an enormous activity pool with

The rides at the Zoom Flume Water Park are fun for everyone in the family. GREENE COUNTY TOURISM several slides of all sizes, a game area, and a toddler section for one- and two-year-olds. The Black Vortex Speed Slide takes three at a time through an exciting water adventure that older kids will appreciate. The Wave Pool, a new addition to the water park, will appeal to children of all ages. There are nature trails, scenic overlooks, and waterfalls—as well as a restaurant with an observation deck and a sizable outdoor food court with picnic areas.

Facilities: Restrooms, changing areas, picnic areas, restaurant, food court, lockers.

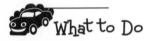 What to Do

CANOEING AND KAYAKING

CD Lane Park. 281 CR 56, Maplecrest 12454; 518-734-4170; www.town ofwindham.com. Free.

The small lake here has a sandy beach area and the town park itself offers soccer and baseball fields, a picnic pavilion, and a beautiful environment the kids will love. You should bring your own canoe or kayak to

GREENE COUNTY TOURISM

the lake; there are no rentals available. Do note that there isn't swimming here unless there is a lifeguard on duty.

North and South Lake State Park. CR 18, Haines Falls 12436; 518-589-5058; www.dec.ny.gov. Admission. There are canoe and rowboat rentals here; the lakes both have beach areas with lifeguards on duty during the summer swimming season.

FISHING

There are approximately 60 streams with wild trout in the county, as well as lakes, ponds, and of course the Hudson River. NY 23A passes Rip Van Winkle Lake in Tannersville, Schoharie Creek, and the Schoharie Reservoir, all easily accessible and great places to fish with young children. NY 145 leads to Lower Catskill Creek, Upper Catskill Creek, and Ten Mile Creek; while NY 296 offers easy access

GREENE COUNTY TOURISM

to the Batavia Kill boat launch and the East Kill Trout Preserve. Yellow signs mark public fishing places in the county and most have designated parking areas. Permits and licenses can be obtained at most bait and tackle shops or town clerk offices. For more detailed information, contact the **Department of Environmental Conservation** at 845-256-3000.

Fins and Grins. 5571 Cauterskill Road, Catskill 12414; 518-943-3407. They offer fishing charters as well as scenic rides on the Hudson River. Captain Bob Lewis supplies all the equipment you need for the excursion. Call in advance to make arrangements.

Reel Happy Charters. 518-622-8670. Captain R. E. Booth has 30 years of experience navigating the Hudson River. He charters a 21-foot boat with room for three people to fish comfortably on the river. April and May is striped bass season and June through October there are other bass varieties, along with catfish. Fly-fishing excursions are also offered. Equipment and bait are supplied. Call in advance to make arrangements.

HIKING

Cohate Preserve. NY 385, Athens 12015; 518-622-3620. This nature preserve (with a self-guided tour) on trails that run along the Hudson River is a perfect gentle hiking spot, even with young children. You can easily see the sign for the preserve on the right side of the highway if you are heading from Catskill toward Athens.

Four Mile Point Preserve. Four Mile Point Road (off NY 385), Coxsackie 12051; 518-731-2727. This preserve is about 8 miles north of the Rip Van Winkle Bridge, a 7.6-acre riverfront area that offers picturesque shoreline vistas and a tranquil inland pond. There are nature trails, and this is a wonderful place to observe several types of birds. Kids will be comfortable on the gently sloping terrain.

Rams Horn–Livingston Sanctuary. Grandview Avenue (off US 9W), Catskill 12414; 518-678-3248. Go 2.5 miles south of the Rip Van Winkle Bridge on US 9W; then make a left onto Grandview Avenue; the parking area is 0.5 mile up the road. Here there are 480 acres of the Hudson's largest tidal swamp forest, which is a breeding ground for shad and bass. There are about 3 miles of trails that can be easily hiked by even the youngest children. A bonus is that bald eagles are often seen in this area.

HORSEBACK RIDING

Bailiwick Ranch/Catskill Equestrian Center. 118 Castle Road, Catskill 12414; 518-678-5665; www.bailiwickranch.com. Open year-round. In business for over 40 years, there is riding here for all ages and abilities. Scenic mountain trail rides are offered for either one or two hours or a half day. For those who would like something more intensive, there are all-day mountain trips and overnight camping excursions. The youngest kids will have fun on the pony rides and playing in the petting zoo. (**See Additional Attractions, pg. 176**). There are both English and Western riding lessons offered in the indoor and outdoor riding arenas.

K&K Equestrian Center. 5203 CR 67, East Durham 12423; 518-966-4829; www.kandkequestrian.blogspot.com. A family-owned and -operated business for over three decades, they offer guided scenic trail rides, pony rides, lessons, and overnight trips. There is an informal atmosphere here, so everyone feels comfortable and welcomed.

Tanglewood Ranch. 438 Cornwallville Road, Cornwallville 12418. Open year-round. This ranch offers scenic trail rides with a five-state view (on a clear day!), pony rides, and horse-drawn hayrides. Depending on what you want to experience, there are half-day, full-day, and overnight camping trips available by advance reservation. Both Western and English riding styles are accommodated.

PERFORMING ARTS

Catskill Mountain Foundation. 7950 Main Street (NY 23A), Hunter 12442; 518-263-4908 x. 202 (weekdays), 518-263-5157 (weekends); www.catskillmtn.org.

This nonprofit organization has revitalized the town of Hunter. Stop in at the performing arts center or bookstore/gallery/organic café and market, all on Main Street, and pick up a current schedule of events that include children's programs, concerts, dance performances, art exhibits, films, festivals, and more. There is a green market open year-round, featuring local organic produce, pasta, grains, eggs, cheeses, and other gourmet specialty foods. Across the street, the foundation also houses the **Doctorow Center for the Arts**, a performance venue showcasing children's theater, puppet shows, musical performances, and the **Pleshakov Piano Collection**—a small piano museum of interest to children studying music. The foundation is definitely the place to find out what is happening culturally in the mountaintop region. Do check their Web site if you are planning a visit and want to include some cultural events. They sponsor the **Sugar Maples Center for Arts and Education** in Windham, which includes classes with state-of-the-art facilities for ceramics, fiber arts, and painting (in addition to hotel accommodations).

Dutchman's Landing. Catskill Point, Main Street, Catskill 12414; 518-943-3223.

This area once served as a boat landing for the Hudson River craft, and today visitors can enjoy spectacular views of the river and eastern shore. There is often musical entertainment here during the warm weather; a farmer's market and craft market operate summer through fall on weekends; and there are also displays of the cultural history of the Catskills, travel information, a picnic and dining area, and riverfront festivals. This is a wonderful place to hang out with the kids with easy access to the Hudson River while enjoying a picnic supper.

Greene Room Players. 518-589-6297. This theater group has been presenting professional musicals, revues, children's shows, comedies, and drama for nearly two decades. The performances are given year-round and take place in various venues throughout the county. There is no Web site, but feel free to call for a schedule.

SKIING AND SNOWBOARDING

Hunter Mountain. NY 23A, Hunter 12442; 518-263-4223, 1-800-486-8376; www.huntermtn.com. (From exit 21 on the New York State Thruway, the trip is approximately 24 miles. Take NY 23 east to US 9W south, then NY 23A west—or it's 18 miles from exit 20 by taking NY 32 north to NY 32A north to NY 23A west.)

STEVE LAING

Hunter Mountain offers challenges for skiers of all ages and abilities.

STEVE LAING

Hunter Mountain has a reputation for being the snowmaking capital of the East and it's well deserved. There are three mountains—Hunter One, Hunter West, and Hunter Mountain—and all offer skiers of all skill levels a chance to test themselves on over 55 trails. Runs at Hunter can extend over 2 miles, with a 3,200-foot summit elevation and vertical drops of 1,600 feet; there are some extremely difficult areas, even for expert skiers. Double, triple, and quadruple chairlifts (there are now 11 lifts) cut some of the lines down to size, but this is such a popular area there are always crowds on weekends and holidays. The Kaatskill Flyer, a six-passenger high-speed lift—the only one of its kind in New York State—was installed in 2010. Do check out the special discounts during weekdays (residents of the local counties get a substantial discount on Tuesdays) when there are no lift lines. They offer early season deals on both lift tickets and lodging as well.

The PlayCare program is for children 6 months old through 6 years of age on Fridays through Sundays. The trained staff entertains the youngest children who are getting ready to ski and ride the lifts. The Three-Year-Old Program gets the little ones out for a half-hour session on the snow while enrolled in a half or full day of PlayCare. The Explorers and Mountaineers program is for children ages 4–12. Here young skiers will learn to improve their turns and build confidence in small groups. Lift tickets, equipment rentals, and lessons are included for all programs.

Hunter offers ski and snowboard lessons for all levels of ability. There is a terrain park for snowboarders with a 1,000-watt stereo system that blasts music, and snowshoeing and snow tubing areas as well.

Facilities: Restrooms, café, restaurant, food court, deli, BBQ, ski school, ski shop, rentals, lockers, babysitting.

Windham Mountain. NY 23, Windham 12496; 518-734-4300, 1-800-SKI-WINDHAM; www.windhammountain.com.

With its 46 trails ranging from beginner to expert serviced by 10 chairlifts, including two high-speed quad lifts, Windham has all the ingredients for great family fun. The summit elevation is 3,100 feet with a base elevation of 1,500 feet: 30 percent of the trails can be easily navigated by beginner skiers. Snowmaking covers 98 percent of all terrain. The Snow Sports School is organized for lessons by age and ability. The First Class Program consists of first-time skiers. Children may progress to Junior Instructor level up to the Racing group, if they excel. Those between the ages of 2–7 who do not wish to ski can spend the day in the learning center with activities such as arts and crafts and games; lunch is included.

There are entertaining special events and activities at Windham Mountain after the snow melts. GREENE COUNTY TOURISM

Younger skiers (ages 4–7) can join the Mini Mogul program for lessons, and children from the ages of 8–12 can take a half day or full day of lessons with the Mountain Master program. Windham Mountain is a great place to take the family and enjoy group activities, particularly snowshoeing, which offers an entirely different way to explore the mountain—even the youngest family members can participate. Night skiing is offered on weekends and holidays; there is an extensive snowboarding area, and a fully equipped tubing park (**see Windham Mountain Adventure Park, pg. 178–179**).

Facilities: Restrooms, cafeteria, lodge, ski shop, rentals, lockers, children's learning center, snowshoeing, snow tubing park, ice rink.

Mountain Trails Cross-Country Ski Center. NY 23A, Tannersville 12485; 518-589-5361; www.mtntrails.com. (Located 0.5 mile west of the traffic light on NY 23A in the village of Tannersville.) Always call before going; weather conditions are continually changing.

Cross-country ski enthusiasts will want to visit Mountain Trails. There are 21 miles of state-of-the-art Snowcat-groomed and track-set woodland trails (beginner to expert) in the beautiful Catskill Mountains. There are also snowshoe and pull-sled rentals. Lessons are available with certified instructors. The trails are patrolled on weekends and during holiday weeks by the ski patrol.

Facilities: Restrooms, snack bar, lodge, ski shop, rentals.

SWIMMING

North and South Lakes. CR 18 (off NY 23A), Haines Falls 12436; 518-589-5058, 518-943-4030; www.dec.ny.gov. Admission (with extra charge for campsites).

This recreational area has breathtaking scenery and a multitude of activities. The highlight of a visit here is swimming in the mountain lakes with their clean, sandy beaches. Boat rentals and fishing are also available, making this a wonderful spot for a family outing. A short hike from North Lake is Kaaterskill Falls, one of the highest waterfalls on the East Coast and a popular subject for Hudson River School artists. The area also has a campground with hook-ups for recreational vehicles. On summer weekends the place gets very busy; if you plan to stay overnight, make reservations early.

Facilities: Restrooms, changing areas, picnic areas, showers, boat rentals, campsites, beach areas with lifeguards.

FAMILY RESORTS

Greene County is an area filled with old-fashioned family resorts owned by the same families for generations. It is impossible to include all the excellent establishments in this book, but I've chosen some of my favorites.

Hull-O Farms. 3739 CR 20, Durham 12422; 518-239-6950; www.hull-o .com. Open year-round.

A stay at this farm is an authentic experience that will be long remembered by your children. You can live the country life on this 300-acre working farm that has been in the same family for seven generations. Milk a cow, collect chicken eggs, feed pigs and baby calves, go fishing, or take a nature walk. The hands-on experience is fun for everyone. There are pumpkins to be picked and hayrides in the autumn, as well as BBQ dinners during the warm-weather months with all-natural

A farm vacation, where children collect chicken eggs and feed pigs, will long be remembered.

meats from the farm and fresh vegetables. There are three cozy guesthouses on the premises and home-cooked meals are served family-style at the enormous dining room table where guests have a chance to meet at the end of a busy day. Nightly rates include a full breakfast and dinner. Children under the age of 2 stay free; those 2–12 are less than half price. There is a two-night minimum stay.

Sunny Hill. 352 Sunny Hill Road, Greenville 12083; 518-634-7642; www.sunnyhill.com.

The Nicholsen family has run this resort since 1920 and several guests return year after year for decades. Surrounded by the Catskills, the facilities here include two 18-hole golf courses, two ball fields, swimming pools, basketball, volleyball, a lake with paddleboats and canoes, indoor miniature golf, and organized outings to points of interest in the area. Together with its scenic location and variety of recreational activities, this makes a wonderful spot for a family reunion. The resort has a capacity of 350 and there are a variety of accommodations available; rates include three meals daily. Do check out their two "Kids R Free" weekends in June and September.

Facilities: Golf courses, ball fields, swimming pools, basketball courts, volleyball courts.

Thompson House. 19 NY 296, Windham 12496; 518-734-4510; www .thompsonhouse.com. Open year-round.

Since 1880 the Thompson family has been offering memorable vacations for families at this picturesque resort with breathtaking views of the Catskills at every turn. South Mountain provides the dramatic backdrop for the resort and the adjoining Windham Country Club where golfers will enjoy the 18-hole course. Kids will be delighted with the huge playground, tennis courts, and large swimming pool with inflatable slide. The pool is heated from May to early September. There are daily scheduled activities for all age groups in addition to nearby bicycling, hiking, horseback riding, and evening entertainment. Breakfast and

GREENE COUNTY TOURISM

dinner are included in the rates, while lunch is served in the coffee shop à la carte. During the winter months, guests at The Evergreen at the Thompson House can enjoy the private lighted ice rink and sledding hill while being only a few minutes drive away from Windham Mountain.

Facilities: Golf course, tennis courts, swimming pool, coffee shop.

Winter Clove Inn. Winter Clove Road, Round Top 12473; 518-622-3267; www.winterclove.com. Open year-round. Group rates.

This is a great family vacation resort that has been run by the same family for four generations. Located in Winter Clove, a deep valley that holds the winter snows until early spring, guests are housed in an old-fashioned (but comfortable) lodge, which has been updated and restored to provide all the modern amenities. Escape to the charm of the country, a place where time moves at a more leisurely pace. Indoor and outdoor pools, tennis courts, volleyball, golf, bowling alleys, and a game room are all on the premises, so that there is always something fun going on for every age group. Kids will love the country picnics, hayrides, movies, and bonfires that are offered in the warm-weather months. During summer evenings, visitors can enjoy the inn's large front porch, complete with rocking chairs. Visitors are welcome to enjoy the many beautiful pools and waterfalls that surround Winter Clove. The chef prepares three meals daily, and the choices on the menu include children's entrées. During the winter, access to cross-country ski trails and equipment are included in the room rate. The Catskills offer many exciting recreational activities nearby.

Facilities: Bowling alley, swimming pools, tennis courts, golf course, hiking trails.

DELAWARE COUNTY

▼▲▼▲▼▲▼

D elaware County, with more than 64,000 acres that are state owned and proclaimed "forever wild," is an ideal place to go for families that enjoy outdoor recreation. The region is filled with places to fish, canoe, kayak, horseback ride, bike, and hike. And at the end of an activity-packed day, visit one of the county's charming villages, which seem as if they were plucked from a 19th-century picture book. This is a county that cherishes its past and a visit here brings back a sense of community celebration that is hard to find in 21st-century life.

Any itinerary to Delaware County should include some special places children will particularly appreciate. There is no better way to sample the fun of old-time travel than to hop aboard any of the vintage trains on the **Delaware & Ulster Railride,** which begins in Arkville. Kids will love the whistles, the bells, and the *click-clack* of the train as it weaves along the tracks, through meadows, and up mountains. **Hanford Mills** in East Meredith is a restored sawmill and woodworking shop where kids will be able to watch as waterpower is harnessed to produce wood products and animal feed. A huge 10-foot water-wheel is still used to make the machinery run and visitors are guided through the rambling mill to watch the antique

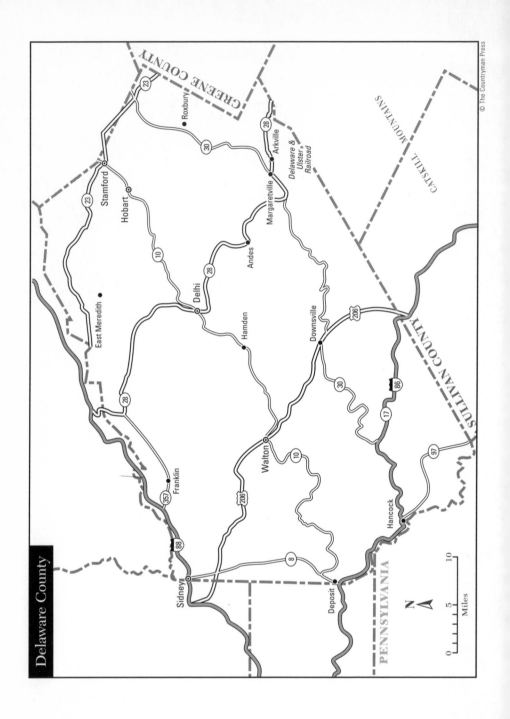

Delaware County

machines. **Plattekill Mountain** in Roxbury is known for its big mountain skiing terrain (and biking during the warm-weather months) and small mountain charm. Family-owned and -operated, the area caters to what they know best—families.

DELAWARE COUNTY TOURISM

Since Delaware County is still a rural area, the special events here tend to take place during the "better weather" months, from late spring through summer. June brings the **Meredith Dairy Fest,** complete with exhibits, games, tractor pulls, music, crafts, hayrides, butter making, ice cream, and all things dairy. **Firemen's Field Days,** a July tradition in Margaretville, features carnival rides and entertainment, along with games of skill and chance. The second week of August is the **Delaware County Fair** in Walton, where the emphasis is on agriculture. On Labor Day Sunday, **Turn of the Century Day** brings vintage baseball to Kirkside Park in Roxbury. The clock is turned back to 1898 and all the pursuits of Victorian times are offered, including period dress, croquet, sack races, horseshoes, a barbershop quartet, and a chicken BBQ. This event commemorates the renowned Roxbury Nine's last baseball game of the season.

For further information, contact the **Delaware County Chamber of Commerce**, 5½ Main Street, Delhi 13753; 607-746-2281, 1-800-642-4443; www.delawarecounty.org.

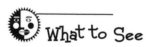

What to See

MUSEUMS AND HISTORIC SITES

Delaware County Historical Association. NY 10, Delhi 13753; 607-746-3849; www.dcha-ny.org. Library and exhibits are open year-round. Admission. Group tours are available by advance reservation.

Kids who love the past will enjoy becoming a part of it when they visit this historic site. The Frisbee House, which is on the grounds, was the birthplace of Delaware County's government, but the site itself is much more than dry history. In the house, kids will get a chance to see a children's room from the mid-19th century as well as a selection of old toys, clothing, furniture, and a tavern from the 1800s. Out in the barn, a permanent exhibit introduces viewers to the rhythm and patterns of 19th-century farm life. A dog churn might interest children. (The name is derived from the common practice at the time of harnessing dogs to

power a wheel that churned butter.) There is also an enormous collection of wagons and large farming tools like rakes, flails, and apple presses. Also on the grounds are the blacksmith shop, a gun shop, a one-room schoolhouse, a tollhouse, and a small family cemetery. Young nature lovers will enjoy walking the short trail that begins at an old farm path and winds down to Elk Creek. The plants and flowers are marked, and lucky observers may even spot a raccoon or two.

The Frisbee House in Delhi at the Delaware County Historical Association.

DELAWARE COUNTY TOURISM

Even the youngest visitors will be able to complete this trail so don't hesitate to take the walk, especially in the summer. Special events at the site are well suited to children's interests. Additionally, teachers may want to inquire about the program called "The Butcher, The Baker, The Candlestick-Maker." The education director will give a 30–60 minute presentation at your school, depending on what length is requested.

Facilities: Restrooms, picnic areas, gift shop. Pets are not allowed. Most of the buildings are wheelchair accessible.

Hanford Mills Museum. Intersection of CR 10 and CR 12, East Meredith 13757; 607-278-5744; www.hanfordmills.org. (The museum is located 10 miles east of Oneonta.) Admission. Group tours at special rates available by advance reservation.

The pastoral Hanford Mills Museum complex on Kortright Creek is a great place for a picnic.   DARREN MCGEE, NYSDED

Once a busy, noisy sawmill, gristmill, and woodworking shop, this pastoral site has been restored to its original use, and visitors will be able to watch as waterpower is once again harnessed to produce wood products and animal feed. Situated alongside a serene millpond, the buildings reflect the pace and industries of a century ago. A huge 10-foot waterwheel is still used to make the machinery run, as Kortright Creek provides the power. Visitors are guided through the mill building to watch the waterwheel and the antique woodworking machines. The staff is friendly and will answer questions about procedures; the tour will interest adults and children, who never seem to tire of watching the waterwheel grumble and roar its way around in circles. Outside, 15 other notable structures include barns, lumber sheds, and an icehouse; there are also fly-fishing clinics at the millpond. Hanford Mills is well known for its special children's events. On Independence Day, an old-fashioned celebration features traditional music, homemade ice cream, games, and rides. The museum is also open the first Saturday in February for its annual ice harvest, when visitors of all ages can try their hands at sawing and harvesting ice.

Facilities: Restrooms, picnic areas (the pond is a lovely place to have lunch, but bring your own, there are no nearby restaurants or stores), gift shop (children's games and books are available, as well as local food products). Pets are not allowed. There are gravel paths here, but it would be difficult to maneuver a stroller inside the buildings. The mill, some exhibits, and restrooms are wheelchair accessible.

ADDITIONAL ATTRACTIONS

Delaware & Ulster Railroad (DURR). 43510 NY 28, Arkville 12406; 845-586-DURR; www.durr.org. Entrance to the site and depot is free, but admission is charged for the ride. Children under three ride for free. Group rates are available by advance reservation.

All aboard for a two-hour ride on the old Doodlebug, a self-propelled mail and freight car that was used more than 70 years ago on the Catskill rail lines! Painted bright red, the car is one of several pieces of old railroad stock that have been restored to provide fun rides for all ages. Even the youngest children will be delighted with the whistles, the bells, and the *click-clack* of the train as it weaves along the tracks through meadows and up mountains. Along the way, the friendly train crew points out interesting sites and tells stories of what travel was like before automobiles. The Catskill Mountains were once a daily stop for tourist and milk trains from New York City, but when the service stopped in the 1960s many believed the echo of the train whistle was gone forever from the region. But the rail ride has resurrected some of the favorite trains that once rattled along the tracks. Try to visit the DURR on a special-events weekend that caters to kids. Sometimes costumed train robbers stop the train to hold up the crew and passengers. Occasionally, fiddlers and storytellers entertain everyone with songs and tales. There are Halloween ghost trains and foliage runs during the autumn months. The Web site has a complete timetable and listing of special events.

Travelers take in the scenery on the Delaware & Ulster Railroad ride that wends its way through the Catskill Mountains. PETER FINGER

Facilities: Restroom, gift shop, snack caboose. Wheelchair and stroller accessible.

Pakatakan Farmers Market. Round Barn, 46676 NY 30, Halcottsville 12438; www.pfmarket.org. Free.

Kids will enjoy a stop at this farmer's market, which is likely to yield a shopping bag full of local vegetables, fruits, and crafts. The market is housed in a historic round barn that was designed to make maintaining the stock less work. Indoor and outdoor vendors provide the best in produce, much of it organically grown, complete with free samples at many booths and a chance to chat with a farmer about their life and work. There are a number of prepared food vendors as well and lots of picnic areas where you can enjoy lunch or a snack. Special events, which take place just about every week through the summer, have included musical performances, dances, visits from farm animals and raptors, and the famous cow-pie derby. This is a fun way to spend a country morning, and a great way to experience rural life that continues to survive in Delaware County.

Facilities: Restrooms, picnic areas. No pets are allowed. Strollers can manage on the grounds, but wheelchair accessibility may be a problem, especially in inclement weather.

Stone and Thistle Farm. 1211 Kelso Road, East Meredith 13757; 607-278-5773; www.stoneandthistlefarm.com. There is a small fee for the tour and both the brunch and tour are $15. School tours for 25 or more children are welcome.

Grass-fed and organic-raised beef, lamb, goat, pork, poultry, and rabbit are the business of this family farm in a pastoral valley at the foothills of the Catskills. A visit here is a great way to introduce children to antibiotic- and hormone-free foods. The farm is also home to the Kortright Creek Creamery, which produces certified organic grass-fed goat's milk and yogurt. Farming is a family adventure and Tom and Denise Warren along with children Riley, Katey, and Shane are all involved in the enterprise. The family also has border collies and horses that visitors will be able to see up

Children have a chance to spend time with the animals at Stone and Thistle's "Farmer for a Day" program.
DELAWARE COUNTY TOURISM

close. For those children who want more time here, there is a "Farmer for a Day" program. Join the family and milk goats, collect eggs, move sheep with the border collies, and tend the vegetable gardens. Included is a delightful meal using the products gathered from the farm.

Facilities: Restrooms, restaurant, gift shop.

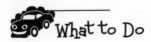

What to Do

BICYCLING

Catskill Scenic Trail (CST). 607-652-2281; www.catskillscenictrail.org. This 19-mile trail is great for off-road trips and can be accessed at various points where there are designated parking areas. One place to get on the trail is the historic Stamford Depot at the intersection of Railroad Avenue and South Street in the village of Stamford. There is also a parking lot north of NY 10, just east of the village of Bloomville. The CST is marked with octagonal signs that show the distance to the trailhead in the direction you are facing. There is only a 400-foot change in elevation over the entire 19 miles, which makes it a pleasant, relatively easy ride for all. Stamford is the peak, and it is downhill in both directions from that point, so I suggest you begin the tour there. The Web site contains detailed information about the trail.

A group of mountain bikers takes a rest at Bike Plattekill Mountain Resort.

DELAWARE COUNTY TOURISM

Bike Plattekill Mountain Resort. 469 Plattekill Mountain Road, Roxbury 12474; 607-326-3500; www.plattekill.com. This mountain biking center offers rentals, instruction, and 60 miles of trails in the surrounding valleys and mountains. There are also hiking and chairlift rides. If you are a first-timer, this is a great place to go to try out the sport. However, there is a variety of terrain to suit all levels of ability.

CANOEING AND KAYAKING

Al's Sport Store. At the junction of NY 30 and NY 206, Downsville 13755; 607-363-7740; www.alssportstore.com. Al's is a clearinghouse for canoe, kayak, and fishing information; they rent equipment and have tours in season.

CHRIS OLNEY

Canoeing the Delaware River is a popular way to explore the county—and get out of the car!

Catskill Outfitters. 7 North Street, Walton 13856; 1-800-631-0105; www.catskilloutfitters.com. This shop is able to supply everything you need to rent for a canoe or kayak outing.

FISHING

Delaware County is home to the East and West branches of the Delaware River, the Susquehanna River, and the Beaverkill stream; it is served by the Cannonsville, Pepacton, and Schoharie reservoirs, making fishing a popular sport in this region. The Beaverkill is probably the most famous trout fishing stream in America, the birthplace of fly-fishing—so if your family wants to try the sport, this is one of the best places anywhere to start. New York State fishing licenses are required. They are easy to purchase in most towns; check with the town clerk or at the village offices. For reservoir fishing, special permits are required—call the Department of Environmental Conservation regional office (607-652-7366) for information on permits and maps. Brown and yellow wooden signs along the streams and rivers indicate fishing areas open to the public. Most of these places offer off-road parking. Detailed maps are available where you purchase your fishing license and at town offices. Riverfront property may be posted off-limits as part of the New York City watershed, so the maps should be consulted; heavy fines could result from illegal fishing. Further information on specific fishing areas can be obtained by calling 1-800-642-4443.

HIKING

Catskill Forest Preserve. 65561 NY 10, Stamford 12167; 607-652-3698; www.dec.ny.gov. The regional office of the preserve is a good place to get information regarding the more than 300 miles of trails that vary in length from 0.5 mile to almost 100 miles. Even novice hikers will find comfortable trails, whether for a day trip or an overnight experience. Trail brochures are available upon request.

Catskill Scenic Trail. Railroad Avenue, Stamford 12167; 607-652-2821; www.catskillscenictrail.org. This trail has a marked 19-mile stretch with a hard-packed surface and gentle grade perfect for hiking, biking, and cross-country skiing. This is an excellent choice for those with young children.

Spring is a great time of year to hike or bike the Catskill Scenic Trail.
DELAWARE COUNTY TOURISM

Kirkside Park. Main Street, Roxbury 12474; 607-326-3722. This historic 11-acre treasure was formerly the estate of Helen Gould-Shepard, daughter of railroad magnate and Roxbury native son Jay Gould. Rich in natural beauty and history—and restored to its glorious splendor—Kirkside has rustic Adirondack-style bridges, graceful paths along the east branch of the Delaware River, and lush plantings to admire in the warm-weather months.

Painting at Kirkside Park.
DELAWARE COUNTY TOURISM

Oquaga Creek State Park. 5995 CR 20, Bainbridge 13793; 607-467-4160; www.nysparks.state.ny.us. There are 6.5 miles of marked hiking trails here that will delight those of all abilities. The park itself is actually in three counties—Delaware, Broome, and Chenango.

SUNY Delhi Outdoor Education Center. NY 28, Delhi 13753; 607-746-4051; www.delhi.edu. This facility, 2 miles south of the village of Delhi, offers woods walks and educational excursions in a nature preserve with marked trails, making it an excellent place to introduce children to hiking.

HORSEBACK RIDING

Broken Spoke Stables. 874 Narrow Notch Road, Hobart 13788; 607-538-9651; www.brokenspokestables.com. Reservations required.

This 87-acre property with miles of trails has been in the same family for over 130 years. In addition to trail rides, they offer lessons (both English and Western style riding) and boarding. The surrounding countryside is a beautiful area to explore on horseback.

Stone Tavern Farm. 2080 Upper Meeker Hollow, Roxbury 12474; 607-326-3600; www.stonetavernfarm.com. Reservations required.

The beautiful stone tavern from which this stable derives its name was built in 1803; formerly an inn, it is the oldest building in Roxbury. This is a wonderful place to go out on the trail with experienced guides. Children must be 10 years of age to handle a horse on their own. Those 6–9 need to have a guide walk with them (at an extra charge). The 4- and 5-year-olds may enjoy pony rides. The stable also offers guided picnic lunch trail rides (2.5 hours) and dinner excursions (3 hours), complete with a full spread from the grill cooked at a streamside location.

PERFORMING ARTS

The Open Eye Theater. 960 Main Street, Margaretville 12455; 845-586-1660, 845-586-2727; www.theopeneye.org. There are new plays and classics for all ages here as well as a youth theater workshop and arts in education program. Call or check the Web site for a current schedule of performances.

Facilities: Restrooms. Wheelchair and stroller accessible.

DELAWARE COUNTY TOURISM

ALEC WALKER

Roxbury Arts Group. 53484 Main Street, Roxbury 12474; 607-326-7908; www.roxburyartsgroup.org. This cultural organization features a wide variety of arts, entertainment, and education programs year-round at three venues (Roxbury, Stamford, and Denver Vega Valley). There are concerts, puppet shows, workshops, and arts programs for children. Call or check the Web site for a schedule.

Facilities: Restrooms. Wheelchair and stroller accessible.

Stamford Performing Arts Center. 76 Main Street, Stamford 12167; 607-652-3121. There is the full range of performance art here—plays, concerts, mime, and children's theater. They don't have a Web site, so call for a schedule of events.

Facilities: Restrooms. Wheelchair and stroller accessible.

West Kortright Centre. 49 West Kortright Church Road, West Kortright 13757; 607-278-5454; www.westkc.org. Enjoy everything from Bach to bluegrass and zydeco at this cultural center, which sponsors performance workshops, concerts, art exhibits, and community gatherings in a historic country church. Concerts are held both outdoors, in the green fields, and indoors—where guests sit in unique rounded pews. The intimate setting makes all events delightful. There are usually performances in both theater and dance that will appeal to young people; call or check the Web site for a schedule.

Facilities: Restrooms. Wheelchair and stroller accessible.

SKIING AND SNOWBOARDING

Ski Plattekill Mountain Resort. 469 Plattekill Mountain Road (two miles off NY 30), Roxbury 12474; 607-326-3500; www.plattekill.com.

Plattekill Mountain has been called the Catskills' best-kept secret, and is known for its big-mountain terrain and small-mountain charm. This family-owned and -operated resort caters to families. There are 35 trails and three lifts serving 1,100 feet of vertical drop. The mountain has something for everyone, from 2-mile-long beginner cruising runs to some of the steepest double-black-diamond slopes in the region. The resort also offers a full-service ski school with lessons in skiing and snowboarding, and a special children's program called Snowkidding for those under the age of eight. This program is geared to teach youngsters the fundamentals of skiing in a relaxing, fun atmosphere. A racing program and freestyle mogul camp are also available for more advanced skiers. Plattekill is a fine place to escape overcrowded slopes on weekends and enjoy a laid-back, family-friendly atmosphere.

Facilities: *Restrooms, cafeteria, ski school, retail shop, nursery (hourly and day rates available).*

SWIMMING

Bear Spring State Park. 512 East Trout Brook Road, Downsville 13755; 607-865-6989.

Launt Pond is beautiful and this state park offers beaches, boat rentals, and a campground. However, make sure to call in advance to check if lifeguards are on duty (beaches are closed when they are not).

Big Pond Little Pond State Park. 549 Little Pond Campground Road, Andes 13731.

The 13-acre pond in this park is open for swimming when lifeguards are on duty. There are also rowboat, paddleboat, kayak, and canoe rentals available.

East Sidney Recreation Area. 4659 NY 357, Franklin 13775; 607-829-3528.

In addition to a lovely beach, there are playgrounds, picnic areas, campgrounds, and a boat launch at this recreation area on the Ouleout Creek between Franklin and Unadilla. It's a good choice for families with young children who will find many activities to keep the kids entertained.

OTSEGO COUNTY

▼▲▼▲▼▲▼

O tsego County is a timeless place where heritage and natural beauty merge in the rolling foothills of the northern Catskills, the land of James Fenimore Cooper's *Leatherstocking Tales*. If you love baseball, you will love Cooperstown, the heart of the county and the birthplace of the sport. Folklore has it that Abner Doubleday, on an afternoon in 1839, was inspired to invent a game that soon became our national pastime. The county is well known for its maple syrup production, and during the season many farms throughout the area invite visitors to watch the sap being boiled into syrup— before going indoors to enjoy a hearty pancake breakfast.

Otsego is a place where past meets present, from hands-on history museums and Native American art to baseball games and soccer tournaments. The **National Baseball Hall of Fame** is a must-see for baseball lovers of all ages. Three floors are filled with thousands of pieces of baseball history—memorabilia, clothing, photos, cards, and equipment. Everyone in the family will appreciate the **Farmers' Museum,** a "village" assembled during the last 50 years by importing buildings from across central New York State. A highlight is the Cardiff Giant, known as America's greatest hoax. The **Science Discovery Center** at the State University of New York at Oneonta has

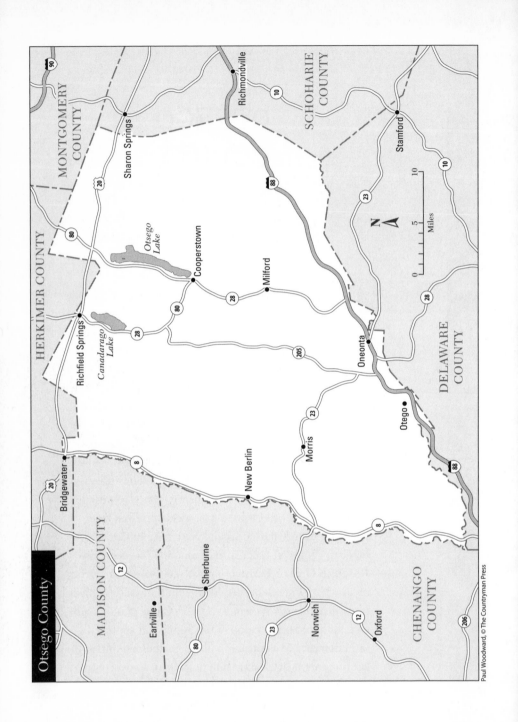

Otsego County

Paul Woodward, © The Countryman Press

more than 80 hands-on exhibits for kids, who marvel at the array of gadgets and gizmos. **Glimmerglass State Park** is a great place to spend time swimming, fishing, or camping overnight. James Fenimore Cooper called Otsego Lake "Glimmerglass" because of its serene beauty; it's the perfect place to end a busy day of sightseeing.

Try to coordinate your visit to Otsego with one of the many special events in the region. In mid-July, the Hall of Fame induction ceremonies are held at the National Baseball Hall of Fame. Cooperstown is bustling during the summer, and it's an exciting time to visit. The county celebrates its traditions every August at the annual county fair in Morris. And in September, the **Fly Creek Cider Mill** hosts its annual **Antique Tractor Festival.**

For further information, contact **Otsego County Tourism,** 242 Main Street, Oneonta, NY 13820; 607-643-0059, 1-800-843-3394; www.otsegocounty.net and www.thisiscooperstown.com.

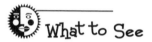 What to See

MUSEUMS AND HISTORIC SITES

Baseball Wax Museum. 99 Main Street, Cooperstown 13326; 607-547-1273; www.baseballwaxmuseum.com.

Here you will find the only wax museum featuring baseball greats and a virtual-reality exhibit featuring Roger Clemens's fastball. Some of the wax figures include Lou Gehrig, Ty Cobb, Joe DiMaggio (and Marilyn Monroe), Jackie Robinson, and dozens more. The place is filled with autographed items and features Tom Catal's *Tribute to Mickey Mantle.*

Facilities: Restrooms, gift shop, café.

Farmers' Museum. 5775 NY 80 (Lake Road), Cooperstown 13326; 607-547-1450, 1-888-547-1450; www.farmersmuseum.org. (The

Kids love to strike the same pose as the lifelike players at the Baseball Wax Museum.
THISISCOOPERSTOWN.COM

museum is located 1 mile north of the village of Cooperstown.) Admission (children under the age of six are admitted free). Group rates and tours available by advance reservation.

Although this "village" looks as if it has been in Cooperstown forever, it was really assembled during the last 50 years by importing buildings from across central New York State. Split rails and stone fences guard the landscape, heritage breeds of animals grace the farmyard, and children have a wonderful time in this 19th-century historic village and farm. You enter the site through the huge stone barn that houses several exhibit galleries worth the price of admission by themselves. Four exhibit areas highlight aspects of life in rural upstate New York, including hops production, traditional handcrafts, and architectural styles. The family activity center provides parents and children with exciting learning opportunities.

Housed in his brightly striped tent is the Cardiff Giant, known as America's greatest hoax. It is a huge stone carving that was buried by night, and then dug up by an enterprising con artist/farmer who publicized it as a petrified giant of biblical times. P. T. Barnum eventually bought the giant.

Outside, the village itself has much to explore and see; the buildings house enough to keep all ages interested. There is a printer's shop, where much of the village's printing is still done; a doctor's office; a pharmacy; a blacksmith shop with working smith; a tavern; a church; eight heritage gardens including a children's garden; and more. Heritage breeds of farm animals include Devon cattle, chickens, ducks, sheep, pigs, turkeys, and a patient pair of oxen. Special weekend events highlight the season including a Spring Festival in May, Independence Day in July, Harvest Festival in September, and a Candlelight Evening in December. Kids should not miss a stop at the village green, where they can try walking on stilts or rolling a hoop along the grounds.

Facilities: Restrooms, picnic areas, restaurant, gift shop. Strollers can manage here, and the paths can be negotiated by a wheelchair, but call ahead if access is a concern.

Fenimore Art Museum. 5798 NY 80 (Lake Road), Cooperstown 13326; 607-547-1400; www.fenimoreartmuseum.org. Admission (children under the age of six are admitted free).

This museum houses one of the most outstanding collections of folk art in America. Children and their families will enjoy learning about art and history with a truly hands-on approach here. The galleries reflect and complement permanent and temporary exhibits in the museum and encourage learning through visual, tactile, and auditory activities. Children are encouraged to relax, sit back, and interact in gallery spaces constructed especially for them. The labels for many paintings have corresponding text for kids—and at their eye level. There is even a corner where children can stop and create artwork of their own, which is posted on one of the gallery walls.

The museum also houses the Thaw Collection of North American Indian Art, one of the finest private collections in the country, now accessible to all. Children will be intrigued by the colorful powerful art created by Native American tribes, including huge paintings on hides, carved kachina dolls, and striking beaded clothing.

Facilities: Restrooms, restaurant, gift shop (with a wonderful selection of books and activity kits for children). Stroller and wheelchair accessible.

National Baseball Hall of Fame. 25 Main Street, Cooperstown 13326; 607-547-7200, 1-888-HALL-OF-FAME; www.baseballhall.org. Admission (children under the age of six are admitted free). Group rates available by advance reservation.

This is it—the promised land for baseball lovers of any age! Three floors are filled with thousands of pieces of baseball history—memorabilia, clothing, photos, cards, and equipment. From the time you enter—where the hand-carved lifelike wooden statues of Babe Ruth, Ted Williams, and other greats greet you—until you leave, everything you see is related to great and not-so-great moments in America's favorite pastime. Pictures of current players and the uniforms from all the modern major leagues in the Today's Highlights room will gain the attention of young fans, as will the large baseball gum and tobacco card collection on display. The Hall of Fame gallery holds the plaques of inductees; there is a section devoted to the early African American leagues; and the new wing's state-of-the-art theater offers a short film all about the excitement and tradition of baseball. Kids who love statistics will enjoy the Records room, filled with memorabilia and displays concerning the records set by the greatest players—and a chronological history of baseball displays with many bats, balls, and gloves that were involved in the

greatest plays. The museum's
interactive exhibits let kids call
up information on the Hall of
Fame members, and additional
displays focus on women in baseball, umpires, and the World
Series. Throughout the summer,
a series of baseball films is
screened in the Library Building,
which faces Cooper Park. The
National Baseball Hall of Fame
is a comfortable museum, especially on a hot summer afternoon,
but be aware that it is always
crowded on Independence Day and when the annual Hall of Fame
induction is held (also in July).

THISISCOOPERSTOWN.COM

*Facilities: Restrooms, gift shop (with lots of baseball memorabilia).
Strollers can manage here and the museum is wheelchair accessible.*

ADDITIONAL ATTRACTIONS

Clark Sports Center. 124 CR 52, Cooperstown 13326; 607-547-2800;
www.clarksportscenter.com. Admission for daily pass (additional charge
for use of Nautilus equipment).

An outstanding stop for families, this sports center is state-of-the-art
and open to the public. There is an indoor swimming pool, a bowling
alley, indoor running tracks and climbing wall, and the area's only Out-
ward Bound–designed adventure ropes course and climbing wall. For a
rainy day, this action-filled stop will keep the kids busy. Not all the facilities are available for use all the time, so if the kids have a special interest,
check the Web site or call ahead for the schedule. Classes and workouts
are available as well.

Facilities: Restrooms, lockers, towels.

Cooperstown and Charlotte Valley Railroad. 136 East Main Street, Mil-
ford 13807; 607-432-2429; www.lrhs.com. Admission.

Take a ride along the scenic Susquehanna River with the Leatherstocking Railway Historical Society's rail journey back in time. The two-

hour, 16-mile round-trip train ride occasionally features special events that will delight the kids.

Facilities: Restrooms.

Cooperstown Family Campground. 230 Petkewec Road, Cooperstown 13326; 607-293-7766, 1-800-959-CAMP; www.cooperstownfamilycamp-ground.com. (Take NY 28 2.5 miles south from Cooperstown; turn right onto CR 11, and go 4 miles.) Watch for signs. Admission.

This is a large (100-unit) campground that offers a great deal to families. The campsite is only minutes away from the village of Cooper-stown, so visitors can enjoy the outdoors and still be near all the muse-ums and attractions. On summer evenings children will love the free pony rides and hayrides. The small working farm on the premises allows kids to help milk the cows in the morning, feed the chickens, and get up close to the animals—which include peacocks, deer, cougar, and many miniature mammals. There are on-site fishing ponds and a pool for swimming. The youngest hikers will enjoy the short marked nature trail, and afterward can play miniature golf, ride in a paddleboat, or play games in a recreation hall in the event of rain. This is a busy place, and it's one of the few campgrounds that offer such a variety of activities. It is necessary to make reservations in advance on summer weekends.

Facilities: Restrooms, snack bar.

Cooperstown Bat Company. 118 Main Street, Cooperstown 13326; 607-547-2415; www.cooperstownbat.com. Free.

This company specializes in making custom and fine bats and bat accessories, such as display racks. They issue commemorative bats, per-sonalized bats, and even autographed bats. Each one is handmade, and you can watch the staff working on a custom order if you visit during the summer months. Do call in advance and ask what hours there will be bat turning!

Facilities: Restrooms.

Doubleday Batting Range. 135 Main Street (next to Doubleday Field), Cooperstown 13326; 607-547-1852; www.doubledaybatting.com. No admission (but there is a charge for the pitching machines and video games).

The batting range is not connected with the Hall of Fame—but it is an interesting, fun commercial stop for baseball-hungry kids. Here you can use the same pitching machines used by the pros and check your throwing speed with radar gear. It's the only place in the village where kids can actually throw a baseball!

Facilities: Restrooms, snack bar.

Fly Creek Cider Mill and Orchard. 288 Goose Street, Fly Creek 13337; 607-547-9692; www.flycreekcidermill.com. (Located 3 miles from the village of Cooperstown; follow the signs from NY 28 and NY 80.) Free.

This site offers visitors a chance to see apple cider produced as it was a century ago, with one of the oldest water-powered mills in the state. Built in 1856, the mill is still run with a 1924 engine for the grinder and an 1889 hydraulic apple press. Mill-made fudge, cheese, and cider samples are offered to visitors, and the last weekend in September is the big Applefest—with baked goods, kids activities, and (of course) apples, apple wine, and cider for sale. The mountain views are lovely in autumn, and you may want to combine a stop at the mill with a day in nearby Cooperstown.

Facilities: Restrooms, snack bar (featuring gourmet specialty foods), gift shop. The ground floor of the mill is accessible to strollers and wheelchairs.

Science Discovery Center of Oneonta. Physical Science Building, State University, Oneonta 13820; 607-436-2011; www.oneonta.edu. Free. Group tours by special arrangement.

This unique center places the emphasis on practical science; kids will have a chance to test and explore more than 80 interactive exhibits. They can learn about sound, electricity, magnetism, and chemistry; make noise; or just watch as the gadgets and gizmos prove that science is for everyone.

Facilities: Restrooms. Wheelchair accessible.

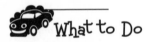 What to Do

BOAT CRUISES

Lake Otsego Boat Tours. 1 Fair Street, Cooperstown 13326; 607-547-5295. Admission.

Cooperstown lies at the foot of Otsego Lake, and there is no better way to see the lake and surrounding landscape than from the water. Lake tours take you past scenes from James Fenimore Cooper's novels: Kingfisher Tower (a small water tower from the 19th century built in the shape of a castle), well-manicured lakeside estates, Sunken Island (which disappears when the water is high), and James Fenimore Cooper's home. Older children will love the stories of pioneers and Native Americans told by the boat guides, and the lake is beautiful on a summer afternoon. I recommend you bring along sun hats and sweaters, especially if it is a breezy day. Boat tours leave from the bottom of Fair Street, near the Baseball Hall of Fame. The *Glimmerglass Queen* is a beautiful vessel, and older children may even feel they have been whisked back in time during the tour!

Facilities: Restrooms, snack bar.

Sam Smith's Boatyard. 6098 NY 80, Cooperstown 13326; 607-547-2543; www.samsmithsboatyard.com. (Located 2.5 miles north of the village of Cooperstown.)

This is where you can rent a kayak or canoe for an outing on the lake, far from the bustle of Main Street. The nautical gift shop is a fun place to check out and fisherkids can select their own tackle here as well.

MAPLE FARM TOURS

Otsego County is well known for its maple syrup production, and at many farms throughout the county visitors may watch the sap being boiled down into syrup. The sap houses are usually small affairs that are steamy, hot, and sweet, and there is nothing like the taste of warm maple syrup to usher in spring for you and the kids. Tours consist of a stop in the sugar bush (the maple trees), a visit to the sap house, and (sometimes) the candy-making area. The tours are usually informal, and I suggest you put on boots and a hat before you venture out into the woods and the mud of an Otsego County March. Make sure to call before you go since the season is highly weather dependent. The following farms offer tours in maple season, which usually runs from March to mid-April: **Brodies Sugarbush,** 2959 CR 34, Westford 13488; 607-264-3225. Take NY 165 to CR 34 and go 1 mile up the road, watch for signs; **Captain's Grove Maple Products,** 654 US 20, West Winfield 13491; 315-822-5835; **Millers Mills Maple,** 258 Huxtable Road, West Winfield 13491; 315-822-5283.

PARKS

Gilbert Lake State Park. 607-432-2114; www.nysparks.state.ny.us. (The park is located between NY 205 and NY 51, 12 miles northwest of Oneonta.) Fee for camping. Groups and camping by reservation only.

This 1,600-acre state park is located in one of the loveliest areas of central New York State. Lush forests and open meadows surround Gilbert Lake—with its sandy beach, where kids will enjoy swimming and boating. There are children's play areas in the park, and several marked nature trails and hiking trails will tempt the adventurous. A special recreation program is held in the park through the summer, and there are occasionally storytellers and other entertainers to amuse the youngsters. Camping is available on-site, in either campgrounds or cabins, but note that the cabins must be reserved several months in advance. The action doesn't stop at Labor Day, however—cross-country ski trails, snowshoeing, and snowmobiling are all popular sports at this park during the winter.

Facilities: Restrooms, picnic areas, snack stand in summer. Strollers are not recommended here. The beach is wheelchair accessible, with a ramp down to the lake, and several of the bathrooms have access as well.

Glimmerglass State Park. 1527 CR 31, Cooperstown 13326; 607-547-8662; www.nysparks.state,ny.us. (The park is located 7 miles north of Cooperstown on the east side of Otsego Lake.) Open year-round. There is a small use fee charged. Group visits and overnight camping are permitted by advance reservation only.

James Fenimore Cooper called Otsego Lake "Glimmerglass" because of its serene beauty, and you can see why at this delightful park—where you can spend the day or camp overnight. Swim and fish from lakeside spots, watch sailboats go by, or enjoy some time with the kids in the children's playground areas. There are extensive hiking trails throughout the 600-acre park, as well as a shorter trail for young naturalists. A picnic area is complete with fireplaces and covered pavilions for bad weather, but make sure to note: Because of the small number of campsites (only 40) and the popularity of the lake, this campground fills up quickly in the summer. Even day-trippers should bring along their own portable chairs and tables. If you are in Cooperstown on a weekend during the winter months, there is a lot to do in the park—including snow tubing (the tubes are free), cross-country skiing, ice skating on the lake (bring your own skates), and snowshoeing. About 3 miles of trails snake through the park and the skiing is free, but you must bring your own equipment.

Hyde Hall Mansion, a covered bridge, and several outbuildings are contained within a 15-acre historic site within the park. The 50-room mansion, a restoration in progress, is considered one of the finest surviving examples of classical revival architecture in the country. There are occasionally concerts on the grounds, so inquire about any special events when you enter the park.

Facilities: Restrooms, picnic areas, snack stand, fireplaces, campsites, playground. On winter weekends, the restrooms are open, and there are hot drinks and snacks for sale. The park has limited access areas for strollers and wheelchairs, although six of the campsites are accessible to the disabled.

PICK-YOUR-OWN FARMS

Ingall's Berry and Vegetable Farm. 4663 NY 28, Cooperstown 13326; 607-547-5481. There are seasonal harvest delights here, ranging from asparagus in May to apples in autumn. You can pick berries, tomatoes, and a variety of other crops. Call in advance to see what is ripe for picking. Children will love the corn mazes and hayrides.

Willy's Farm and Cider Mill. 349 Badeau Hill Road, Schenevus 12155; 607-547-2186. This family-owned and -operated cider mill and pumpkin farm is located on 100 scenic acres with lots of room for the kids to run around. It is definitely a terrific place to visit during autumn harvest time when there are special events on weekends, including pumpkin painting and pumpkin rolls. In addition, there are crops to pick, hayrides, a corn maze, and home-baked pies and other tempting treats for sale.

SCHOHARIE COUNTY

▼▲▼▲▼▲▼

S choharie County history has been entwined with the history of emerging America from the beginning. The Schoharie Valley was so important to the Revolutionary cause that the U.S. Army's first cavalry charge took place here. General George Washington stationed several regiments of Continental soldiers—troops he could ill afford to spare—to protect the valley's harvest, which supplied his army.

What is now known as the **Old Stone Fort Museum** withstood a fierce attack by the British during the Revolutionary War. Located in the village of Schoharie, it first opened its doors to visitors in 1889. Today, children enjoy touring the 18th-century Dutch barn and 19th-century one-room schoolhouse. At the **Iroquois Indian Museum** a self-guided tour takes visitors through a series of interactive displays that include an archaeological dig and tell the story of the earliest people who lived along the Cobleskill Creek some nine thousand years ago. Kids will also learn about the Mohawks who had a village in the Schoharie Valley in the 1700s. No visit to the area would be complete without a trip through the fantastic subterranean worlds of the county. Two popular and spectacular caves—**Howe Caverns** and **Secret Caverns**—offer visitors a unique underground adventure filled with winding

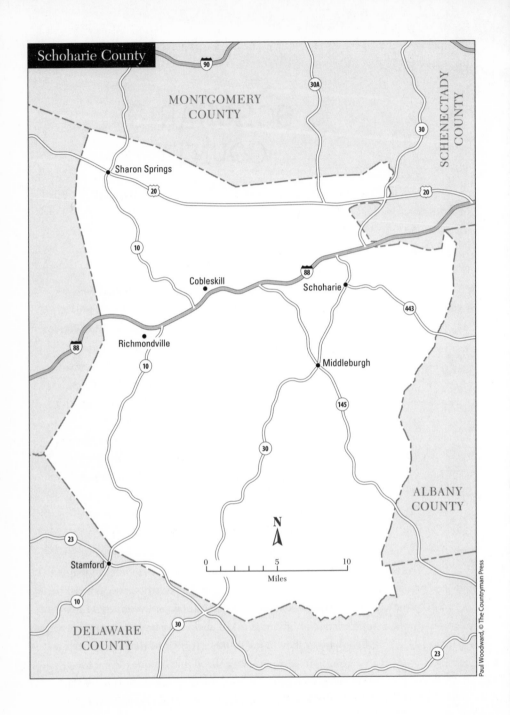

Schoharie County

MONTGOMERY COUNTY

SCHENECTADY COUNTY

Sharon Springs

Cobleskill

Schoharie

Richmondville

Middleburgh

ALBANY COUNTY

N

0   5   10

Miles

Stamford

DELAWARE COUNTY

Paul Woodward, © The Countryman Press

passageways and massive geologic formations. There's plenty of fun aboveground at the New York Power Authority's **Blenheim-Gilboa Power Project Visitors Center.** Housed in a 19th-century dairy barn, the state-of-the-art exhibits and interactive displays show kids how hydropower is created and used.

With rolling hills, waterways, and wide-open spaces, Schoharie County offers visitors a vast outdoor recreational area. With two state parks, three state forests, and miles of nature trails, it is paradise for families who love to hike, bike, and camp. The 500-acre **Mine Kill State Park** offers a relaxing site for picnicking, softball, volleyball, basketball, and water sports. Winter activities include tobogganing, sledding, snow-shoeing, and cross-country skiing. For something a little different, visit the **Landis Arboretum** in Esperance to see one of the Northeast's most magnificent collections of trees and shrubs. The 200-acre public garden is the perfect place for kids who are curious about plants, animals, and natural history. The grounds contain ponds, a wetland, open fields, trails, and phenomenal views.

A number of kid-friendly special events take place year-round and reflect the way of life in the county. The fourth weekend in April is the annual **Maple Festival** in the village of Schoharie. The **Strawberry Festival** takes place at the Old Stone Fort on the last Wednesday in June. For six days beginning on the first Tuesday in August, enjoy the **Cobleskill Sunshine Fair,** which is filled with activities for children of all ages. Labor Day weekend brings the annual **Iroquois Festival** to the museum, and Haunted Howe Caverns is scheduled just before Halloween.

For further information, contact **Schoharie County Tourism,** 335 Main Street, Middleburgh 12122; 518-827-3900; www.schoharie chamber.com.

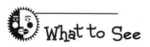 What to See

MUSEUMS AND HISTORIC SITES

Iroquois Indian Museum. 324 Caverns Road, Howe's Cave 12092; 518-296-8949; www.iroquoismuseum.org. (Take exit 22 off I-88, and follow signs on NY 7 for 1 mile. Go left at the Howe Caverns sign on Caverns

Road, then continue 1 mile to the museum entrance.) Admission. Group rates and tours available by advance reservation.

This colorful museum has won awards for its design, which evokes the longhouses of the Iroquois nation, and it contains a marvelous collection of ancient and modern Iroquois art and artifacts. The Iroquois were the most powerful tribe of native peoples in the region and included the Six Nations: Mohawk, Oneida, Onondaga, Cayuga, Seneca, and Tuscarora. The self-guided museum tour takes visitors through a series of displays that include an archaeological dig, Iroquois creation myths, crafts, and artwork. There are shelves and displays filled with beadwork, basketry, paintings, soapstone carvings, cornhusk weavings, and costumes. Silverwork glints in another section, and there are ceremonial objects like pipes and clothing. Changing exhibits highlight living Iroquois artists and their works, and a visit here on a summer weekend will often include the delights of a traditional storyteller or doll maker, or the chance to join in a community dance. In the lower section of the museum, the children's section offers visitors a chance to participate in hands-on crafts demonstrations or try on Native American clothing. The gift shop deserves special mention, since it stocks only Iroquois arts, crafts, and publications, and there are lovely gifts for all ages and budgets. Outside, there are nature trails and an Iroquois log cabin and garden to explore. Special festivals are held every Memorial Day and Labor Day weekend and include entertainment, educational displays, craftspeople, and traditional foods. School groups may request special programs about the modern Iroquois, but any young visitor will come away from this museum knowing more about the Native American heritage.

Facilities: Restrooms, picnic areas, gift shop, snack stand. Wheelchair and stroller accessible.

Old Stone Fort. 145 Fort Road (off NY 30), Schoharie 12157; 518-295-7192; www.schohariehistory.net. Admission (children under the age of five are admitted free). Group tours available by advance reservation.

The Old Stone Fort is a marvelous museum complex that gives young visitors a glimpse into Schoharie County's past. First of all, there is the fort itself, which withstood an attack by the British during the American Revolution in an unsuccessful attempt to rout 200 settlers. The exhibits are done up in the old-curiosity style—rows of glass cases alternate with open displays of some odd and quirky items. An old hand-pump fire wagon from the 18th century is shown (it was built before George Washington was born), as are foot warmers, bear traps, musical instruments, specimens from a nearby fossil forest, and tools from pre-historic cultures. Also in the complex is a blacksmith shop, farming equipment, a law office, a barn, and an 18th-century house. There is a complete one-room schoolhouse where kids can sit at the desks and try out the slates and other sample lessons, as well as the century-old car owned by the first female mayor in New York State, Eleanor Taylor. Kids can even try on period clothing here. The Scribner Exhibit of 20th-Century Communications features radios, cameras, projectors, recording devices, and a television set that dates back to 1947. Children appreciate the unstructured feeling of this museum and the jumble of collections here. Their annual visitor-interactive Columbus Day weekend event features music, old-fashioned foods, and costumed militiamen. It is a true living history event that will please children of all ages.

Facilities: Restrooms, picnic areas, gift shop.

ADDITIONAL ATTRACTIONS

Blenheim-Gilboa Power Project Visitors Center. 1378 NY 30, North Blenheim 12131; 1-800-724-0309; www.nypa.gov. (Watch for signs on NY 30.) Free. Group tours available by advance reservation.

Housed in a 19th-century dairy barn, the Blenheim-Gilboa Power Project Visitors Center is filled with state-of-the-art exhibits and interactive displays that demonstrate how power is made and used. Video and computer technology help explain the science of energy and electricity to both children and adults. The hands-on computerized displays make kids part of the action. They can hop on a bicycle generator and turn pedal power into electricity, or test their energy smarts with a touch-screen video quiz. The Power Authority provides some of the lowest-cost electricity in the state; it operates 17 generating facilities and maintains more than 1,400 miles of transmission lines. The project supplies more than one million kilowatts of energy at times of peak demand by recycling water between two reservoirs. Each of the reservoirs—one atop Brown Mountain, the other at its foot—holds five billion gallons of water. When generating power, the water cascades down a vertical shaft five times taller than Niagara Falls. When storing water—usually at night or on weekends—the process is reversed and water is pumped back up the shaft for storage. A recent addition to the displays here is a turbine from a generator displayed on the front lawn.

Next to the visitors center is Lansing Manor, an early American country estate built in 1819 by John Lansing, a New York State delegate to the 1787 Constitutional Convention. The manor house was restored by the Power Authority in 1977 and fully refurbished in 2002. It is filled with authentic furnishings from the first half of the 19th century, and showcases the simple yet gracious lives of the families that first lived there. After a tour, take a stroll along the 2.5-mile Bluebird Trail, so named because of efforts to restore populations of New York's state bird. The trail traverses a rolling hillside between the visitors center and nearby Mine Kill State Park. There is also a 2-acre wetlands area that serves as an outdoor classroom to explain the function and benefits of wetlands to air and water quality.

Facilities: Restrooms, picnic areas. Wheelchair accessible.

Caverns Creek Grist Mill. 259 Caverns Road (one mile off NY 7), Howe's Cave 12092; 518-296-8448; www.cavernscreekgristmill.com. A nominal admission is charged for the mill tour. Group tours available by advance reservation.

A restored 1816 gristmill, this charming, bright-red working "museum" still grinds corn with a 1,400-pound water-powered millstone. There are three floors of exhibits here, all related to the history and art of milling—including stone dressing, grinding, and waterwheels. The miller on duty can answer questions about the operation of the mill, and there is a short tour of the site. Children will enjoy watching the wheels go round and listening to the rush of water as it pours into the mill through the elaborate series of gutters and races. Outside, there is a lovely picnic area along the millpond, and a series of short hiking paths leads along the millrace. The overshot waterwheel is located at the side of the mill and is just as fascinating to younger visitors as the mill itself.

Facilities: Restrooms, picnic areas, gift shop stocked with locally ground flours. Overall not suitable for strollers or wheelchairs, although the grounds have some accessible paths.

Cobleskill College Agricultural Tour. NY 7, Cobleskill 12043; 518-255-5700; www.cobleskill.edu. Free. Group tours available by advance reservation.

This college is part of the State University of New York (SUNY) system. It contains more than 50 buildings over a 550-acre campus, which includes a 300-acre working farm. Cobleskill has a national reputation as a fine agricultural college, and a tour of the campus can introduce children to the workings of a modern farm. Tour stops include visits to the cattle barn, a greenhouse (with crops and flowers), the plant science building, the horse barn, and the dairy barn. Kids love the farm machinery that's on view, especially the tractors—and although this is a walking tour, children as young as four should be able to manage it easily. There is a small fisheries and wildlife museum on campus, with displays and exhibits of local plants and animals. Because many of the tour stops are actual work areas, you may have a chance to see milking or harvesting in progress—but what you see depends upon the season and the time of day. The campus is lovely, and this is a nice stop for kids interested in farm life.

Facilities: Restrooms, picnic areas, gift shop in the student center. Strollers and wheelchairs can manage fine on the campus.

Cooper's Ark Farm. 145 Ark Lane, Schoharie 12157; 518-295-7662; www.coopersarkfarm.com. Admission includes a tour and hayride.

This beautiful working farm is home to over 400 laying hens, several llamas, an alpaca, a donkey, and dozens of goats. Children will enjoy the tour and can get involved in farm tasks like grinding corn and learning to use various farm tools. The owners invite families to bring a picnic and spend a fun-filled educational day here.

Facilities: Restrooms, picnic areas, farm shop.

George Landis Arboretum. 174 Lape Road, Esperance 12066; 518-875-6935; www.landisarboretum.org. Open year-round. Free. Group tours by advance reservation.

This 163-acre public garden is home to hundreds of rare shrubs and trees from around the world. It is on the site of a 19th-century farm, the home of Fred Lape—the arboretum's founder, an amateur botanist, poet, English professor, and writer—who established the arboretum in 1951 as a memorial to George Landis, a faculty colleague at Rensselaer Polytechnic Institute (RPI) and fellow amateur botanist. There are plantings, gardens, and pathways lined with trees from Russia, Japan, China, and other exotic lands—as well as common trees native to the area. There are several hiking trails and a short walking path that is perfect for a family stroll. The plants are all well marked, so you may enjoy spending some time identifying plants and trees with the kids. It's really peaceful and lovely here on a summer afternoon, and the kids will enjoy running around and letting off some steam. The arboretum offers special children's workshops in botany and nature studies during the summer months, but call ahead for a schedule.

Facilities: Restrooms, picnic areas, barn, greenhouse, and meeting-house. This site is not recommended for wheelchairs or strollers, although the restrooms and parking area are accessible.

The Gilboa Fossils. 122 Stryker Road, off NY 990V, Gilboa 12076; 607-588-9413; www.gilboafossils.org. (The exhibit is next to the Gilboa Town Hall, 3 miles north of the intersection of NY 30 and NY 23 at Grand Gorge.)

These fossils were discovered in the Gilboa area in 1920 but date back to 380 million years ago, during the Devonian period. They are the oldest tree fossils in the world and will surely intrigue those kids interested in what life was like in the times of the dinosaurs.

Howe Caverns. 255 Discovery Drive, Howe's Cave 12092; 518-296-8900; www.howecaverns.com. (Take exit 22 from I-88 and follow the signs.) Admission. Group rates, private tours, and "lantern tours" are available by advance reservation.

One of the oldest "tourist" caves in the Northeast, Howe Caverns has been introducing people to the underground since the 19th century; a local farmer, Lester Howe, discovered the site in 1842. Today you can still see what millions of years have created underneath your feet. The tour begins with an elevator ride from the visitors center, which descends 156 feet to the subterranean walkway that takes you through the

Howe Caverns, with a year-round temperature of 52 degrees, is a great place to escape the heat on a hot summer day.

ALBANY COUNTY CONVENTION & VISITORS BUREAU

lighted caves. The year-round temperature is a constant 52 degrees, and the array of formations is fascinating to see. Children will enjoy the Bridal Altar, with its heart-shaped stone (more than 500 weddings have taken place here), and the unique wall formations—including the Old Witch and the Chinese Pagoda in Titan's Temple. But the best part of the tour is the boat ride on the underground Lake of Venus, where tour guides turn off the lights and let you experience total darkness. The cave is brightly and safely lit. Bring a sweater or a light jacket, because the cave is damp and the tours last about one hour. In general, kids enjoy the rock formations, tunnels, and (in particular) the Winding Way's narrow passages. The rock hounds in the family can purchase bags of mining rough and wash away the soil to reveal semiprecious gems, which are theirs to keep; they can also watch as the geode they select is cut in half to reveal its prized contents!

Facilities: Restrooms, picnic areas, snack bar, restaurant, retail shops, motel, and homemade fudge. The caves are not stroller friendly or wheelchair accessible. Note that backpacks and other large bags are not allowed in the cave.

Mine Kill Falls Overlook and Environs. NY 30 between Mine Kill and Blenheim. Free.

You can park and walk along a path to the overlook, where the falls drop dramatically to the stream. This is not a good walk for very young sightseers, since it is a 0.25-mile trek that climbs uphill on the return trip. If you want to picnic at an unusual site, try to find the longest single-span covered bridge in the world, which is located just north of the Blenheim-Gilboa Power Project Visitors Center entrance in Blenheim (the bridge is on your right).

Secret Caverns. 671 Cavern Road, Howe's Cave 12092; 518-296-8558; www.secretcaverns.com. (The caverns are 5 miles east of Cobleskill, between NY 7 and US 20 on Cavern Road.) Admission. Group tour rates available by advance reservation.

These caverns are a totally different underground experience from neighboring Howe Caverns. The two cave companies have been competing for years, and Howe wins hands-down as the more sophisticated tourist attraction. However, if you and the older kids are looking for somewhat more adventure and Tom Sawyer–like experiences, then by all means visit Secret Caverns; don't bring younger kids unless they like to walk. The tour begins not with an elevator ride but instead with a walk down more than 130 steps to the cave floor. Then you trek alongside the underground river to see wonders such as Alligator, the Cavern's Monster, City of the Future, and Wonderland. The rock formations are all lighted, and a misty 100-foot waterfall is impressive. Kids will love the stalagmites and stalactites—the latter "stick tight" to the ceiling—and the colorful wall deposits called flowstone. The caverns are a constant 50 degrees, so bring along a sweater for the 45-minute tour.

Facilities: Restrooms, picnic areas, restaurant, motel. This site is not stroller or wheelchair accessible.

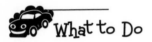 What to Do

MAPLE SYRUP FARMS

Many of the maple syrup producers and sap houses in Schoharie County are run on an intermittent basis; however, there are a few places that have been in business for many years and welcome visitors year-round.

Buck Hill Farm. 185 Fuller Road, Jefferson 12093; 607-652-7980; www .buckhillfarm.com. (Take NY 10 to Jefferson and watch for signs to the farm.) Open year-round. Free.

This farm has a complete maple production setup, including a candy-making area. There are tours of the sugarbush, sap house, and shop during maple season, and the staff will be glad to mail maple gifts to your friends or feed you a pancake breakfast during certain seasons. The sap season runs from March to mid-April but is weather dependent, so call ahead.

Maple Hill Farms. 107C Crapser Road, Cobleskill 12043; 518-234-4858; www.maplehillfarms.biz. (This farm is located 3 miles northeast of the town of Cobleskill.) Open year-round.

The best time to visit this farm is when they are boiling the sap in maple season. They produce syrup the old-fashioned way with a woodburning evaporator, a tradition in the Putnam family—owners for five generations. The maple weekends are usually the last two weekends of

March—when the farm is bustling with activity—but call ahead to check. They sell maple products in a lovely country store on the premises.

Stone House Farm. 305 Lynk Road, Sharon Springs 13459; 518-284-2476. (From Sharon Springs take US 20 west 1.5 miles; make a right on Lynk Road. The farm is on the left about 1 mile up the road.) Open year-round.

This small family farm has 30 Jersey cows and a 3,000-tap maple operation. You'll find pure maple syrup, cream, candy, and sugar on sale year-round, and pancake breakfasts in the sap house in maple season.

PARKS

Max V. Shaul State Park. 3075 NY 30 (watch for signs), Fultonham 12071; 518-827-4711; www.nysparks.state.ny.us. Open year-round. Admission. Group rates and camping available by advance reservation.

This small, wild state park is only 57 acres, but it packs a lot into its space. The park straddles Schoharie Creek, which is renowned for fishing, and this is the perfect recreational stop for a summer's day when you are traveling with the kids. Campsites are available for overnight use, and there are BBQ pits for day-trippers as well. Short nature trails let you take kids on a walk through the woods on quiet paths filled with plants and birds. There are playgrounds on the site and cross-country skiing trails are opened in winter, but you must bring your own equipment. I recommend this park as a nice place for a picnic, or to get away from the summer tourist bustle in some of the larger towns in the region. If you don't want to stop here for a picnic, just travel north 1 mile or so above the park on NY 30; there is a charming picnic and rest stop on the left, which is set along the creek and has covered table sites.

Facilities: Restrooms, picnic areas, campsites. The restrooms are wheelchair accessible.

Mine Kill State Park. 161 Mine Kill State Park Road (off NY 30), North Blenheim 12131; 518-827-6111; www.nysparks.state.ny.us. Open year-round. Admission, depending on season.

This is an excellent day-use park (no overnight camping allowed) that is often quiet, even on holiday weekends. Located on Schoharie Creek, which is part of a reservoir system, the park overlooks the water and provides many hiking trails, picnic areas, and other seasonal delights. The summer offers pool swimming—complete with locker rooms, a snack bar, and sunbathing areas. A boat launch for the reservoir is open from May through Labor Day, and the park has cross-country skiing and snowmobile trails in the winter. Kids will enjoy walking the trails, which wind down through the forest to the water's edge.

Facilities: Restrooms, picnic areas, snack bar, athletic fields, playgrounds, locker room. Wheelchair accessible.

Vroman's Nose Nature Preserve. Mill Valley Road, Middleburgh 12122; 518-827-5747; www.schoharievalley.org. Open year-round.

This preserve has a 1.5-mile walking trail through woodlands that brings you out to a cliff facing the lovely Schoharie Valley, a view you will always remember. This is a nice place to stop while driving through the county. Look for directional signs on NY 30.

Facilities: Restrooms, picnic areas.

PICK-YOUR-OWN AND OTHER FARMS

Barber's Farm. 3621 NY 30, Middleburgh 12122; 518-827-5454; www.barbersfarm.com. Located 3.5 miles south of Middleburgh.

GEORGE CHERNILEVSKY, HTTP://COMMONS.WIKIMEDIA.ORG

You can pick your own tomatoes, peppers, and eggplants here and the kids will enjoy visiting the cows in the dairy barn. During the autumn there is a corn maze, and a retail market on the premises sells an array of plants starting in spring. This farm has been family owned and operated since 1857 and is a wonderful place to show children farm life. Call or check the Web site to see what crops are ready for picking.

Facilities: Restrooms, picnic areas.

Pick a Pumpkin Pumpkin Patch. 2716 Creek Road, Esperance 12066; 518-868-4893; www.pickapumpkin.com.

Jim and Lois VanDerwerken began farming here in 1955 and it makes a wonderful place to visit in autumn. The kids will love the free hayrides out to the fields to pick pumpkins and gourds. There is a Three Story Tree House and Storybookland as well as specialty foods, including fabulous cider doughnuts.

Facilities: Restrooms, picnic areas.

Schoharie Valley Farms/Carrot Barn. 5605 NY 30, Schoharie 12157; 518-295-7139; www.schoharievalleyfarms.com.

The enormous carrot barn here is what initially attracts many visitors to this large, bustling farm. Although this isn't a place where visitors can pick crops, it is well worth a stop. In season there is asparagus, tomatoes, corn, peppers, and squash grown here along with other vegetables from neighboring farms. The greenhouses are stocked with seasonal plants and there is an excellent selection of hearty sandwiches for those who opt for lunch at the farm.

Facilities: Restrooms, farm store, gift shop, café.

Sharon Orchards. 573 Chestnut Street, Sharon Springs 13459; 518-284-2510. (From US 20 west in Sharon Springs, turn left onto Chestnut Street; the orchard is on the right 2 miles ahead.)

The orchards here produce apples, cherries, peaches, pears, and plums, and visitors can pick their own or buy from the farm stand. This particular orchard is unusual for the variety of fruit offered. Call before you go to see what's ready to be picked; they have no Web site.

Facilities: Restrooms, picnic areas.

Terrace Mountain Orchard. 158 Apple Blossom Lane, Schoharie 12157; 518-295-7755; www.terracemountainorchard.com. (In Schoharie turn onto Bridge Street; the next right is Terrace Mountain Road, and the orchard is 2 miles ahead on the right.)

There are 16 apple varieties offered here—as well as excellent cider, doughnuts, pies, and specialty foods available in the shop on the premises.

Facilities: Restrooms, picnic areas.

Wellington's Herbs and Spices. 649 Rickard Hill Road, Schoharie 12157; 518-295-7366; www.wellingtonsherbsandspices.com. Tours by advance arrangement.

While you cannot pick your own crops here, this family-friendly place is a nice oasis. There are spectacular hillside views, a 2,500-square-foot country store, lovely herb and flower gardens, a children's petting zoo, ponds, and a tearoom.

Facilities: Restrooms, picnic areas.

THE CAPITAL REGION
Albany, Schenectady, and Rensselaer Counties

▼▲▼▲▼▲▼

T he city of Albany is the oldest chartered city in the United States, and long before the city received its charter in 1686, the settlement was an important river stop and trading center. Henry Hudson discovered the area in 1609 while seeking a route to the Far East. Gradually, the Dutch settled here, attracted by the area's fertile farmland and abundant game. Trade and industry burgeoned, since the city was located where the navigable Hudson River ended and the Erie Canal began. Today the capital region is a dynamic place where you can revisit the past with a trip to a children's museum; stop at a planetarium; enjoy an outing at a state park; or watch lawmakers at work in the state capitol building. The region is firmly rooted in history, which provides a strong foundation for its continuing growth in the 21st century.

A tour of Albany is best begun at the city's **Heritage Area Visitors Center,** which offers a spectacular orientation show, suggested walking and driving tours, and a planetarium. During the summer this is the starting place for city trolley tours of the capital's attractions. One of the best places to take kids in Albany is the **New York State Museum.** The changes in the state over the centuries are

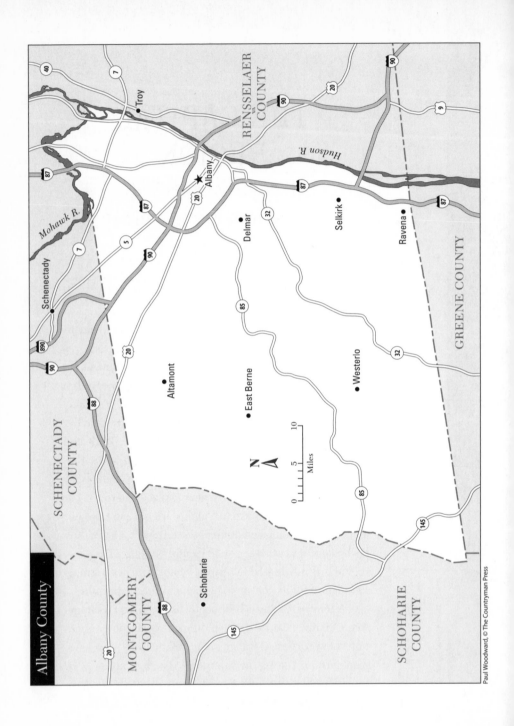

Albany County

RENSSELAER COUNTY

SCHENECTADY COUNTY

GREENE COUNTY

MONTGOMERY COUNTY

SCHOHARIE COUNTY

Troy

Albany

Schenectady

Delmar

Selkirk

Ravena

Altamont

East Berne

Westerlo

Schoharie

Mohawk R.

Hudson R.

N

0 5 10
Miles

Paul Woodward, © The Countryman Press

displayed in a series of realistic, life-like dioramas. Mastodons, wild birds, bear, and deer are shown in their natural habitat, while street scenes of old New York show subways, fire engines, and shops of the past. Don't miss a tour of the **New York State Capitol,** one of the most beautiful government buildings in the world. Some of the art most appealing to kids can be found on the famous staircases here. Older kids will enjoy watching the lawmaking process from the Senate galleries if you happen to visit when a legislative session is taking place.

Sailing past the city of Albany on a Hudson River outing.

For a break from sightseeing in the city, head out to **Grafton Lakes State Park** for year-round sports and outdoors activities. Over 2,000 acres provide a full range of playgrounds, ball fields, and picnic areas, and four lakes may be enjoyed in the park—with swimming at Long Pond, which has a lovely sandy beach. Another recreational gem, the **Hudson-Mohawk Bikeway,** is one of the capital region's most popular features, a 41-mile path traveling along the Hudson and Mohawk rivers and connecting Albany, Schenectady, and Troy.

Heading over to Troy, the **Children's Museum of Science and Technology** is a must-see with its fantastic Exploring Hudson River Life exhibit. Kids can follow all 315 miles of the Hudson River in this 75-foot interactive display. The **Schenectady Museum and Planetarium** is a hands-on museum featuring interactive exhibits that tell the story of the city's role in world-changing innovations such as refrigeration, radio, and television.

To enliven your stay, check out a few of the special events that coincide with your visit. Seasonal celebrations abound and there are many that are perfect for families. Every May in Albany's Washington Park, the annual **Tulip Festival** features arts and crafts, children's games, and live entertainment. In June, the **Annual Kids' Arts Festival** takes place at Proctor's Theatre in Schenectady with lots of activities for the preschool set. In October, the **Annual Apple Festival at Goold Orchards** in Castleton-on-Hudson is a day filled with festivities and apple-picking.

For further information, contact the **Albany County Convention and Visitors Bureau,** 25 Quackenbush Square, Albany 12207; 518-434-1217, 1-800-258-3582; www.albany.org.

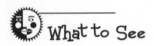 What to See

MUSEUMS AND HISTORIC SITES

Spring flowers in bloom in Albany's Washington Park.

Albany Heritage Area Visitors Center and Henry Hudson Planetarium. 25 Quackenbush Square, Albany 12207; 518-434-1217, 1-800-258-3582, 518-434-0405 for the planetarium; www.albany.org. There is a nominal charge for planetarium shows.

This site offers visitors a series of changing exhibits, as well as interactive displays that highlight history and culture in the capital city and provide an overview of the region. The planetarium features star shows about once a month for both children and a general audience. There are special programs during the summer months and at other school vacation periods throughout the year.

Facilities: Restrooms, gift shop.

You need 3-D glasses for the show at the Henry Hudson Planetarium.

Albany Institute of History and Art. 125 Washington Avenue, Albany 12210; 518-463-4478; www.albanyinstitute.org. Open year-round. Admission (children age five and under admitted free). Group tours by advance reservation.

This museum was founded in 1791 as a repository for science and history materials. Today the Albany Institute of History and Art

(AIHA) celebrates five centuries of the history, art, and culture of the upper Hudson Valley. It is housed in a complex of three historic buildings connected by a glass atrium. The Museum Explorers Gallery, a special hands-on museum experience for families, offers a great introduction to the AIHA. Activities include Crack the Code (how to read and understand museum labels), the Minimuseum (design and install your own exhibition in a scale model of a museum gallery), Guess the Mystery Object (discover the stories original objects can tell), and Try on History (dress up in 18th-century clothing). Kids will also enjoy exercising their imagination in the art-making corner or at the computer station.

The first floor of gallery space is dedicated to temporary exhibitions, with the exception of three galleries that highlight AIHA's permanent collections: the Entry Point Gallery, the Open Storage Viewing Room, and the Sculpture Gallery. On the second floor, visitors experience the best of AIHA's permanent collections, including The Landscape That Defined America: The Hudson River School, which features some of AIHA's finest landscape paintings from the first American school of painting. Other permanent exhibits focus on trading culture and 18th- to 19th-century painting and sculpture. Kids will especially enjoy the Ancient Egypt gallery, which is like entering an ancient tomb. Albany's own beloved mummies have the place of honor among objects that explore the themes of the Nile, daily life, and the afterlife.

Special programs and workshops for children and families are an important part of the museum's activities. Kids can make their own valentines or try their hand at creating Egyptian art. Teachers should note that special lectures can be arranged for classes if reservations are made in advance.

Facilities: Restrooms, gift shop, café. Wheelchair and stroller accessible.

The Children's Museum of Science and Technology. 250 Jordan Road (in Rensselaer Technology Park), Troy 12182; 518-235-2120; www.cmost .com. Open year-round. Admission. Groups by advance reservation.

Where can you see the 315 miles of the Hudson River in an impressive 75-foot exhibit, complete with waterfalls and live animals? In this museum's fantastic Exploring Hudson River Life exhibit, of course. Kids will enjoy following the waterway from an Adirondack tributary to estuary and salt-marsh tanks, then to a tidal pool. They will feel as if they

were right at the river's edge watching live trout, bass, catfish, puffer
fish, and a snapping turtle. At the
seawater-filled tide pool, a museum
educator shares fascinating facts
about the starfish, horseshoe crabs,
and sea urchins that live there. The
museum also has a wonderful bee
exhibit. The hands-on learning
experience Operation Wild gives
young visitors the opportunity to
touch live reptiles and giant
insects—including turtles, geckos,
and snakes. There is a complete
weather station, electron micro-
scope, computer lab, and exhibits
on light and optics. The museum's
planetarium with digital dome
offers multimedia shows on space
exploration, constellations, and

Kids enjoy hands-on activities at the
Children's Museum of Science and
Technology, a great place to visit on a
rainy day. ALBANY COUNTY CONVENTION & VISITORS BUREAU

molecules. Exciting interactive exhibits and shows fill this award-winning
museum. Workshops, group tours, overnights, and school-break camp
programs are listed on the Web site and are available by advance
arrangement.

*Facilities: Restrooms, restaurant (Eatery in the Park, serving lunch
and snacks). Wheelchair and stroller accessible.*

Crailo State Historic Site. 9 Riverside Avenue, Rensselaer 12144; 518-
463-8738; www.nysparks.state.ny.us. (From I-787, take US 20 east to
Rensselaer; at the first traffic light, turn right and go one block further to
the site.) Admission. Groups welcome by advance reservation only.

Crailo was a Dutch-fortified farmhouse built circa 1704 by the Van
Rensselaer family. It soon became the center of a vast estate, which contained more than 700,000 acres. Although the building has undergone
many changes over the past 300 years—serving at various times as a
home, a boarding school, a church rectory, and even a cinder-block factory—today the restored building contains exhibits about the history of
Dutch culture in the upper Hudson Valley. Young visitors will see how

the Dutch lived, slept, worked, and ate (school groups can arrange for a cooking demonstration), and they also can see the two gun ports that were cut into the walls in the 1700s. There are displays of art and furniture, and while the museum is lively enough, very young children will not be entertained unless they have a strong interest in history or everyday life of long ago. Archaeological artifacts from the Fort Orange area are on display and are used in conjunction with the tours to explain the historical significance of the Dutch influence in present-day New York State. There is a new addition to the site, the award-winning video *A Sweet and Alien Land*, which should not be missed. If the weather is warm, make sure to wander around outside. It is here, legend says, that in 1758 a British surgeon composed a funny song about American soldiers and then set the words to an old drinking tune. The result is the still-popular song known as "Yankee Doodle"!

One of the guides in period dress at historic Crailo, where the song "Yankee Doodle" was composed.
ALBANY COUNTY CONVENTION & VISITORS BUREAU

Facilities: Restrooms, picnic areas. Strollers are difficult to maneuver in the house, but the museum is accessible to wheelchairs.

Empire State Aerosciences Museum. 250 Rudy Chase Drive, Glenville 12032; 518-377-2191; www.esam.org. Admission.

The mission of this facility is to educate but also to entertain and excite young people with experiences of air and space. The museum consists of nine buildings on 27 acres located at the western perimeter of the Schenectady County Airport (where Charles Lindbergh landed in 1927). Visitors will learn about the history of flight, as well as New York State's importance in the development of aviation. There is an impressive collection of aircraft on display outdoors that includes a F-14A Tomcat, a A-6E Intruder, a A-4F Skyhawk II, and a Huey helicopter. The main galleries contain some of the more fragile aircraft, detailed models, dioramas, historical artifacts, memorabilia, and photographic displays. The Amelia Earhart exhibit should not be missed. There are a few hands-on exhibits, including a mock-up of a 1910 Von Pomer airplane and a simulated-reality vehicle (SRV), which treats kids to a video and "ride" that makes them feel as if they were part of the action. Aviation Adventure programs are held during school vacation weeks, as well as throughout the summer. Check the Web site or call for a schedule.

Facilities: Restrooms, cafeteria, gift shop. Wheelchair and stroller accessible.

Empire State Plaza. Albany 12242; 518-474-2418; www.empirestateplaza.org. (Located off exit 23 of the New York State Thruway (go through the tollbooth to I-787 and take the Empire State Plaza exit) and bounded by Swan, Madison, State, and Eagle Streets.) Free.

Empire State Plaza in Albany.
ALBANY COUNTY CONVENTION & VISITORS BUREAU

Popularly called the Plaza, this is really a government complex that includes office buildings, a convention center, a performing arts center known as the Egg, a concourse, and the state museum. Built at a cost of more than two billion dollars and finished in 1978, the Plaza fulfilled Governor Nelson Rockefeller's dream of a government center that would draw people in, an urban park for all seasons. It has achieved world renown as an outdoor arts center. There is enough open space that kids can enjoy the outdoors, and all family members will find something to amuse them. Scattered across the plaza (or the esplanade) are a series of reflecting pools where kids can ice skate in the winter; in warmer weather they can roller-skate on the walkways. Along the mall are plantings and modern sculpture, fountains, waterfalls, and an excellent play area known as the Children's Place—which has outdoor activity areas, a sandbox, and a separate toddler area. Next to the play area is the environmental sculpture called the Labyrinth, where you can sit on benches and take a break from walking. The New York State Vietnam Memorial, at the courtyard in the Justice Building, is a quiet park with memorial panels for the people from New York State who served in the war. Inside the concourse you will find fine examples of modern art on permanent display, which can introduce older kids to colorful canvases by great masters. For a bird's-eye view of it all, head to the observation deck on the 42nd floor of the Corning Tower. From the deck, which is free, you can see the Catskills, the Adirondacks, and the Berkshires in the distance on a clear day. At the end of the mall, near the huge stairway that leads up to the New York State Museum, concerts, a farmer's market, and special events are held throughout the summer—including a Tulip Festival.

Facilities: Restrooms, cafeteria, food concessions, gift shop, skate rental. There are many shops inside the concourse. Stroller friendly and wheelchair accessible.

New York State Capitol. Washington Avenue and State Street, Albany 12224; 518-474-2418; www.assembly.state.ny.us/tour. (From I-787, take the Empire Plaza exit; the plaza is bounded by Swan, Madison, State, and Eagle Streets; the capitol is on State Street, at the northern end of the plaza.) Free. Group tours available by advance reservation.

Happy children on the Capitol steps.

The New York State Capitol Building is considered one of the loveliest government buildings in the world, and rightfully so. Built between 1867 and 1899, the intricate carvings and decorative motifs are still as fresh and fascinating as they were almost a century ago. The tour is designed to introduce children to the workings of the state legislature, and, along the way, they have a chance to see architecture, art, and even some live lawmakers at work! Surprisingly enough, some of the art most appealing to children can be found on the famous staircases. The Senate Staircase is also called the Evolutionary Staircase because of the wonderful carvings of animals that decorate its sides, a variety of wildlife from single-cell creatures to lions. The Great Western Staircase is the most elaborately carved and is also known as the Million-Dollar Staircase for both the cost of its construction and its wealth of carvings. In fact, many of the carvings are of famous people, including Abraham Lincoln, Ulysses S. Grant, and Harriet Beecher Stowe—and the stonecarvers included their own portraits as well. The East Lobby holds a fine collection of flags that date back to the Civil War, as well as changing exhibits. Older kids will enjoy watching the lawmaking process at work from the Senate galleries (call before you go to see when sessions are taking place). There is enough to see for all ages, and the capitol is always buzzing with activity, so this is not a boring tour. Outside, parks at either end of the building offer magnificent flower gardens and great spots for picnic lunches and rest stops.

Facilities: Restrooms, cafeteria. Wheelchair access; strollers are welcome, but the building has many staircases.

New York State Museum. 3023 Cultural

Education Center, Empire State Plaza, Albany 12230; 518-474-5877; www.nysm .nysed.gov. (To reach the plaza, take exit 23 off the New York State Thruway; pick up I-787, and get off at the Empire Plaza exit.) Free. Group tours available by advance reservation.

This is by far one of the best places to take kids in the Albany region. The chang-

One captivating diorama at the New York State Museum includes a model of the Cohoes mastodon, a creature that roamed the upstate region in prehistoric times.

ALBANY COUNTY CONVENTION & VISITORS BUREAU

Empire State Plaza, with its lovely fountains, plantings, and picnic tables, is a great place for kids to run around after a museum visit or tour of the Capitol.

ing life and history of New York State over the centuries is shown in a series of realistic, lifelike dioramas. Mastodons, wild birds, bear, deer, and other wildlife are shown in their natural habitat, while street scenes of old New York show pushcarts, subways, fire engines, and shops of the past. A popular stop for younger kids is the original *Sesame Street* set, with a video featuring Oscar the Grouch, Kermit, County Von Count, and Big Bird. A Native American section has displays of everyday life as experienced by a variety of New York tribes. The Discovery Place offers children a spot to explore hands-on learning projects with a science theme. Rotating exhibits like Prehistoric Mammals provide a unique and fun approach to education. The famous Cohoes mastodon is a special attraction, and a moving September 11 exhibit was installed in 2002. There are a number of shows given in the museum's theater. Special events are scheduled throughout the year; you may get to enjoy a Victorian holiday or visit with an American artist.

Facilities: Restrooms, cafeteria, gift shop. Wheelchair accessible and stroller friendly.

Scotia Glenville Children's Museum. 303 Mohawk Avenue, Scotia 12302; 518-346-1764; www.travelingmuseum.org.

This is a truly unusual children's museum—you don't go to it; it comes to you, in the form of a museum teacher and tote bags filled with objects, artifacts, and project materials. The museum travels to 12 counties within a 50-mile radius of Scotia, and if you are a teacher or a leader of a children's group, you can make arrangements to have your own museum visit for a day. There are also birthday party visits, with special programs for such celebrations. Founded by three women who believed that museums should offer hands-on participatory exhibits, the

The Schenectady Museum is chock-full of interactive exhibits, like this one that shows how electricity works.

museum has traveling programs for schools, fairs, festivals, summer recreation sites, and after-school programs. The exhibits are more than just displays; children are encouraged to become involved as geologists, explorers, musicians, and artists.

Schenectady Museum and Planetarium. 15 Nott Terrace Heights, Schenectady 12308; 518-382-7890; www.schenectadymuseum.org. (Located off NY 5 in the downtown area.) Open year-round. Check Web site or call for a complete schedule and special school break programs. Admission. Group tours by advance reservation.

This Schenectady treasure celebrates the region's creativity in both technology and culture. The museum is notable for the strength of its collections, including artifacts and photographs from the history of General Electric (GE) and the Marjorie Bradt Foote Costume Collection, with approximately 6,000 costumes. The collection of 1.5 million photos covering GE's history ranks among the top 10 private collections in the nation. Permanent exhibits invite visitors to celebrate the birthplace of radio and television by testing the technology of a variety of items from a light bulb to a refrigerator. There are also changing exhibits of art, history, and technology.

MVP Kid's Place is a permanent exhibit that focuses on community life and is geared to kids between the ages of four and nine. Children can step into the role of a GE scientist (Schenectady is the home of GE), try on clothes at Barney's Department Store, and put on their own puppet shows in the WRGB puppet theater. They will also encounter a child-sized kitchen, a soapbox derby car from the 1950s, and a full-size model of a Mars Rover developed at nearby Rensselaer Polytechnic Institute. The exhibits combine hands-on activities and objects from the museum's collection to help young children discover their own communities and to give new meaning to the diverse people, places, and things around them.

The Suits-Bueche Planetarium, renovated and reopened in 2003, has been automated with state-of-the-art computer technology—including dozens of brand-new projectors, two video projectors, and an amazing sound system. In addition, the Spitz A3P Star Projector, the workhorse of the planetarium, continues to display some of the most spectacular views of the stars. The planetarium has a lighting system that shows off magnificent sunrises and sunsets, a wraparound silhouette of the capital-district skyline, and plush new carpeting. Two 42-inch plasma screen video monitors showing astronomical images—from the latest Hubble pictures to NASA TV footage—flank a fiber-optic star curtain and futuristic display welcoming visitors to an unforgettable show.

Facilities: Restrooms, gift shop.

ADDITIONAL ATTRACTIONS

Albany Aqua Ducks and Trolleys.

Broadway and Clinton Avenue, Albany 12207; 518-434-0405; www.albanyaquaducks.com. Admission. Group tours by advance reservation.

The Albany Aqua Ducks are U.S. Coast Guard–certified, state-of-the-art Hydra-Terra vehicles and the operators are licensed captains in the Coast Guard. This 90-minute tour combines land (trolley) and water vehicles and offers a great way to see the historic sites of the city. There are

The Albany Aqua Ducks take visitors on kid-friendly city tours that combine both trolleys and water vehicles. ALBANY COUNTY CONVENTION & VISITORS BUREAU

City Tour: Schenectady

If you are in the Schenectady region, you may want to take a self-guided walking tour of the historic Stockade District, which has been described as one of the region's most extensive collections of 18th-century architecture. While touring the stockade, visit the **Schenectady County Historical Society** (32 Washington Avenue, Schenectady 12305; 518-374-0263) and pick up a brochure about the area. Older children with an interest in architecture will enjoy this, and the Stockade area has many interesting shops and eateries. In the Village Square, make sure the kids see "Lawrence the Indian," a statue that memorializes one of the earliest Native American friends of the settlers. **Union College**, on Union Street, is renowned as one of the first architecturally designed campuses in America. Adults and children will want to see the 16-sided **Nott Memorial** building, a National Historic Landmark and a prime example of high Victorian Gothic architecture on the campus.

also daily conductor-narrated historic trolley tours during the summer months (June through Labor Day) that stop at 20 locations in the city; it provides an excellent way to get oriented upon arrival in Albany.

Facilities: Restrooms, gift shop.

AMTRAK Train Station. 525 East Street, Rensselaer 12144; 1-800-USA-RAIL; www.amtrak.com. (Located just over the Dunn Memorial Bridge.) Open year-round. Free (but there is a charge to ride the train).

Kids love trains, and from this conveniently located station in the capital region you can take a short train ride to Saratoga Springs, Schenectady, Hudson, or Rhinecliff. The views along the Hudson River are magnificent any time of year, especially when the boats and ships are chugging upriver and downriver—but try to schedule a trip for autumn, when the foliage is spectacular. Even if you don't take a train ride, you can watch the trains come and go from the observation area near the tracks, and kids will enjoy getting up close to the tracks, seeing the bustle and color of the train crews, and listening to the whistles and bells. Note that you should time your visit not to coincide with morning and evening rush hours.

Facilities: Restrooms.

The Costumer. 1020 Barrett Street, Schenectady 12305; 518-374-7442; www.thecostumer.com. Open year-round. Both individuals and groups must make advance arrangements to take a free tour.

The chance to go behind the scenes at this business is a real treat, and school-age children will be delighted with the magnificent costumes and mascots here. The Costumer specializes in costumes for school theatrical and musical productions as well as commercial work. On display are costumes from *Annie, The King and I,* and *The Music Man*—as well as dozens of period costumes. The kids can watch while these costumes are created and stored. A retail shop is filled with all kinds of makeup kits, gadgets, and items for magic tricks.

Facilities: Restrooms, retail shop.

Discovery Center/Albany Pine Bush.

195 New Karner Road, Albany 12205; 518-456-0655; www .albanypinebush.org. Open year-round. Free.

The 3,010 acres of pine bush in this preserve is one of the best remaining examples of an inland pine-barrens ecosystem in the world. The sand plain here is also home to a unique diversity of plants and animals and the environmentally green building at the Discovery Center shows some of these flora and fauna. Children can walk under the life-size 25-foot pitch pine tree hanging from the ceiling and investigate life in its root system with an ultraviolet viewer. They can play I Spy with binoculars to spot pine bush animals, insects, and plants. This area even includes a giant glacier to be examined close-up. A Sand Lab lets kids visit with the ant lion who captures and devours ants. They can use radio

Children enjoy learning a variety of ways to improve the environment at the innovative Discovery Center.

waves to track a life-size model coyote, see a hognose snake, and touch the fur of a deer. In the Conserve This World section, kids can manage the habitat, and be a burn boss to decide if weather conditions are satisfactory for a controlled burn. In addition to dozens of hands-on exhibits like these, the Discovery Center offers an array of educational programs featuring birds of prey, turtles, and snakes. There are photography classes, guided hikes, wildflower walks, and field trips. This is a site that will show children ways to improve the environment and demonstrate how they are part of a global ecological community.

Facilities: Restrooms, gift shop. Wheelchair and stroller accessible.

Five Rivers Environmental Center. 56 Game Farm Road, Delmar 12054; 518-475-0291; www.dec.ny.gov/education. (Located 7 miles south of Albany, off NY 443 in Delmar; watch for signs.) Open year-round. Free. Groups are accommodated by advance reservation only.

A unique nature center, Five Rivers offers a wide variety of programs, hikes, and tours for both adults and children. Named after the five large rivers in the general area of the center, this is an excellent place to spend hours exploring the outdoors. A series of self-guided nature trails are specially designed for younger children. Wooden walkways let you explore pond areas, trees, marshes, and woodlands; there are guide brochures for each walk, which vary in length from 0.125 mile to 2-mile loops. The trails include stops at woodlots, orchards, fields, wildflower meadows, and stream banks, and the brochures include information about animal habits and ecosystems. A butterfly and hummingbird garden is designed to attract wildlife on the wing. Inside the interpretive center, kids can see exhibits about local wildlife, including many samples that are touchable—a rare feature in many other museums. Aristotle the owl is a special favorite with kids here, and many events are held in the center all year long. Weeklong Family Fun programs run all summer and offer guided walks, special projects, and bird-watching. The center participates in the annual New Year's Day bird count, and visitors are welcome to bring their binoculars and participate. In the winter, activities include maple sugaring, snow tracking, cross-country skiing, snowshoeing, and signs of the season; in the fall, there are "wetlands wanders" and nature's harvest workshops; the spring and summer bring animal identification, pond visits, and tree identification classes. When you are in the center, don't forget to ask for copies of nature worksheets and game pages for the kids to use on the trails.

Facilities: Restrooms, picnic areas. Both are wheelchair accessible. The site is stroller friendly along most of the trails, and there is wheelchair access both inside and outside the interpretive center; two short trails are wheelchair accessible. There are large-print and Braille trail guides available.

Hoffman's Playland. 608 New Loudon Road (US 9), Latham 12110; 518-785-3842; www.hoffmansplayland.com. (Located 1 mile south of Latham Circle.) Free, but there is a charge for the rides.

This amusement park has been in business since 1952, and it is a tradition in the Albany area. Hoffman's offers a nice place to escape with kids two years old and older for an afternoon of fun and rides (there are 18 of them here). The youngest children will enjoy the carousel, bots, bumper cars, Ferris wheel, helicopters, train, small roller coaster, and caterpillar. Older kids will appreciate the Tilt-A-Whirl, Scrambler, and Paratrooper—as well as the large arcade area. There is a miniature golf course adjacent to the site (there is an additional charge for this). This clean, enjoyable park is nicely landscaped and offers a refreshing change from the atmosphere of the mega-amusement parks.

Facilities: Restrooms, snack bars.

Hudson River Way. Albany; www.albany.org. This magnificent pedestrian walkway opened in August 2002, and extends from Broadway at Maiden Lane over I-787 to the Albany Riverfront Park at the Corning Preserve. It is designed to connect downtown Albany to the shores of the historic Hudson River and to tell the story of Albany through a series of paintings depicting historical artifacts. Created by mural artist Jan Marie Spanard and her talented crew, the paintings adorn the two staircase landings and the 30 lampposts that line both sides of the bridge. The story begins hundreds of millions of years ago, when Albany was at the bottom of a prehistoric sea. As you progress over the bridge, the story continues through time, and includes the early Dutch merchants and other scenes of historic importance. There are two large murals on the landings that divide the three flights of the grand staircase. The paintings are done in a permanent liquid stone paint called "keim" that will not fade or peel for decades. Although this isn't a walk for those with very young children, older kids will enjoy walking over the pedestrian bridge to the park. Be aware that river breezes can be quite brisk in the cool-weather months.

Facilities: Restrooms (in the park).

Stratton Air National Guard Base. 1 Air National Guard Road, Scotia 12302; 518-344-2103; www.dmna.state.ny.us. (Located at the Schenectady County Airport.) Open year-round. Free. Tour arrangements must be made in advance due to security considerations.

This air base is home to the world-famous Skibirds, the only C-130 aircraft operating on skis in the world. The unit that rescued Dr. Jerri Nielsen from the South Pole when she was stricken with breast cancer came from Stratton. A highlight of a visit here is a chance to get inside one of the aircraft that is on-site, but you will also see the firehouse, fire trucks, and even the life-support systems that are used in the event of a plane going down. A slide presentation on Antarctica is shown (this is a military base that supports other bases throughout the world), and the tour includes a question-and-answer session.

Facilities: Restrooms. Stroller and wheelchair accessible.

USS *Slater* Destroyer Escort-766. 141 Broadway, Albany 12210; 518-431-1943; www.uss slater.org. Admission includes a one-hour tour of the ship.

During World War II, 563 destroyer escorts battled Nazi U-boats in the North Atlantic, protecting convoys of soldiers and supplies. In the Pacific, they stood first in line to defend naval task forces from kamikaze attacks. Today only one remains afloat.

Step back in time aboard the only destroyer escort warship still in World War II battle configuration. Moored in the Hudson River in downtown Albany, see how the crew lived and carried out its mission of antisubmarine warfare. The armament, combat information, radio rooms, pilot-house, galley, mess hall, officer's quarters, and crew's sleeping

The kids can board and explore the USS *Slater*, the only destroyer escort warship still in World War II battle configuration.

area are all authentically restored. Older children interested in military history will enjoy this stop.

Facilities: Restrooms, gift shop. Strollers are not permitted on the ship.

Watervliet Arsenal Museum. 1 Buffington Street, Watervliet 12189; 518-266-5805; www.wva.army.mil. (Take I-87 to I-787 north (exit 23), then exit onto Broadway (NY 32), and follow signs.) Free.

The arsenal does not offer tours for security reasons, but the museum is a unique and interesting stop for children over the age of six. The main exhibit traces the history of cannons in the United States and has several fascinating examples on display, including one of George Washington's cannons and several Civil War cannons. There is a re-creation of a 19th-century machine shop, which will delight kids interested in gadgets. Photos and a video describe the cannon manufacturing process—and outside, a full-size tank is on display. While this stop is not for everyone, children who are interested in the military and military history will love it.

Facilities: Restrooms.

 What to Do

BICYCLING

Albany Riverfront Park at the Corning Preserve. 1-800-258-3582 and 518-434-2032; www.albany.org. The best section of this park for biking lies along the west bank of the Hudson River, where you pick up the Mohawk-Hudson Bike Trail. To get there, take exit 23 off the New York State Thruway; pick up I-787, and get off at exit 4. Follow signs for Colonie Street. This is a delightful park where strollers will enjoy walking along the river and the bikeway is accessible. To obtain a map of this 30-mile bike trail, call 1-800-962-8007.

Downtown Bike Tours. There are two city bicycle tours in downtown Albany—one runs from Quackenbush Square to the New York State Capitol, and the other goes from Washington Park to the Empire State Plaza. A brochure and map of these tours may be obtained at the Albany Heritage Visitors Center.

BOAT CRUISES

Dutch Apple Cruises. 139 Broadway, Albany 12201; 518-463-0220; www
.dutchapplecruises.com. Admission. There are two-hour sightseeing
cruises and three-hour dinner cruises available on a 65-foot, double-deck
tour boat that holds 145 people. The price is reasonable and there are
discounts for children, seniors, and groups. You will see historic Dutch
mansions, tiny hamlets, and oceangoing vessels in the Port of Albany.

ICE SKATING

Albany County Hockey Facility. 830 Albany-Shaker Road, Loudonville
12211; 518-452-7396; www.albanycounty.com/hockey. Open for both
figure skating and hockey. There are both freestyle and public sessions
for figure skating. Call or check the Web site for a schedule. Snack bar
on premises.

Clifton Park Ice Arena. 16 Clifton Common Road, Clifton Park 12065;
518-383-5440; www.cliftonparkarena.com. Open year-round for both
figure skating and hockey. There is a snack bar, video arcade, and skate
rentals as well.

Schenectady County Recreational Facility Ice Skating Rink. 5 Tower Road,
Scotia 12302; 518-384-2445; www.schenectadycounty.com. This indoor
rink is open year-round. There are public sessions for figure skating as
well as freestyle times and hockey sessions. Call or check the Web site
for a schedule.

Swinburne Park Skating Rink. Clinton Avenue at Manning Boulevard,
Albany 12206; 518-438-2406; www.albanyny.org. This is an outdoor
skating rink; call or check the Web site before you go for the time of the
sessions. The schedule is weather-dependent here.

PARKS

Central Park. Central Parkway (off State Street, NY 5), Schenectady
12309; 518-382-5151. Open year-round. Free.

This 372-acre city park is a gem, complete with lake, playing fields,
swimming pool, tennis courts, duck pond, and playgrounds. Young children enjoy the playground with toddler-sized equipment, a train ride,

the swimming pond, and the chance to feed the numerous ducks (bring your own bread). Older kids like the boats that can be rented for rides on the pond. All ages can appreciate the exquisite rose gardens, where 4,500 rosebushes bloom (there are over 200 varieties) on a 3-acre garden site. Try to visit in June, when the roses are at their peak. During the summer months you may be able to see a concert at the Music Haven Stage in the park.

Facilities: Restrooms, picnic areas, snack bar. Strollers and wheelchairs can manage on the pathways.

Grafton Lakes State Park. 61 North Long Pond Road, Grafton 12082; 518-279-1155; www.nysparks.state.ny.us. (Located 12 miles east of Troy.) Open year-round. Admission during certain months.

This 2,357-acre state park offers a variety of year-round sports and outdoor activities for children of all ages. This is one of the best parks in the Albany area for a day trip, since there is so much to keep the kids busy and parents will enjoy the beautiful lakes and forests. The park contains a range of playgrounds, ball fields, and picnic areas. There are four lakes and the Dunham Reservoir, but swimming is only permitted at Long Pond, which has a lovely sandy beach and rentals of paddleboats, rowboats, and canoes. Visitors are welcome to bring their own canoes or sailboats to use on any of the lakes. Three of the four lakes are stocked with trout, bass, and pickerel, so be sure to bring fishing poles along; you do need a license to fish here, however. There are over 25 miles of groomed trails for hiking, mountain biking, horseback riding, and orienteering in the summer months. Special events for kids at this time of the year include crafts, games, and story time. There is also a miniature golf course. During the winter the trails are used for cross-country skiing, snowshoeing, and snowmobiling. Snowshoes may be rented in the park office, but bring any other equipment.

Facilities: Restrooms, picnic areas, lockers, bathhouse, food concessions (summer only). Strollers and wheelchairs can maneuver in some areas of the park. The bathrooms, Long Pond Beach, and a trail in its vicinity are all wheelchair accessible.

John Boyd Thacher State Park. 1 Hailes Cave Road, Voorheesville 12186; 518-872-1237; www.nysparks.state.ny.us. Open year-round. Free to enter (but parking fee).

Thacher Park is unusual in one respect: It is one of the richest fossil-bearing areas in the world. The park itself is well equipped for a day of fun: There are extensive hiking trails along the escarpment and through beautiful wooded areas. Hikers may also explore sections of the Long Path that runs through Thacher Park. In addition, there are 500 acres of open meadow that are perfect for hiking. The most popular trail is the Indian Ladder Trail, which descends 100 feet down along the escarpment and is rich in geological fossils and historical significance. The views along this trail are magnificent. There is an Olympic-sized swimming pool as well as a number of picnic areas and playgrounds. In the winter months, cross-country skiing and snowshoeing are popular here, with several areas suitable for beginners. Snowshoes are available for rental (but bring your own skis), and there are guided snowshoe walks on many winter weekends. Call for a schedule of educational programs offered at the park throughout the year.

Facilities: Restrooms, picnic areas, snack bar (during the summer months). Wheelchair accessible.

Washington Park. Madison Avenue (between State Street and Madison Avenue), Albany 12210; 518-434-2032; www.albany.org. Open year-round. Free.

This park has served as a gathering place for the public since the 17th century, and it is still one of the most beautiful parks to visit in any city, in any season. The 5-acre lake has paddleboats for rent, and the ducks enjoy a handout or two. There are several small play areas throughout the site, some of which include equipment designed for toddlers. The park offers special events throughout the warm-weather months, including the **Albany Tulip Festival** in April that takes advantage of the colorful plantings throughout the park and features costumed performers. Children will love the horse-drawn cabs that are available for hire, and the rose gardens offer a perfect spot to rest. In the winter, ice skating is allowed on the lake and the trails and hills come alive with cross-country skiing and sledding (bring your own equipment). Be sure to plan a stop in Washington Park, especially if you are going to spend the day taking in other Albany sights; the park is a quiet and restful place for kids to refuel at any time of year.

Facilities: Restrooms, picnic areas, snack bar. Strollers can manage on many of the paths, but wheelchair access can be a problem in some areas.

About 2 miles from Thacher State Park is **Thompson's Lake State Park**, 68 Thompson's Lake Road, East Berne 12059; 518-872-1674; www.nysparks.state.ny.us; which offers seasonal overnight camping facilities and has a sandy beach for swimming on Thompson's Lake. The park is open year-round. This lovely lake is actually an ancient sinkhole formed over one million years ago in fossil-rich Onondaga Limestone. Ice fishing is popular here in the winter.

Also nearby is the **Emma Treadwell Thacher Nature Center**, 87 Nature Center Way, Voorheesville 12186; 518-872-0800; www.nysparks.state.ny.us. Open year-round. Located near the shore of Thompson's Lake. Inside the nature center, kids will find lots to do; they may enjoy exploring a large geological model of the Helderberg Escarpment, watch a working honeybee colony, see an array of natural history exhibits, or participate in exciting natural history programs offered year-round. The nature center also offers several miles of trails for hiking, cross-country skiing, and snowshoeing.

PICK-YOUR-OWN FARMS

Altamont Orchards. 6654 Dunnsville Road, Altamont 12009; 518-861-6515; www.altamontorchards.com. (Their fields are located on NY 146, about 1.5 miles before the Altamont Fair entrance.)

This is a nice place to gather strawberries in June and apples in the fall. Do bring your own containers for gathering the crops here.

Goold Orchards. 1297 Brookview Station Road, Castleton 12033; 518-732-7317; www.goold.com. Farm store, bakery, and winery open year-round. School tours by special arrangement.

This is the oldest apple farm in the capital region; they celebrated 100 years in business in 2010. You can pick strawberries in June, raspberries in September—and in autumn, several varieties of apples of course! The bakery creates fresh homemade cider doughnuts, fruit pies, and cookies daily, and the farm store sells fresh-pressed cider and apple wine. The annual **Apple Festival** is held on Columbus Day weekend, a marvelous celebration of arts, crafts, and agriculture with food vendors and special activities for the kids—including a haunted house. This is a terrific family-friendly stop.

Indian Ladder Farms. 342 NY 156, Altamont 12009; 518-765-2956, 1-866-640-PICK; www.indianladderfarms.com.

This farm specializes in pick-your-own apples and pumpkins in the fall as well as strawberries, blueberries, and raspberries throughout the summer months. On several summer weekends there are demonstrations of beekeeping, sheepshearing and cider making. Children will enjoy seeing the farm animals here as well. The Yellow Rock Café serves lunches created from locally produced meats, dairy, and vegetables.

SKIING AND SNOWBOARDING

Maple Ridge. 2725 Mariaville Road, Schenectady 12306; 518-381-4700; www.mapleskiridge.com. (Take I-88 north to exit 25. Make a left onto NY 7 (east), a left onto NY 337, and another left onto NY 159 (west); the ski center is 3 miles ahead on the left.)

For over 45 years this family-owned and -operated ski center has offered a warm, friendly atmosphere to both skiers and snowboarders. It is a small center with just eight different runs ranging from beginner to expert. It's a good place for the youngest skiers to learn the basics. The Ski Tykes program is specifically for four- and five-year-olds who have never skied; the Snow Stars program is for six- and seven-year-olds who have never been on skis. There is also a snow tubing park adjacent to the ski area.

Facilities: Restrooms, cafeteria, ski school, retail shop, full equipment rentals.

THEATER AND ENTERTAINMENT

Capital Repertory Theater. 111 North Pearl Street, Albany 12207; 518-462-4531, 518-445-SHOW; www.capitalrep.org. Open year-round. Admission. Theater lovers will enjoy the performances here; Capital Rep has been offering first-rate entertainment for nearly 30 years. The company employs professional equity actors and designers from New York City. There are usually six productions over the course of the year—which include musicals, comedies, dramas, and family-oriented productions. Several student matinees are also offered in conjunction with the education department. Check the Web site for a complete schedule.

The Egg. 518-473-1061, 518-473-1845 (box office); www.theegg.org. This marvelous venue includes year-round modern dance, theater, concerts, storytellers, and other musical performances. Visitors may enjoy a virtual cornucopia of entertainment at this half-round building constructed on a pedestal, one of the most architecturally unique theater venues in the world. There are two theaters inside, as well as a wraparound lounge that offers an excellent view of the plaza. Children's programming in the past has included *The Pied Piper, Peter Pan,* and *Sleeping Beauty.* The Web site contains a complete current schedule.

Proctor's Theater. 432 State Street, Schenectady 12305; 518-346-6204; www.proctors.org. This theater was completed in 1926 and is furnished in the gilt-and-marble grandeur of the old vaudeville world. The performance season includes touring productions of Broadway shows like *South Pacific.* There are also silent films accompanied by Wurlitzer organ music and a complete selection of children's theater programs year-round. The Web site lists a complete schedule of offerings.

Times Union Center. 51 South Pearl Street, Albany 12207; 518-487-2000; www.timesunioncenter-albany.com. This sports and entertainment complex is home to several athletic teams, but it is also where you can see a range of entertainment from Stars on Ice and Bob Dylan to Bon Jovi and Sesame Street. There are car shows, regional basketball playoffs, and more. Check the Web site for a complete schedule.

SARATOGA COUNTY AND ENVIRONS

▼▲▼▲▼▲▼

S ince the 18th century, when natural medicinal springs were discovered in the region, Saratoga has played host to visitors from around the world. Today the county's world-class horse racing, performing arts center, several museums, charming architecture, fabulous shops, and fine restaurants make it a great choice for a vacation getaway. Over one thousand buildings in the county are listed on the National Register of Historic Places. There are acres of parks and woodlands on one side of town, and there's an elegant racetrack with a splendid Victorian grandstand on the other. Saratoga Springs may give the appearance of a small town, but it offers all the culture of a big city with lots of family-friendly activities.

The **Children's Museum at Saratoga** should be on the itinerary of all visitors with youngsters between the ages of two and nine. The location of the museum in the downtown area makes it an easy stop to combine with shopping or a visit to Congress Park, where kids can run around. At the lake, parents can sit and watch the ducks while the young ones play along graveled paths. The **Saratoga Performing Arts Center (SPAC)** offers a broad range of entertainment—including jazz, rock, dance, and country—in a unique outdoor setting. While

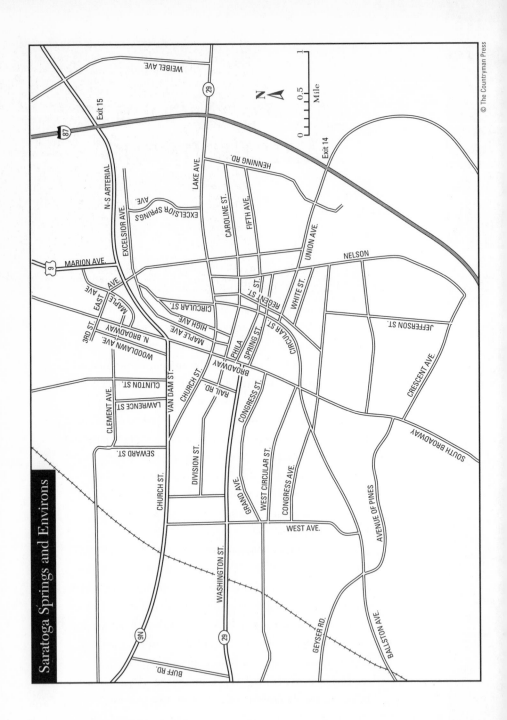

Saratoga Springs and Environs

© The Countryman Press

most of the performances are oriented toward adults, if your children enjoy a special type of music or dance, you can purchase lawn tickets that allow you to sit on blankets off to the side—where the views of the stage are still fairly decent. In summer, make sure to stop at **Brown's Beach** on Saratoga Lake, a great place to relax with the family; the shallow swim area is perfect for little children. In Ballston Spa, 7 miles south of Saratoga Springs, kids may be entertained by the

WWW.STOCKSTUDIOSPHOTOGRAPHY.COM

National Bottle Museum, which is devoted to the history of the handmade bottle. The permanent collection boasts nearly two thousand bottles, and there's a working glass studio. The nearby **Double M Arena** holds rodeos on Fridays during the summer. Kids can marvel at the bareback riding, barrel racing, bull riding, and calf roping—while the rodeo clowns do their best to make everyone laugh. **Saratoga National Historical Park** in Stillwater appeals to older children who have studied the famous three-pronged attack of the American Revolution. A battlefield tour begins at the visitors center, where elaborate displays of maps, miniature soldiers, battle arrangements, and slide shows guide the viewer through this turning-point battle in the war.

The summer season is when Saratoga comes alive with an array of celebrations geared to families. While the city's clear, crisp winter days are perfect for cross-county skiing and ice skating in the Spa State Park, most travelers prefer the warm-weather months in this part of the world. July brings the **Independence Day celebration at Saratoga National Historical Park,** an event filled with games and activities for children. **The Saratoga County Fair** is another July happening with exhibits, food, rides, shows, animals, and live entertainment. The month of August brings **Travers Festival Week,** a celebration around the racecourse's midsummer derby, the **Travers Stakes.**

For further information, contact **Saratoga County Chamber of Commerce,** 28 Clinton Street, Saratoga Springs 12866; 518-584-3255; www.saratoga.org.

 **What to See**

Saratoga Springs.   JOHN R. DILLON

MUSEUMS AND HISTORIC SITES

Children's Museum at Saratoga. 69 Caroline Street, Saratoga Springs 12866; 518-584-5540; www.childrensmuseumatsaratoga.org. Admission. Groups welcome by advance reservation.

This unique museum offers children aged two to nine a chance to explore the world, from the local community to the international level. Interactive exhibits allow kids to run a general store, make giant bubbles, and "freeze" their shadows. A tree house, fire truck, science section, movie theater, and two toddler areas are also popular with young visitors. Special events have included art workshops and magic shows. The museum is centrally located in town, so that a visit can be combined with shopping or stops at the Canfield Casino Museum and park.

Facilities: Restrooms. Wheelchair and stroller accessible.

National Bottle Museum. 76 Milton Avenue (NY 50), Ballston Spa 12020; 518-885-7589; www.nationalbottlemuseum.org. (The museum is 7 miles south of Saratoga Springs on NY 50.) Donations appreciated.

This museum focuses on the history of the handmade bottle; until 1903 glass bottles were handmade, not manufactured. The permanent collection consists of approximately two thousand bottles, but there are also changing exhibits that borrow from collections throughout the nation. Make sure to stop at the working glass studio across the street that is owned by the museum; there are classes in glassblowing and workshops with internationally renowned guest artisans. Every June the museum has a bottle show and sale, featuring antique-bottle dealers from throughout the East Coast.

Facilities: Restrooms, research library (available during museum hours).

National Museum of Dance. 99 South Broadway, Saratoga Springs 12866; 518-584-2225; www.dancemuseum.org. Admission. Group tours available by advance reservation.

Balletomanes and children who are fascinated by dance will undoubtedly want to spend an hour here. Changing exhibits focus on the history and glamour of dance in America—as told through photos, videos, costumes, and music. The multimedia Hall of the Fame, a permanent exhibit, pays tribute to the founders and shapers of American professional dance—from Fred Astaire and Alvin Ailey to Bill "Bojangles" Robinson and others. There is also a children's wing that is equipped with a stage, wardrobe, and artwork. In July, kids may see performances by students of the New York State Summer School of the Arts programs, and modern dance students are in residence during August.

Facilities: Restrooms, gift shop. Strollers are welcome here; wheelchair accessible.

National Museum of Racing and Hall of Fame. 191 Union Avenue, Saratoga Springs 12866; 518-584-0400; www.racingmuseum.org. Open year-round. Admission (children under the age of five are admitted free).

This museum is one of the most technologically advanced sports museums in the country, and it will entertain any child who has ever shown an interest in horses. The first stop should be the video *Race America,* which introduces the viewer to the excitement of a day at the races—its noise, music, movement, and color are all rolled into a package with lots of visuals and not too much information to confuse younger viewers. In the museum galleries, hands-on exhibits let the viewer participate in such activities as walking through a starting gate, watching a jockey go through a race, and listening to commentaries of famous trainers and jockeys. An elaborate display of costumed mannequins shows 19th-century Saratoga at its most elegant, and another shows a reproduction of a famous horse "portrait" painter's studio. Interactive computers in the Hall of Fame let kids call up information on jockeys, horses, and trainers, and the Anatomy Gallery houses a full-sized horse skeleton. During the school year there is a discovery room with hands-on activities, including a place for kids to design their own racing silks.

Facilities: Restrooms, changing tables, gift shop (this is one of the best shops for horse lovers, with gifts for all ages). Wheelchair and stroller accessible.

Saratoga Automobile Museum.
Spa State Park (off US 9), Saratoga Springs 12866; 518-587-1935; www.saratogaautomuseum.org.

This museum is housed in a restored 1930s Saratoga water-bottling plant in the park. Dozens of classic cars are on display, including a 1928 sedan once owned by Charles Lindbergh and a 1931 Dusenberg Model J Roadster.

Facilities: Restrooms, gift shop. Wheelchair and stroller accessible.

An outdoor exhibit at the Saratoga Automobile Museum.

Saratoga National Historical Park.
648 NY 32, Stillwater 12170; 518-664-9821; www.nps.gov. The visitors center is open year-round. Admission. Group tours by advance reservation.

Anyone who has ever studied the famous three-pronged plan of the American Revolution or hissed at the memory of Benedict Arnold will enjoy a visit to this

Saratoga National Historical Park makes the American Revolution come alive.

park. The battlefield tour begins at the visitors center—where elaborate displays of maps, miniature soldiers, battle arrangements, and an orientation video guide the visitor through this all-important battle of the American Revolution. From the center, you can take a two-hour drive-and-stop battlefield tour, where 10 stations offer overlooks and descriptive markers about the days leading up to the battle. The most interesting stops include the monument dedicated to Benedict Arnold's heroics (before he became a traitor) and Schuyler House, which contains memorabilia of General Philip Schuyler and his wife. Younger children enjoy the special events held throughout the summer in the park, which include musketry displays, soldiers' encampments, and old-fashioned craft demonstrations. While the battlefield park is interesting, the tour is a long one, and is not suitable for car-weary children or those who have no interest in Revolutionary War history.

Facilities: Restrooms, picnic areas, gift shop.

Tang Teaching Museum. Skidmore College, 815 North Broadway, Saratoga Springs 12866; 518-580-8080; www.tang.skidmore.edu. Open year-round. Admission.

In addition to fine art, the Tang has a few peripheral exhibits (including films and performances) in progress and some intriguing auditory treats, such as collaborative exhibits with Skidmore's science and history departments. The museum aspires to promote interdisciplinary learning through art for all age levels. There are a variety of educational tours as well as periodic Family Saturday programs that involve art projects for both children and their parents.

Facilities: Restrooms, gift shop. Stroller and wheelchair accessible.

ADDITIONAL ATTRACTIONS

Breakfast at the Clubhouse at Saratoga Racetrack. 267 Union Avenue (NY 9P), Saratoga Springs 12866; 718-641-4700 (months other than August), 518-584-6200 (during August); www.nyra.com (months other than August) and www.saratogarace track.com (during August). Group rates are available by advance reservation.

Breakfast at Saratoga Racetrack has been a tradition for more than a century, when elegant carriages brought ladies and gentlemen to the trackside tables. Today you can still combine breakfast and an exciting look at thoroughbred horses as they work out each morning at the racetrack. Children love to watch the horses gallop around the track. A trackside announcer explains

For over a century, families have enjoyed the tradition of breakfast at the Saratoga Racetrack.

which horses are working out and who is riding them. Each morning features a starting-gate demonstration that shows how horses are "loaded" into the gate and how they must wait for the bell and the cry of "And they're off!" before they speed around the track. After dining, take a free tour of the paddock area, where the horses live during their stay at the track. Visitors ride through the area on small "people trains" to watch the grooms, owners, trainers, and jockeys as they go about the very busy and expensive routine of caring for racehorses. Visitors must leave the track area after breakfast ends and before the track reopens for the races, when admission is charged.

Facilities: Restrooms, picnic areas, gift shop. The breakfast area is fine for wheelchairs and strollers, but do not attempt to take them on the paddock tour.

Canfield Casino, Congress Park, and the Springs. 315 Broadway, Saratoga Springs 12866; 518-584-6920; www.saratoga-springs.org or www.saratoga.com. Admission.

When Saratoga was the "Queen of Spas," the truly elegant would take the waters at the local springs and then walk in Congress Park. In the evenings, the casino would open for gambling and dining, and both the infamous and the famous—like Lillian Russell and Diamond Jim Brady—would attend. Today's visitors can still enjoy the same throwback atmosphere. A walk through the park brings you to hidden pools and fountains surrounded by flowers. My favorites are two puffy-cheeked Tritons nicknamed Spit and Spat, who spew water at each other across a small pool. At the lake, parents can sit and watch the ducks or let the kids play along the graveled paths. Just outside the park, look for the famous Saratoga flowerbeds, which are planted in the shape of horses and horseshoes. The city has its own watering trucks to ensure that the flowers stay fresh all through the summer. The original redbrick casino is now a charming museum that offers vignettes of early Saratoga life, costumes, toys, a gambling room, and various small collections of everything from rocks to Chinese shoes. Across the street from the casino, on Spring Street, is one of the original Saratoga springs, where you can take a cup of natural water for whatever ails you.

Facilities: Restrooms (for paid visitors), gift shop. Strollers are perfect for the park, but there is a steep flight of stairs up to the casino museum. The site is now wheelchair accessible.

Rodeo at the Double M Arena. 678 NY 67, Ballston Spa 12020; 518-885-9543; www.doublemwestern.com. (Take the Northway to exit 12; follow NY 67 west 1 mile to the arena.) Admission.

A visit to a rodeo is exciting for adults and children alike, and this is the oldest professional weekly rodeo in the United States. Cowboys and cowgirls participate in bareback riding, barrel racing, bull riding, and calf roping—just like the Western shows. Rodeo clowns do their best to make you laugh and protect the cowboys by attracting the bulls' attention. Trick riding and roping demonstrations are also given. The action takes place in a well-lighted outdoor arena, with excellent close-up views from the grandstand.

Facilities: *Restrooms, picnic areas, snack bar. Strollers and wheelchairs can manage here.*

Saratoga Performing Arts Center (SPAC). 108 Avenue of the Pines, Saratoga Spa State Park, Saratoga Springs 12866; 518-587-3330; www.spac.org. Tickets for performances can be purchased through major ticket services.

One of the premier performance centers in America, SPAC offers an amazingly broad range of entertainment in a unique setting. Choose among jazz, rock, folk, dance, opera, country, orchestral, and other music and dance performances throughout the season. While most of

The lawn seating at SPAC provides an ideal way for families with young children to enjoy a music or dance performance.

the entertainment is suitable only for adults, if your child enjoys a special type of music or dance, then by all means purchase lawn tickets the afternoon of the performances. Covered seats are available, but the lawn seating lets you sit on blankets or chairs under the trees off to the side—or anywhere you like, and the views of the stage are fairly decent. If you like to see every movement of the performance, then bring binoculars. Even if your child falls asleep, you can still enjoy the performance and babysit under the stars at the same time. Some excellent food stands in the park are open during the concerts, but you are not allowed to bring food into the covered seating area.

Facilities: Restrooms, restaurant, snack stands. SPAC is fine for strollers, but be aware that if you attend a popular concert, you may have to walk quite a distance from the parking area to the lawn site.

Saratoga Springs Public Library. 49 Henry Street, Saratoga Springs 12866; 518-584-7860; www.sspl.org. Open year-round. Free.

This library is worth a stop if you want to take a break from sightseeing in the city. They have a huge children's room, with several computers that have Internet access and educational games. There is also an extensive calendar of children's programs featuring puppet shows, videos, storytellers, and musical groups. While the kids are busy, parents can use computers themselves or enjoy reading from the extensive magazine offerings available here. Check the Web site or call for a schedule of special programs.

Facilities: Restrooms, café. Stroller and wheelchair accessible.

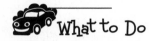 What to Do

BOATING, CANOEING, AND KAYAKING

Fish Creek Marina. 251 NY 67, Saratoga Springs 12866; 518-584-1901; www.fishcreekmarina.com. You can rent canoes, kayaks, or rowboats here. A nice feature is that there is a large pavilion available on the premises for BBQs and campfires. Great sunsets can be seen from this spot on the lake and people come from all over Saratoga to watch the sun go down here!

Point Breeze Marina. 1459 NY 9P, Saratoga Springs 12866; 518-587-3398; www.pointbreezemarina.com. This is a place to rent several different types of craft including canoes, kayaks, rowboats, pontoon boats, speedboats, and fishing boats. They have it all.

Saratoga Boat Works. 549 Union Avenue, Saratoga Springs 12866; 518-584-BOAT; www.saratogaboatworks.com. At the north end of Saratoga Lake, this full-service marina is a good place to rent a powerboat or pontoon boat. If you want to waterski, this is where you can rent the necessary equipment.

HIKING

Bog Meadow Nature Trail. Saratoga Springs 12866; 518-587-5554; www
.saratogaplan.org. From Broadway, make a right onto NY 29 east. Go
through the traffic light at Weibel Avenue; the trail entrance is about 500
feet farther on the right. Open year-round. Free. This 2-mile nature trail
is ideal for those traveling with small children. It is fairly flat and goes
through the wetlands just outside the city. You can walk in the warm
weather or cross-country ski in the winter months. There is a parking area.

East Side Recreation Field. Lake Avenue, Saratoga Springs 12866; 518-
587-3550; www.saratoga-springs.org. From
downtown Saratoga, make a right turn onto Lake
Avenue and go about 1.5 miles. The field is on
the right side, just after the East Avenue light.
Open year-round. Free. This 20-acre park has an
excellent skateboard area. There is also a wading
pool for small children as well as tennis courts, a
playground, basketball courts, and a 0.25-mile
paved circular track that's great for inline skating
and running.

Saratoga Spa State Park. 19 Roosevelt Drive (1
mile south of town off US 9), Saratoga Springs
12866; 518-584-2535; www.saratogaspastate
park.org. Open year-round. The park is free,
although there is a small charge for swimming
and the bathhouses. This 2,000-acre park is a
gem: clean, wide open, full of activities to keep
visitors busy. There are several streamside trails
for walking that make perfect short hikes for
those with children.

Saratoga Spa State Park,
open year-round, is a
winter wonderland—the
perfect place for a brisk
walk. JOHN R. DILLON

ICE SKATING

Saratoga Spa State Park. 19 Roosevelt Drive (1 mile south of town off
US 9), Saratoga Springs 12866; 518-584-2535; www.saratogaspastate
park.org. There is a lovely outdoor rink here in season, weather permitting. Call or check the Web site for hours, which change depending on

the weather conditions. Kids may participate in both hockey and figure skating here.

Saratoga Springs Ice Rinks. 32 Weibel Avenue, Saratoga Springs 12866; 518-583-3462; www.saratoga-springs.org. Call for a schedule which varies from week to week. There are two rinks here and they accommodate both hockey and figure skating. The Weibel rink is Olympic-sized and the Vernon rink is smaller. Both offer family skate sessions, public skates, and hockey sessions. Call for a current schedule.

PICK-YOUR-OWN FARMS

Saratoga County has long been famous for its horses and for its sweet summer cantaloupes (called hand melons), but several farms offer pick-your-own fruits and vegetables as well.

Ariel's Vegetable Farm. 194 Northern Pines Road, Gansevoort 12831; 518-584-2189. They are located 5 miles north of Saratoga Springs. Call for hours. Here you will find luscious strawberries, asparagus, raspberries, beans, and peas for the picking.

Bowman Orchards. 107 Van Aernam Road, Malta 12020; 518-885-8888; www.bowmanorchards.com. Open year-round. The orchard fruit is available for visitors to pick during September and October. There are a variety of fresh baked goods for sale in the market.

Hand Melon Farm. 533 Wilbur Avenue (NY 29), Greenwich 12834; 518-692-2376. The farm is located 13 miles east of Saratoga Springs. The melons here are usually ready to be picked from late July through mid-September. They are sweet and resemble cantaloupes. You can also pick your own strawberries here in June, and raspberries in September. A farm stand is also open, depending on the season. Do call to see what is in season before heading out there.

Riverview Orchards. 660 Riverview Road, Clifton Park 12065; 518-371-2174; www.rivervieworchards.com. Open daily during apple season; at other times call or check the Web site for hours, which vary. They offer pick-your-own apples (there are several varieties) as well as an orchard tour and special autumn events and demonstrations that will delight the kids. Don't miss the "donut robot" in the bakery!

SWIMMING

Brown's Beach. 511 NY 9P (on Saratoga Lake), Saratoga Springs 12866. Take exit 12 off the Northway; make a right and go 3 miles. At the lake, make a right and go north 1 more mile; the beach is on the left side of the road. Admission. This 250-foot-long, 25-foot-wide, and only 4-foot-deep public beach area has a terrific shallow swimming area that is great for small children. The adjacent marina offers kayak, canoe, and paddle-boat rentals. There is a snack bar on the premises.

Peerless Pool. Saratoga Spa State Park; 518-584-2000; www.saratogaspa statepark.org. Admission. This Olympic-sized pool is a great place to cool off after a day of walking around the city. However, the Victoria pool is a better choice if you have very young children.

Victoria Pool. Saratoga Spa State Park; 518-584-2000; www.saratogaspa statepark.org. Admission. There is a small children's pool here in addition to a larger swimming pool.

YMCA. 290 West Avenue, Saratoga Springs 12866; 518-583-9622; www.ymcasaratoga.org. Open year-round; check Web site or call for information on public swimming sessions, which change daily. There are family swim times here; a great rainy-day activity. The pool is 25 yards long and 5 lengths wide; the water temperature is usually around 84 degrees.

THEATER

Home Made Theater. The Spa Little Theater in Saratoga Spa State Park, 19 Roosevelt Drive, Saratoga Springs 12866; 518-587-4427; www.home madetheater.org. This theater is open during a calmer time of year in Saratoga Springs. Families will enjoy the full range of children's theater in this venue. Classes are offered for children as well. Check the Web site or call for a current schedule.

WARREN COUNTY
The Lake George Region and Southern Adirondacks
▼▲▼▲▼▲▼

Travelers will feel the change almost immediately as they cross the county line into Warren—the cooler climate, the aromatic blend of mountain air and hometown atmosphere, the magnificent open spaces of the Adirondack landscape. Ever since the end of the Revolutionary War in 1783, visitors have flocked to Lake George, drawn by its spectacular natural beauty. Still to this day, water, wilderness, and fun combine to make the Lake George area a summer paradise for family vacationers. Chock-full of activities kids love—theme parks, arcades, train rides, garnet mining, and miniature golf—this is a place where it's easy to spend quality family time. And if you have never been a fan of winter, Warren County is an excellent place to try your first trek on snow-shoes or cross-country skis; miles of trails await you. When the old-fashioned way of sliding in the snow with a toboggan or tube isn't enough, try downhill skiing or snowboarding at Gore Mountain; you can even end the day with a horse-drawn sleigh ride.

No family trip to Warren County is complete without a visit to the **Great Escape and Splashwater Kingdom** in Lake George. Once upon a time, this was a tiny park called Storytown; today it is the largest theme park in New York State, with six roller coasters and 125 total

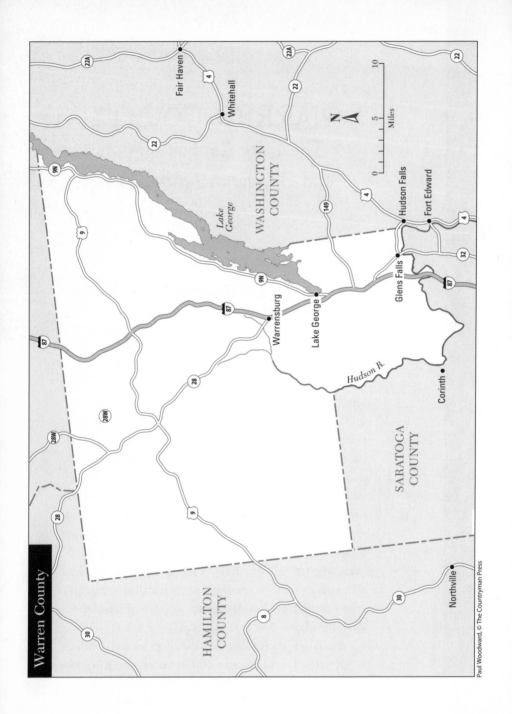

Warren County

rides. The park combines the old and new, the adventurous and the tame, so that everyone enjoys the visit. For an unusual and fun afternoon, don't miss the **Barton Garnet Mines** in North Creek—the oldest continuous garnet-mining operation in the world, producing a major portion of the world's industrial garnets. Lake George offers history as well as thrills; **Fort William Henry,** situated magnificently overlooking Lake George, is a huge restored site with interactive displays that bring the Colonial period to life. With the arrival of winter, kids who ski start to imagine piles of deep snow and fun-filled days schussing down the slopes. **Gore Mountain,** the largest state-run ski area in New York, is a ski center that offers a variety of skiing and snowboarding programs, and all are geared to providing a great mountain experience for young guests.

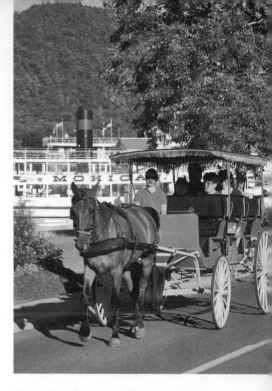

The entire family will enjoy a carriage ride through Lake George Village.
WARREN COUNTY TOURISM DEPARTMENT

There are a multitude of seasonal events in Warren County that will enrich your family getaway. In April several maple sugar producers open their establishments to the public. Kids will delight in watching the transition from sap to syrup before enjoying a sumptuous pancake breakfast where they can taste what came out of the trees! July brings the **County Youth Fair** to Warrensburg. Every Thursday night in July and August there are fireworks over Lake George. September is when the colorful **Adirondack Hot Air Balloon Festival** is held in Queensbury. **Oktoberfest** and **Frightfest** at the Great Escape are marvelous traditions on fall weekends at the amusement park. If you are in the region during the winter, try to coordinate your stay with the **Warrensburg Sled Dog Races** or the **Lake George Winter Carnival** in February.

For further information, contact the **Warren County Department**

of Tourism, 1340 US 9, Municipal Center, Lake George 12845;
1-800-95-VISIT, x. 143; www
.visitlakegeorge.com.

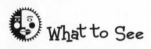 **What to See**

MUSEUMS AND HISTORIC SITES

Fort William Henry. 50 Canada Street (Beach Road at US 9), Lake
George 12845; 518-668-5471; www.fwhmuseum.com. Admission. Group
tours by reservation.

Fort William Henry, an important outpost during the tense years of
the French and Indian War, was constructed at the urging of Major General William Johnson. In 1757, the fort was overrun by French troops,
and the massacres that occurred became the basis for the James Fenimore Cooper novel *The Last of
the Mohicans.* Visitors to the fort
will see a large restored site complete with innovative history displays that bring the Colonial
period to life. In the powder
magazine, an underground log
house reached by a long brick
passageway, there are displays
that explain how kegs of gunpowder were stored beneath the
earth for safety. The cemetery
was the final resting place for
more than 2,500 soldiers, and
some of the graves are on view;
they are shown in a historic con-

Fort William Henry offers excellent
views of Lake George.

text, not a sensational manner. The dungeon is under the main museum,
with the remains of the original fireplace and dark, dismal cells—perfect
for kids to see, though not so good for the original prisoners. At the Living History Wall, buttons, bullets, and other artifacts found on-site are

displayed, and a multimedia presentation shows how the artifacts fit into daily Colonial life. Highlights of the Fort William Henry tour are the musket- and cannon-firing demonstrations. There is also a musket-ball molding demonstration. A wonderful interactive kids' program allows children to join the king's army; after each tour the children are given the chance to dress up and march with the "soldiers" and receive paper-work and a "coin" showing their enlistment into the fort's garrison. There are many costumed guides on site in 18th-century dress, and their uniforms are spectacular. The fort itself looks down the length of Lake George, and the view is worth the visit all by itself.

Facilities: Restrooms, picnic areas, gift shop, snack bar. The area is generally good for strollers, but only some parts of the site are wheelchair accessible.

Hyde Collection Art Museum. 161 Warren Street, Glens Falls 12801; 518-792-1761; www.hydecollection.org. Open year-round. Free (charge for guided group tours, which are available by advance reservation).

The Hyde Collection combines the world of fine art and the rich heritage of the Adirondack region. Formerly the home of Louis and Charlotte Hyde, a prominent turn-of-the-century Adirondack industrial family, visitors will enjoy their extraordinary collection of European and American art. The variety of works that cover the walls in this stately Florentine-style villa include paintings by da Vinci, Rubens, Rembrandt, Cezanne, Renoir, Van Gogh, Picasso, Whistler, and Homer. Eight elegant rooms surround a two-story skylighted courtyard studded with sculpture and tropical plants. The Hyde Collection combines the intimacy of this historic house with the sophistication of a larger art museum. Four additional gallery spaces on three floors present a changing schedule of world-class exhibits.

Throughout the school year, the education department offers ART-full Afternoons, a program that runs once a week after school for children aged 2–12. Each week's lesson includes a tour of an exhibit and a hands-on creative art workshop. One Sunday each month families are invited to participate in an art activity at the museum's art studio, which is connected to a temporary exhibition or aspect of the permanent collection. Saturday morning and vacation workshops are held throughout the year, and there is a summer arts camp. This child-friendly museum is a wonderful place to introduce children to fine art.

Facilities: Restrooms, picnic areas, gift shop. Stroller and wheelchair accessible.

Upper Hudson River Railroad. 3 Railroad Place, North Creek 12853; 518-251-5334; www.uhrr.com. Admission.

Just a short drive from Lake George, this railroad adds an exciting dimension to the Adirondack experience, one that the kids will love. The railroad runs seasonal two-hour excursions along an 8-mile (16-mile round-trip) section of the former Adirondack Branch of the Delaware & Hudson Railroad. Visitors board from restored platforms at the North Creek Depot and see breathtaking scenery as the train follows the Hudson River. There is musical entertainment and a "robbery" on just about every ride, which will delight the kids. After arriving at the picturesque Riverside Station, visitors have a chance to explore the museum room, gift shop, and vintage caboose refreshment stand. The railroad line was built at the end of the Civil War by Dr. Thomas Durant of Union Pacific Railroad fame. It terminated at North Creek until World War II, when it was extended to the iron mines in Tahawus to support wartime operations. The D&H continued to operate until 1989, when the mine closed and rail operations ceased. The scenic railroad fulfills the vision of owners John and Jerry Riegel of Delmar, New York, and the company founder, Walter Riegel—whose family has been in railroad construction for decades. The museum at North Creek Depot gives detailed information about the history of the railroad and the Adirondacks; it is open whenever the train is running and is worth a stop.

Facilities: Restrooms, snack bar, gift shop. Stroller and wheelchair accessible.

ADDITIONAL ATTRACTIONS

Barton Garnet Mines. Barton Mines Road (off NY 28, watch for signs), North Creek 12853; 518-251-2706; www.garnetminetours.com. Admission (children under the age of six admitted free). Group rates available.

These mines represent the oldest continuously running mining operation in the United States and produce a major portion of the world's industrial garnets. The New York State gemstone is deep red in color and has long been popular in jewelry. Visitors are taken on a guided tour of the open-pit mines, where blasting and hand digging unearth the gems—which are then graded and polished according to the needs of the user. Kids enjoy digging, so a highlight of this site is the chance for visitors to spend time "prospecting" for their own garnets. Prospectors should bring sun hats, sunscreen, and wear sturdy jeans and shoes for comfort. Bring a pillow to sit on if you are serious about digging all afternoon! There are garnet pockets all over the area, and you can purchase the gems you find. Site guides will answer any questions you have about finding stones. Stop at the mineral shop, which has a great collection of minerals on display and sells an extensive selection of cut and polished gems. Occasionally there are demonstrations of gem cutting and jewelry making—including cabochon cutting, a special way of refining a garnet into a rounded shape.

Facilities: Restrooms, gift shop. This is an accessible site for strollers since the mine floor is firm and flat.

Boston Candy Kitchen. 21 Elm Street, Glens Falls 12801; 518-792-1069; www.bostoncandykitchen.com. Open year-round. Free.

This family-run confectionary and luncheonette, founded in 1902, produces homemade ribbon candies and candy canes in flavors that range from peppermint, wintergreen, and lemon to anise, cinnamon, molasses, clove, and orange. Workers color, pull, knead, shape, and cut the candy into brightly colored ribbons and twists. The luncheonette has its original etched-glass soda fountain backing, a fine marble countertop, and old-fashioned stools that spin. This is a nice, homey place to stop for a snack and show the kids how candy canes actually get their stripes!

Facilities: Restrooms, restaurant, candy shop. Wheelchair and stroller accessible.

The Great Escape and Splashwater Kingdom. 1172 US 9, Queensbury 12804; 518-792-3500; www.sixflags.com. Admission. Group rates available by advance reservation.

There are over 125 rides, shows and attractions, and a full water park in this amusement park spanning 140 acres. Combining elements from the park's days as Storytown USA—when Mother Goose ruled the roost—and today's fast-paced and thrilling roller coasters, the Great Escape is one of the few remaining venues where old and new blend together in delightful harmony, offering something for children of all ages. The park has seven roller coasters—including the Comet, a wooden coaster ranked among the 10 best in the world. The others are the Boomerang, the Coast to Coaster, the Alpine Bobsled, the Steamin' Demon, the Nightmare Indoor Roller Coaster, and the Canyon Blaster. The newest addition, the Proslide Tornado, takes riders through a short section of an enclosed slide before engaging at the top of a giant funnel, simulating an actual tornado. Families who enjoy a more relaxed time can spend the day here watching shows, taking gentler rides, and eating at the many food pavilions. This "escape" is a nice way for kids to have an adventurous day in a bustling amusement park with all the usual amenities.

Facilities: Restrooms, picnic areas, restaurants, gift shops, snack stands, arcades. Stroller and wheelchair accessible.

Magic Forest. US 9, Lake George 12845; 518-668-2448; www.magic forstpark.com. Admission. Group rates by advance reservation.

This is a mellow, almost old-fashioned attraction that is actually set in a forest—so there is plenty of shade, even on the hottest days. Several entertainment "theme" areas offer attractions as diverse as a small Statue of Liberty, Santa's Night Before Christmas display, and a carousel. Younger children will delight in the time spent here as they feed Santa's famous reindeer, pet the baby animals, ride the Magic Forest railroad, and see the magic show. Another treat is watching a horse jump from a low diving platform into a pool. Everything here is geared toward children seven and under. The rides are not too fast or too scary, the colors are bright, and there are lots of places to stop and play make-believe. There are more than two dozen rides (including a 1-mile safari ride) and a fairy-tale trail for the wanderer.

Facilities: Restrooms, picnic areas, snack stand, gift shop. Wheelchair and stroller accessible.

Natural Stone Bridge and Caves. 535 Stone Bridge Road, Pottersville 12860; 518-494-2283; www.stonebridgeandcaves.com. Admission (children under the age of five are admitted free).

During the last ice age an east-west fault exposed this ancient rock to the violent waters from retreating glaciers. The resulting stone bridge is the largest natural marble cave entrance in the Northeast. Children will be intrigued by the self-guided tour, which takes visitors to unusual rock formations—including the Bridge of God, Artist's Gorge, Echo

Cave (yes, there's a real echo), and Cave of the Lost Pool. Two of the caves are lighted for exploration. This unique natural phenomenon is strikingly beautiful and also reveals an extraordinarily rare feature of Adirondack geology.

For an additional fee, there are a few different simulated mining activities. Kids can don a helmet and light and explore the Gold Rush Mine to find iron pyrite and polished gems, treasures they may keep; there is also Gemstone Mining and a Crystal Mine Quest to explore. At the Dino Dig children can uncover buried dinosaur bones; this is a free activity that may be just as appealing to kids as to adults!

Facilities: *Restrooms, picnic areas, gift shop, playground, mineral exhibits, gemstone mining.*

Submerged Heritage Preserve. Lake George 12845; 518-897-1200; www.dec.ny.gov/lands. Information about each site (including directions) is available from the New York State Department of Environmental Conservation (DEC), Region 5, NY 86, Box 296, Raybrook 12977.

This is an unusual site that will intrigue just about anyone interested in shipwrecks. There are actually three shipwrecks in Lake George itself. If you will be in the area and know you want to visit any of the sites, it is best to contact the DEC in advance of your trip. The preserves are pro-tected areas, and damaging them is illegal.

Up Yonda Farm Environmental Education Center. NY 9N, Bolton Landing 12814; 518-644-9767; www.upyondafarm.com. Open year-round. Admis-sion. Group tours welcome by advance reservation.

There are 72 acres of forest, pond, meadows, and streams here with spectacular views overlooking Lake George. No matter what time of year, kids will enjoy a variety of nature programs on plants, wildlife, and topics of seasonal interest. In March there are maple sugaring demon-strations. Kids will also like the wildlife exhibits, which include a diorama with Adirondack mammals and birds in various habitats and seasons. There are hiking trails, perennial gardens, and a butterfly garden from June to September. During the winter months there is snowshoeing (rentals available).

Up Yonda was previously owned by Alice and John Scott (who referred to the farm as the place "up yonda"). During the 1980s, they started to search for an organization that would preserve their farm for

future generations as an education center and eventually decided on the Warren County Parks and Recreation Department. In 1993, the existing buildings were renovated to create an auditorium and natural history museum. Hiking trails were blazed and a curriculum was created to teach visitors about the wonders of nature. Kids who are interested in nature will particularly enjoy this site.

Facilities: Restrooms, picnic areas. Buildings are all stroller and wheelchair accessible.

Make sure to stop at Up Yonda Farm, overlooking Lake George, for a nature walk. WARREN COUNTY TOURISM DEPARTMENT

Warren County Fish Hatchery. 145 Fish Hatchery Road, Warrensburg 12885; 518-623-2877; www.warrencountydpw.com. (Take exit 23 off I-87.) Open year-round. Free. Group tours may be scheduled by advance reservation.

A stop at this hatchery offers kids a chance to view a video presentation on the story of trout, their life cycles and habitats, and then go outside to see trout feeding. Thousands of fish are produced here each season that are used to stock trout ponds and streams throughout the county. Since many children have never caught a fish before, this is an interesting place to visit before or after a fishing expedition. I recommend it for kids who love the outdoors; younger children will probably also enjoy watching the Disney fishing cartoon shown here.

Facilities: Restrooms, picnic areas, canoe access, nature trails. Volleyball and basketball courts are open to the public. Strollers and wheelchairs can manage here.

Water Slide World. US 9, Lake George 12845; 518-668-4407; www.adirondack.net. (Take exit 21 off I-87, and go 0.5-mile south of Lake George Village.) Admission; be aware that there is no refund in the event of inclement weather.

Families with kids who love the water and water fun should plan a day at this amusement park. Water Slide World offers dozens of water activities—including a wave pool known as Hurricane Harbor, where man-made 4-foot waves break over swimmers in a 16,000-square-foot pool. An enormous series of water slides, up to 1,100 feet long, allow older swimmers (no toddlers here) to plunge down watery ramps and splash into pools; one of the slides even has a 360-degree loop and a tunnel. (Kids will enjoy the Blue Tornado slide and the Pirate Ship Cove, where Peg Leg watches over little ones as they slide into the bubble pool.) For an extra charge, kids can ride bumper boats in a confined lake, and parents can relax in hot tubs nearby. Toddlers will enjoy the Toddler Lagoon with its tiny slides, watery rocking horses, and the all-time favorite—water guns. Throughout the park there are places to rent rafts or buy bathing suits and other sun paraphernalia, so even if you don't come prepared, you and the kids can enjoy the park. Outdoor dry play areas offer volleyball and table tennis for a change of pace. This is an excellent park for a hot day, but younger children must be supervised continuously—especially on a crowded summer day when hundreds of people are splashing and sliding. You can enjoy a quieter time by renting a raft and just floating along on the pools or sunbathing in the many chairs and rest areas that surround the pools.

Facilities: Restrooms, restaurant, snack bars, lockers, showers, retail shop (which sells bathing suits and caps).

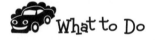 **What to Do**

BEACHES (SWIMMING)

Lake George has been famous for its waterfront for more than three centuries, and although many of the lake's beaches are now privately owned (and so marked), there are still some excellent spots to swim with the kids. Unless otherwise noted, the following beaches are free. Even though this is a resort region, with several private beach areas, remember that day-trippers fill up the parking lots and the best beach spots very early in the day—so plan accordingly.

WARREN COUNTY TOURISM DEPARTMENT

The renowned Million-Dollar Beach at the head of Lake George is one of the few public beaches in the village. WARREN COUNTY TOURISM DEPARTMENT

The famous **Million-Dollar Beach,** so called because of the cost of building it and the ritzy clientele it attracted in the resort's early days, is at the head of Lake George off Beach Road. Park nearby and walk in, since you are not allowed to park on the pier. This beach is particularly family-friendly—with lifeguards on duty, changing rooms, lockers, and a volleyball court. It is part of an extensive system of beaches that run all along the southern end of Lake George. These public beaches include **Shepard Park Beach** (off Canada Street in Lake George Village), which is centrally located near restaurants and shopping. **Ushers Park Beach** (on NY 9L, just past Million-Dollar Beach) is a quieter place and a great choice for parents with very young children, with a large shallow water area as well as a nice playground and picnic area. **Lake George Battlefield Park and Public Campground** on Beach Road is directly in back of Million-Dollar Beach. This 35-acre park includes the remains of an old fort, along with monuments to the men who fought here during the French and Indian Wars and the American Revolution. It's a short walk from the park to the swimming area that has restrooms, picnic areas, and BBQ pits.

BICYCLING

Warren County Bikeway. Warren County Department of Tourism, 1340 US 9, Municipal Center, Lake George 12845; 518-761-6368. You can pick up the bikeway at Glenwood Avenue (US 9), from exit 19 off I-87

(Glens Falls–Queensbury border) and cycle to the Lake George Battle-field Park.

This section of the Warren County Bikeway is known as the Glens Falls Feeder Canal Trail. The Warren County area offers a unique 11-mile trip along this paved bikeway through mostly flat terrain, complete with striking mountain and valley views along the way, ending at the southern tip of Lake George. The one-way trip takes approximately two hours, and follows a marked pathway away from traffic. This is an excursion you may want to plan in advance, and a detailed map of the bikeway is available from the Warren County Department of Parks and Recreation; 1-800-365-1050, x. 2770; www.warrencountydpw.com. If you don't bring your own bikes and you plan on riding the full round-trip, consider renting a bike at **Beach Road Outdoor Supply**, 2239 South Canada Street, Lake George 12845; 518-668-4040.

BOAT CRUISES

Lake George Steamboat Cruises. 57 Beach Road, Lake George 12845; 518-668-5777; www.lakegeorgesteamboat.com. Each of the three cruise boats has its own schedule, so call, check the Web site, or stop by the headquarters on the pier for up-to-date tour information. Admission; children's rates available. Group rates by advance reservation.

This cruise company offers a chance to see Adirondack scenery from a unique vantage point. They run three cruise ships that travel the length of Lake George, on 1-hour to 4.5-hour excursions. You can travel from the Lake George pier to Ticonderoga, or just visit the other end of the lake on the short cruise. I suggest the 1-hour cruise on the *Minne-Ha-Ha,* an authentic paddle-wheeler with steam-engine pistons visible through a glass-paneled engine room. The ship has a piercing steam whistle and is colorful and noisy as it plows through the lake. A tour guide points out famous homes and historic places, although the kids will be enthralled with watching the paddle-wheel and listening to the calliope. This is the oldest boat excursion company in the country and has been offering passengers rides on Lake George since 1817. If you are going to sit out on the deck, it is always windy, and you may want to bring a sun hat and sunscreen; however, there are also enclosed observation areas.

Facilities: Restrooms, snack bar. Stroller and wheelchair accessible.

CANOEING AND KAYAKING

Adirondack Adventures. 4659 NY 28, North River 12856; 1-877-963-RAFT; www.adkadventures.com. If you are interested in planning a kayak, canoe, or raft trip, this outfitter will assist you in getting instruction and equipment and putting the excursion together for either whitewater or lake touring. They also offer lodging packages for overnight trips with New York State–licensed guides.

Lake George Kayak Company. 4973 Lake Shore Drive, Bolton Landing 12814; 518-644-9366; www.lakegeorgekayak.com. Call or check Web site for hours. This outfitter is a good one to contact if you are new to kayaking; they rent kayaks by the hour, half day (4 hours), or full day (24 hours) on Lake George. Some of their double kayaks open up and you can put a third seat in the middle to accommodate a small child.

FISHING

Warren County's 160-plus lakes and ponds and 1,000 miles of streams and rivers offer some of the finest sport fishing in the country. The area is a good place to introduce children to fishing. The Lake George region boasts 11 major game fish: landlocked salmon; lake trout; brown, rainbow, and brook trout; smallmouth and largemouth bass; northern pike; pickerel; sunfish; perch; bluegills; rock bass; and crappies. Trout season begins on April 1; bass season opens the third Saturday in June. You must have a fishing license if you are age 16 or over and one may be obtained at most town and city clerk's offices, as well as most area bait and tackle shops. The Lake George Fishing Alliance is a good source for further local information; they hold clinics for youngsters in the

A father and son enjoy some quiet time fishing from the banks of Lake George. WARREN COUNTY TOURISM DEPARTMENT

spring. The organization may be contacted at www.lgfa.org. The Warren County establishments listed here also offer fishing licenses and will supply just about everything you need for a family outing.

Ann's Bait and Tackle Shop. 8 Norowal Road, Bolton Landing 12814; 518-644-9989.

Beach Road Outdoor Supply. 2239 Canada Street, Lake George 12845; 518-668-4040.

Nemec's Sport Shop. 4036 Main Street, Warrensburg 12885; 518-623-2049.

PARKS AND NATURE TRAILS

Warren County has thousands of acres of public campgrounds and parks, and it would take a lifetime to explore them all. Many of the Lake George–Warren County parks are in wilderness areas, and as such are not always suitable for the young day hiker or novice. I have selected my favorites among those that appeal to younger children as well as older children and parents.

Crandall Park International Trail System. Upper Glen Street (US 9), Glens Falls 12801; 518-761-3813. Open year-round. Free.

This large outdoor nature complex offers approximately 5 miles of fairly flat nature trails for exploration. There is a fishing pond on the site (bring your own poles), as well as picnic areas, recreation fields, and courts for tennis and basketball. A fitness trail has wooden exercise stations complete with use directions for all levels of fitness. Hikers of all ages and abilities will appreciate the extensive trail areas, which lead through pine forests and cross over brooks and waterfalls. The trails are well marked for the hiker, and they are not challenging—so you can walk with the younger set and still have some energy left over for a cookout! (During the winter months, the trails are groomed—and even lighted—for cross-country skiing and snowshoeing.)

Facilities: Restrooms.

Dynamite Hill Nature Trail. NY 8, Chestertown 12817; 518-494-5160; www.northwarren.com. Open year-round. Free. This 0.5-mile, marked trail is an ideal stop for those traveling with young children. There are no restrooms or other facilities here.

Lake George Recreation Park. NY 9N and Transfer Road, Lake George 12845; 518-668-5771. (Located 0.25 mile west of Northway exit 21.) Open year-round. Free. This 364-acre park overlooking Lake George has several marked hiking trails with fairly flat terrain ideal for the youngest hikers.

Facilities: Restrooms.

Pack Demonstration Forest. 276 Pack Forest Road, Warrensburg 12885; 518-623-9679. Open year-round. Free. This 2,500-acre environmental demonstration forest features a well-marked, 1-mile-long, wheelchair-accessible nature trail—as well as ponds, forests, and a small river. Picnic Mountain offers a mild climb and lovely views. Keep in mind there are no restrooms or other facilities on-site here.

SKIING, SNOWBOARDING, AND SLEDDING

Dynamite Hill. NY 8, Chestertown 12817; 518-494-5160; www.north warren.com. Free. There is one trail here with a rope tow that is perfect for beginner and novice downhill skiers. The area is lighted for night skiing, and there's a warming hut. This is a fairly rustic setup, but it's a great find for those with their own equipment and very young kids starting out in the sport. The price can't be beaten anywhere!

Garnet Hill Ski Center. 13th Lake Road, North River 12856; 518-251-2444; www.garnet-hill.com. (Take I-87 to exit 23 and follow US 9 to NY 28 west for 22 miles to North River, where you pick up 13th Lake Road and go 5 miles to the ski center.)

There are 35 miles of trails (16 with set track and 2 that are lit), 6 miles of showshoeing trails, a warming hut, instruction, rentals, and food. Guided tours and lessons are available, as are night ski tours. The kids' ski program, offered on weekends and holidays, makes learning fun for children age 5–12. Younger kids can take a ride in one of the "pulks," a small sled pulled by adults.

Facilities: Restrooms, snack bar, rentals.

Gore Mountain and North Creek Ski Bowl. 793 Peaceful Valley Road, North Creek 12853; 518-251-2411; www.goremountain.com. Ski lift and gondola fees.

Gore Mountain is a huge state-run ski area with a summit elevation of 3,600 feet, 88 trails, and 12 lifts. They have an eight-passenger high-speed gondola and several quad chairlifts. The area offers skiing for all skill levels and complete snowmaking capabilities to keep the fun coming all season. In 2009 Gore took over management of the North Creek Ski Bowl, a winter fun park featuring a snow tubing area, a beginner-rated ski trail, the "Village Slope," and a terrain park with half-pipe. The North Creek Ski Bowl was one of the first commercially operated ski areas in America and the birthplace of the National Ski Patrol. Gore's Bear Cub Den Daycare is open daily for children age six months to six years. There are equipment rentals and lessons for all age groups from toddlers upward. This is a full-service mountain that offers many options to families, as well as some of the steepest trails in the East.

Facilities: Restrooms, restaurant, lodge, ski shop, nursery, rentals, lockers.

Hickory Ski Center. 43 Hickory Hill Road, Warrensburg 12885; 518-623-5754; www.skihickory.net. Lift fee.

This is a small, family-oriented ski area that opened in 1946 and still has an old-fashioned atmosphere. There are 19 trails serviced by three lifts (two Poma lifts and one T-bar). The nice part of this ski center is that it's a homey place with a friendly staff—and children under the age of seven ski free. Lessons are available as are snacks, but there is no nursery or ski rentals here.

Facilities: Restrooms, snack bar.

West Mountain. 59 West Mountain Road, Queensbury 12804; 518-793-6606; www.skiwestmountain.com. Lift fee.

There are 22 slopes and trails and five lifts (a triple chair, two double chairs, and two rope tows) at this busy ski center, which is fairly close to the capital district. They offer instructional programs for alpine, tele-mark, and snowboard enthusiasts. Also available for fun times is the snow tubing park, with two lifts that will bring you up to the level you are most comfortable with on the slope.

Facilities: Restrooms, cafeteria, ski school, rentals.

FAMILY RESORTS

Warren County is filled with family resorts providing delightful getaways for just about every taste and budget. The two resorts included here offer very different vacation experiences; for a complete directory of resorts, contact Warren County Tourism.

Ridin-Hy Ranch Resort. 95 Ridin-Hy Ranch Road, Warrensburg 12885; 518-494-2742; www.ridinhy.com. (Take I-87 to exit 24; bear right, cross the bridge, and take the first left; follow signs 3 miles to the ranch.) Open year-round.

This down-home Adirondack ranch resort has been owned and operated by three generations of the Beadnell family since 1940. There are 700 acres of scenic trails for the riders in the family, but even those who aren't interested in horses will find lots to do here. For those who are new to horseback riding, there is free instruction by experienced wranglers who will make everyone comfortable in the saddle. Activities include rodeos, hayrides, and pony rides for the youngest children. There is also boating on the lake, an indoor heated pool, volleyball, children's arts and crafts, bingo, and entertainment in the evening.

KALLERNA, HTTP://COMMONS.WIKIMEDIA.ORG

Accommodations are varied and include chalet cabins, one-story motel units, and rooms in the lakeside main lodge. All rooms are within easy walking distance of the sandy beach, pool, and main lodge—where three meals are served daily to all guests. There is an informal atmosphere here that will surely make everyone feel welcome and comfortable. A vacation here is like being at summer camp with the entire family!

Facilities: Basketball court, table tennis, swimming pool, boating on the lake, stable.

The Sagamore Resort. 110 Sagamore Road, Bolton Landing 12814; 518-644-9400, 1-800-358-3585; www.thesagamore.com. (Take I-87 to exit 22; turn left onto NY 9N and go 10 miles; turn right onto Sagamore Road.) Open year-round.

Listed on the National Register of Historic Places, the Sagamore combines 19th-century charm with 21st-century sophistication for family vacationers. The hotel opened in 1883 and catered for many years to a select, wealthy clientele that flocked to Lake George during the summer months. In 1981 the Sagamore underwent a $72 million restoration. This world-class resort now offers 350 rooms and suites; the main hotel and lakeside lodge buildings are designed especially for families.

The Sagamore is situated on its own 70-acre island. A great time to visit is between June and August or during a school holiday like President's Week, spring break, or winter recess. The hotel offers family packages with reduced winter rates and the children's program is in full swing during school holidays. Parents may enjoy a relaxing time at the spa or on the golf course, because there are plenty of activities on tap for the kids. The well-organized program is directed by a children's entertainment coordinator and includes such fun-filled activities as face painting, kite flying, dinosaur hunts, and poolside make-your-own-ice–cream-sundae socials. Children must be out of diapers to participate, and those under the age of four may attend only if accompanied by a babysitter (not a sibling). From May to October, there are lake excursions on the *Morgan*, a lovely yacht owned by the hotel. During the winter, the grounds have 10 miles of trails for cross-country skiing and snowshoeing. A free shuttle service runs to and from Gore Mountain (**see Skiing, Snowboarding & Sledding, pg. 287**) for downhill skiers of all ages. If you want to get away with the kids, the Sagamore is an ideal place for everyone to have a great time.

Facilities: *Restaurants, gift shop, golf course, indoor and outdoor tennis, table tennis, indoor pool, salon, spa, fitness room, boating, racquetball, cross-country skiing, snowshoeing, nature trails. Babysitting services can be arranged. Most areas of the main building are wheelchair accessible.*

THE
BERKSHIRES

▼▲▼▲▼▲▼

D ipping your feet in a rushing stream, flying a kite on a spectacular open hillside, skiing down a powder-packed slope, picnicking amid a lush mountain landscape: These are images of family vacations that conjure up powerful memories. Children love rural adventures, but they also require more than such simple pleasures. The Berkshires' mix of breathtaking natural scenery, kid-friendly cultural attractions, and exciting outdoor activities is why so many families visit this part of the world year-round.

A wonderful place to go for a fun family outing is the **Berkshire Museum** in Pittsfield, one of the nation's finest small museums and one of the few where art, history, and the natural world are displayed together. Both the **Clark Art Institute** in Williamstown and the **Norman Rockwell Museum** in Stockbridge hold family days year-round, while Kidspace at the **Massachusetts Museum of Contemporary Art (MASS MoCA)** is an art gallery and studio space designed especially for students, teachers, and families. Children enjoy the drive up to **Mt. Greylock,** the highest point in the state of Massachusetts at 3,491 feet. Now a state reservation, the area comprises 12,000 acres of protected land with spectacular views, alpine forests, and more than 40 rare plant species.

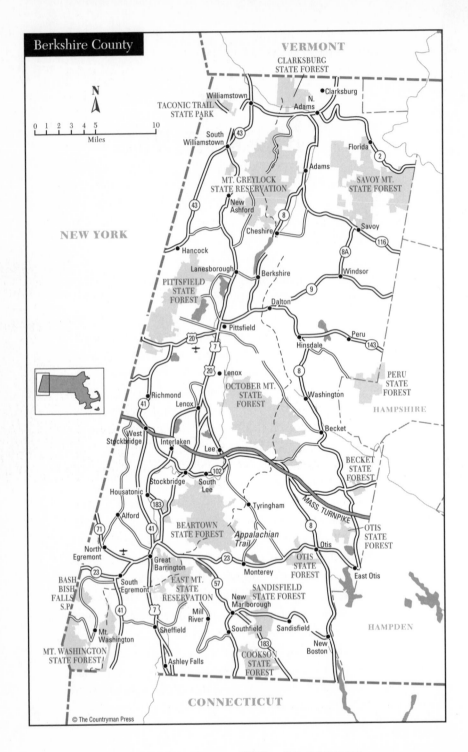

Berkshire County

N

0 1 2 3 4 5   10
Miles

VERMONT

CLARKSBURG
STATE FOREST

Williamstown   N.   Clarksburg
Adams

TACONIC TRAIL
STATE PARK

South
Williamstown   43

43   Florida   2

Adams

NEW YORK

MT. GREYLOCK
STATE RESERVATION

SAVOY MT.
STATE FOREST

New
Ashford   8

Cheshire   Savoy

Hancock

8A   116

Lanesborough   Berkshire   Windsor

PITTSFIELD
STATE
FOREST

9

Dalton

Pittsfield   Peru   143

20   Hinsdale

7   PERU
STATE
FOREST

20   Lenox   8

OCTOBER MT.
STATE
FOREST   Washington

Richmond   41   Lenox   HAMPSHIRE

West
Stockbridge   Interlaken   Becket

Lee

BECKET
STATE
FOREST

102

Stockbridge   South
Lee

Housatonic   183

Tyringham   MASS. TURNPIKE

Alford   71   41

BEARTOWN
STATE FOREST

Appalachian
Trail   8   OTIS
STATE
FOREST

North
Egremont   23   Great
Barrington   23   Otis   East Otis

BASH
BISH
FALLS
S.P.   23   South
Egremont   EAST MT.
STATE
RESERVATION   57   Monterey   OTIS
STATE
FOREST

41   7   Mill
River   New
Marlborough   SANDISFIELD
STATE FOREST   HAMPDEN

Mt.
Washington   Sheffield   Southfield   Sandisfield

MT. WASHINGTON
STATE FOREST   183   New
Boston

Ashley Falls   COOKSON
STATE
FOREST

CONNECTICUT

© The Countryman Press

A worthwhile stop if you are in the Lanesborough area is the **Par-4 Family Fun Center,** which has miniature golf, batting cages, bumper boats, and more. After touring the museums, the kids will especially appreciate all the fun activities here.

Agriculture is still a vital part of county life and several Berkshire farms offer an insider's view of their operations. In Hancock, the 600-acre **Ioka Valley Farm** provides agri-entertainment—including a hay maze, hayrides, and pedal tractors. Guided trail riding and licensed instruction please horse-loving families visiting **Undermountain Farm** in Lenox. Bicycling through the county's rolling landscape has soared in popularity with the construction of the breathtakingly beautiful 11-mile-long paved **Ashuwillticook Rail Trail**. In addition to downhill runs, kids of all ages will enjoy snow tubing and snowshoeing at the area's many fine ski centers: **Brodie, Bousquet, Butternut, Jiminy Peak,** and **Otis Ridge**. Most of these ski areas also offer exciting family activities all summer long, with many special programs and attractions just for kids.

Snow tubing is a popular pastime at many Berkshire ski centers.

There are many wonderful annual events to add to your stay in the Berkshires. Kids are especially interested in the **sheepshearing at the Hancock Shaker Village** held in June. The **Berkshire Arts Festival** in Great Barrington in July features 200 juried artists, music, and activities for the kids. The **Clark Art Institute** in Williamstown puts on a **Family Day** in July with a carnival, acrobats, magicians, and music; they also have a series of free concerts throughout the summer. Every August is the **Berkshire Botanical Garden's flower show,** with special children's classes that will appeal to youngsters who love nature. In September, the annual **Great Josh Billings Run-Aground**—a bike, canoe/kayak, run triathlon from Great Barrington to Lenox—will delight young spectators. October brings the annual **Fall Foliage Festival and Parade** in North Adams and the **Mt. Greylock Ramble.**

For further information, contact the **Berkshire Visitors Bureau,** 3 Hoosac Street, Adams, MA 01220; 413-743-4500; www.berkshires.org.

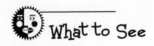 **What to See**

MUSEUMS AND HISTORIC SITES

Berkshire Museum. 39 South Street, Pittsfield, MA 01201; 413-443-7171; www.berkshiremuseum.org. Open year-round. Admission. Group tours available by advance reservation.

A museum chock-full of art, ancient history, and natural science collections, the Berkshire Museum has plenty of appeal for families with young children. There are aquariums filled with freshwater and saltwater fish—along with touch tanks; displays of fossils, gems, and minerals; and a Berkshire Backyard with specimens representing the animals of Berkshire County. A dinosaurs and paleontology gallery, complete with a "Dino-Dig" where kids can look for dinosaur bones, will appeal to younger kids. Innovation Central is a 3,000-square-foot gallery showcasing innovations that have enhanced people's lives around the world. From telegraphs to blogs, plastics to film special effects, children will have fun with several interactive displays in this area. Don't miss the Egyptian mummy, swathed in linen and still holding court surrounded by art and artifacts from ancient civilizations. Older children who appreciate art will like the fine art galleries, including American and European paintings from the 18th and 19th centuries. Of special interest is the Native Peoples Northeast-Northwest exhibit and those featuring replicas of several toys for children designed by Alexander Calder.

Facilities: Restrooms, gift shop (with educational toys and fun items for children). Wheelchair and stroller accessible.

Chesterwood. 4 Williamsville Road, Stockbridge, MA 01262; 413-298-3579; www.chesterwood.org. Admission (children under the age of 18 are admitted free).

This charming site, part of the National Trust for Historic Preservation, was the summer home of Daniel Chester French, the sculptor who created the Lincoln Memorial and the Minute Man statues. A self-guided tour takes you through the studio, residence, and gardens where French spent the summer months. The studio is filled with memorabilia, as well as the tools and plaster casts used to make the Lincoln Memorial. Children will enjoy seeing how sculpture is created, and they can handle some of the tools and reproduction sculptures on display. In the summer, the Saturday Art for Children program introduces kids (over the age of five) to sculpture. Outside, there are lovely gardens and walkways and large sculptures. A short woodland trail that was laid out by French is a pleasant detour for young walkers who enjoy nature.

Facilities: Restrooms, gift shop. There are several buildings on the site and strollers can manage; there is wheelchair accessibility to the studio and barn gallery.

Clark Art Institute. 225 South Street, Williamstown, MA 01267; 413-458-2303; www.clarkart.edu. Open year-round. Admission or free depending on season for adults; children 18 and under, as well as students with identification, are admitted free year-round. Group tours arranged by advance reservation.

One of the best collections of fine art in the region, this museum contains an incredible selection of French 19th-century paintings and sculpture. The colorful paintings by Renoir, Monet, and Degas are a good way to introduce children to fine art, and special activity sheets are available at the information desk. Many of the paintings are well known, and they all depict realistic scenes and people: earthy peasant women, flowers, dancers, and landscapes. Another exhibit hall displays a large collection of silver from the 17th to the 20th centuries; the candlesticks, ewers, and plates are dazzling. This jewel of a museum is rarely crowded and permits children to get up close to fine art. Throughout the year, the Clark offers a variety of public programs—including school programs, concerts, films, and educational courses. Highlights include free summer concerts, lunchtime gallery talks, and year-round family days presented in conjunction with special exhibitions. There are special gallery talks for children that relate to many different areas of the school curriculum—including history, science, creative writing, and literature.

Stone Hill Center, designed by Japanese architect Tadao Ando, opened in 2008. Located on a wooded hillside a short walk from the museum, it houses two new spacious galleries. An enormous terrace area affords wonderful views of the Taconic and Green Mountains. There are trails and walking paths here, making it a good place to go with children after visiting the museum.

Facilities: Restrooms, gift shop, café. Stroller and wheelchair accessible.

Eric Carle Museum of Picture Book Art. 125 West Bay Road, Amherst, MA 01002; 413-658-1100; www.carlemuseum.org. Open year-round. Admission. Group tours available by advance reservation.

Founded in part by Eric Carle, the renowned author and illustrator of more than 70 children's books (including the 1969 classic *The Very Hungry Caterpillar*), this museum is the first one in the country devoted to national and international picture book art. It was built with the aim of celebrating the art we are first exposed to as children. The museum takes children on a colorful journey through the pages of old and new picture book favorites. The museum features three exhibition galleries, a hands-on art studio, a comfortable library for reading and storytelling—and an auditorium for performances, films, and lectures. This is a nice stop for children who are particularly interested in books and their illustrations.

Facilities: *Restrooms, gift shop, café. Stroller and wheelchair accessible.*

Hancock Shaker Village. 1843 West Housatonic Street (US 20), Pittsfield, MA 01201; 413-443-0188; www.hancockshakervillage.org. Admission (children under the age of 12 are admitted free). Group tours are available by advance reservation.

This original Shaker village and farm is a great site for families, especially those interested in American history. The 1,200-acre site was home to the Shakers, a communal religious group, from the late 18th century through 1959. There are 20 historic buildings, most on-site; most are restored to their 1830s appearance, with some structures reflecting early-20th-century life.

The Shakers were a religious community that embraced the tenets of communal living, celibacy, and confession of sin. They followed the teachings of Ann Lee and were socially progressive, believing in the equality of men and women. They were also technologically innovative, inventing or improving on many items in daily use—such as the flat broom. Renowned for their crafts and trades, the Shakers saw their daily work as part of their religious life. "Put your hands to work and hearts to God and a blessing will attend you," said Mother Ann Lee.

There are 20 buildings—points of interest for kids include the famous 1826 round stone barn, which was a model of efficiency and housed 52 dairy cattle; neatly tended herb and vegetable gardens that show dozens of different herbs and heirloom plants raised by the Shakers; the schoolhouse with its "schoolteacher" (a costumed staff person in character) giving lessons on penmanship, spelling, and "how to be a good Shaker"; the 1858 reproduction water turbine, which powers equipment in the laundry and machine shop; and the farm, with heritage breeds of livestock including chickens, cattle, sheep, and swine. There are demonstrations daily of a variety of traditional crafts and trades—such as woodworking, blacksmithing, oval box making, and textile arts—throughout the village. You are able to wander the village at your own pace. In the Discovery Room, children can try their hand at a variety of activities they have seen in the village, including learning to spin wool or weave, trying on Shaker clothes, milking "Mary Jane" (a life-sized replica of a Holstein cow), watching chicks hatch, or playing with 19th-century toys.

Facilities: Restrooms, picnic areas, gift shop, café. Not all buildings are accessible by wheelchairs and strollers.

MASS MoCA. 87 Marshall Street, North Adams, MA 01247; 413-662-2111; www.massmoca.org. Admission. Group tours by advance reservation.

One of the largest museums in the country, with over 300,000 square feet in 26 buildings, this is a welcoming place that encourages the dynamic interchange between making and presenting art. The converted factory space works well for the technically complex sculpture and art on display here, much of which requires huge spaces. The site itself fascinates young visitors with its elaborate system of interlocking courtyards, staircases, and passageways. Interestingly manufacturing began near the site even before the Revolutionary War due to its location at the confluence of two branches of the Hoosic River. Over the past 250 years, the site has had many incarnations—brickyard, sawmill, ironworks, textile factory and electronics manufacturer, and now museum. There are all stages of art production in all its forms, including rehearsals, sculptural fabrication, developmental workshops, and finished works of art. The enormous sculptures are particularly alluring to children. And don't miss Kidspace, a special gallery where kids can create art at their own pace during weekend programs.

Facilities: Restrooms, restaurant, gift shop, café. Stroller and wheelchair accessible in most areas.

Norman Rockwell Museum. 9 Glendale Road (off MA 183), Stockbridge, MA 01262; 413-298-4100; www.nrm.org. Rockwell's painting studio is

also located on the site. Admission (children 18 and under are admitted free). Group tours by advance reservation.

Norman Rockwell was the creator of a special type of American art that celebrated everyday life with all its joys and sorrows, and visitors will appreciate the wealth of art on display here. Set on a picturesque 36-acre estate, the

At the Norman Rockwell Museum, the holiday season brings an array of special events for children, along with enchanting decorations. BERKSHIRE VISITORS BUREAU

museum holds the world's largest collection of original Rockwell works—with over 500 paintings, drawings, portraits, and advertising pieces. Highlights include selections from Rockwell's *Saturday Evening Post* covers, the famous *Four Freedoms* collection, and *Stockbridge Main Street at Christmas*. As a center devoted to the art of illustration, the museum also exhibits the work of contemporary and past masters in the field. While the youngest children may not be enthralled by the large amount of art on view, children age 10 and up will appreciate seeing close-up the images they may see in school and on calendars. Outside, visitors can stroll the grounds and take in the views. Special events and workshops for children, school groups, and families are offered throughout the year; check the Web site or call for a schedule.

Facilities: Restrooms, gift shop. Stroller and wheelchair accessible.

ADDITIONAL ATTRACTIONS

Berkshire Botanical Garden. 5 West Stockbridge Road, Stockbridge, MA 01262; 413-298-3926; www.berkshirebotanical.org. Admission (children 12 and under are admitted free).

If you and your children love gardens and flowers, this is a fine place to spend a few hours. The 15-acre botanical garden is beautifully landscaped with thousands of species and varieties of annuals, perennials, herbs, shrubs, and trees. Specimens from around the world are represented, but the focus is on plants that thrive in the Berkshires. Plantings include colorful perennial and annual gardens, herb and rock gardens, a pond garden, a children's garden, an ornamental vegetable garden, an arboretum, and a greenhouse. Don't forget to check out the woodland interpretive trail. Education programs are offered throughout the year as well. Annual special events include a plant sale, a flower show, the Harvest Festival, and the Holiday Marketplace. First held in 1934, the October Harvest Festival is one of the largest and most renowned community gatherings in the Berkshires. A family-oriented event, it features games, rides, food, arts and crafts, live entertainment, and a giant tag sale. Do check the Web site or call for a complete schedule.

Facilities: Restrooms, picnic areas, gift shop. Wheelchair-accessible pathways serve many areas of the garden.

Berkshire Community College. 1350 West Street, Pittsfield, MA 01201; 413-236-2190; www.berkshirecc.edu. Open year-round.

This community college has a variety of hands-on activities for children throughout the year. In addition to golf and cooking classes during the summer, there are a few innovative and unusual workshops. The robotics workshop will appeal to youngsters interested in high-tech games and science. A circus camp is geared to children ages 8–13 and teaches performance skills like walking a tightrope. The offerings are continually changing and new programs are being added. If you will be in the area for a while, do check the Web site or call for a current schedule.

Facilities: Restrooms. Stroller and wheelchair accessible.

Berkshire Mountain Llama Hikes. 322 Landers Road, Lee, MA 01238; 413-243-2224. All hikes are by appointment only and vary in length between one and three hours. Rates are dependent on how many people are in your party and how long you are out on the trail.

Kids love this unusual experience—spending time in nature on the back of a llama. Known for their sweet dispositions, soft wool coats, and unique personalities, these trusted hiking companions are clever and gentle around children. Led by experienced guides on well-maintained trails, the hikes go into the forests and hills surrounding a pastoral farm.

Facilities: Restrooms.

Berkshire Scenic Railway and Museum. 10 Willow Creek Road, Lenox, MA 01240; 413-637-2210; www.berkshirescenicrailroad.org. Check Web site or call for a schedule. Admission. Group rates by advance reservation.

This two-hour round-trip train ride from Lenox to Stockbridge aboard a train powered by a diesel locomotive from the 1950s (with vintage coaches from the 1920s) will delight everyone in the family. A uniformed conductor narrates the trip, pointing out places of interest. The ride is a fun way to show children the history of railroads in western Massachusetts. There is a museum worth visiting on the premises; admission is included with the price of the rail ride. The Gilded Age exhibition, housed in a vintage 1920s restored Baltimore & Ohio Railroad passenger car, tells the Berkshire story and through photographs and artifacts of the era invites visitors to stop back in time and imagine themselves as part of the Gilded Age.

Facilities: Restrooms, gift shop. The museum is stroller and wheelchair accessible. Food is permitted on the train but bring your own; the only thing available for sale is bottled water.

Bisque, Beads, and Beyond. 370 Pecks Road (Porter Plaza), Pittsfield, MA 01201; 413-442-9300. Open year-round. Charge for the various ceramic pieces.

This paint-your-own-pottery studio and bead boutique provides an enjoyable craft experience, especially in the event of inclement weather. They provide the materials—stamps, stencils, beads, and tools—everything you need to create a hand-painted gift. Even the most artistically challenged will enjoy the relaxed atmosphere here. Children love the array of colors and shapes and those as young as three can participate.

Facilities: Restroom. Stroller and wheelchair accessible.

Dinosaur Footprints Reservation. US 5, Holyoke, MA 01040; 413-532-1631. (Going north on I-91, take exit 17A and follow MA 141 east to Holyoke. Turn north on US 5, then go 2.2 miles. The entrance and parking area are at a small turnout on the right.) Open year-round. Free.

Enormous meat-eating dinosaurs (*Eubrontes giganteus*) more than 20 feet long once lumbered slowly through the mud in this area. They left behind great three-toed footprints 15 inches in length. These remains and fossils are nearly 200 million years old! Kids are fascinated with this site, especially those who are captivated by dinosaurs. In fact, for over a century those who study fossil tracks have acclaimed the Connecticut River Valley for its abundance of specimens. A helpful tip: Bring some water to pour into the tracks and they will be seen more easily. This reservation is worth a detour, but do keep in mind there are no facilities.

Ioka Valley Farm. 3475 MA 43, Hancock, MA 01237; 413-738-5915; www.iokavalleyfarm.com. Open year-round. Hours vary seasonally so call or check Web site. Free. Groups accommodated by advance reservation.

The name *Ioka* is derived from the Indian word meaning "beautiful," and this farm is certainly picturesque. Although this is a working farm, the owners are also dedicated to entertaining visitors and sharing

Children can feed the goats at Ioka Valley Farm, and the petting area includes pigs, sheep, rabbits, and llamas. BERKSHIRE VISITORS BUREAU

the various activities depending on the time of the year. Kids will have a chance to see all aspects of farm life up close; the animal petting area with pigs, sheep, goats, rabbits, chickens, and llamas, will particularly delight the youngest visitors. Each season here brings a different sort of excitement and special events. From mid-February to April the maple barn is in full swing, and kids can watch sap flow from the trees and follow the process until it becomes maple syrup. Delicious waffles and French toast are served in the "Calf-A" as well. From mid-June through July is strawberry-picking time. In the fall, there are pumpkins to be picked, free hayrides, a corn maze to be navigated, and a playground. December is the time to visit the Christmas tree plantation, where you can cut your own tree and then meet Santa. The farm stand sells hormone-free beef, maple products, homemade pies, cookies, and handcrafted gifts. Ioka is truly a place for all seasons and offers agri-entertainment at its best.

Facilities: Restrooms, gift shop, café, farm stand.

Magic Wings Butterfly Conservatory and Gardens. 281 Greenfield Road, South Deerfield, MA 01373; 413-665-2805; www.magicwings.com. (Located off I-91 on scenic US 5 and MA 10.) Admission. Group tours by advance reservation.

Did you know that butterflies taste with their feet as they land on a flower? Did you know almost all butterflies live for approximately two weeks? And like snowflakes, no two butterflies are exactly alike. Children will enjoy this lush tropical butterfly garden inside an 8,000-square-foot glass conservatory with thousands of native and tropical butterflies fluttering around throughout the year. There is a lot to learn about butterfly life cycles, migration, and food sources, and the displays here offer a wealth of fascinating information. There are also outdoor gardens (open seasonally) with iron butterfly sculptures, as well as walking paths among flowers with native butterflies fluttering about. Enjoy the benches, picnic and play areas, and quiet sanctuaries as you explore the grounds. A nature trail at the edge of the woods bordering the conservatory makes for a nice walk. This is a stop that will inspire, educate, and entertain.

Facilities: Restrooms, restaurant, gift shop, nature trail. Strollers are not permitted in the conservatory.

Par-4 Family Fun Center. 20 Williamstown Road (US 7), Lanesboro, MA 01237; 413-499-0051. (Located at the base of Mt. Greylock.) Admission is charged for the various activities.

This is a good place for the kids to let off some steam after sightseeing or traveling in the car for a long distance. There are go-carts, bumper boats, a miniature golf course, batting cages, and more.

Facilities: Restrooms, snack bar. Stroller and wheelchair accessible.

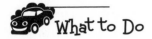 What to Do

BICYCLING

Ashuwillticook Rail Trail. Lanesborough, Cheshire, Adams, MA; 413-442-8928; www.mass.gov/dcr /parks. (From the south, take the Massachusetts Turnpike to exit 2, then US 20 west to US 7 north and MA 9 east to MA 8 north. Signs for parking areas are located on MA 8. From the north, take MA 2 to MA 8 south.) Free.

This 11-mile rail trail, a former railroad corridor, is now a paved 10-foot-wide path that runs parallel to MA 8 through the towns of Lanesborough, Cheshire, and Adams. Phase One, 5 miles long, begins at the Berkshire Mall in Lanesborough and ends at the MA 8 crossing in Cheshire. Phase Two, 6 miles long, begins where Phase One ends in Cheshire and extends to the center of Adams. The rail trail

This 11-mile rail trail offers easy pedaling for the youngest cyclists, despite its difficult name!

BERKSHIRE VISITORS BUREAU

passes through the Hoosac River Valley between Mt. Greylock and the Hoosac Mountains. The Native American word *Ashuwillticook* means "the pleasant river between the hills." As its name implies, there are spectacular views here and the area is home to several species of wildlife. This trail provides a safe and easy ride, perfect for a family outing. Note that children 16 years of age and under must wear a helmet.

Facilities: Restrooms (at the trail parking areas only).

HIKING

Bartholomew's Cobble and the Colonel John Ashley House. Weatogue Road, Ashley Falls, MA 01222; 413-229-8600. (Take US 7 south from Great Barrington and follow MA 7A to Ashley Falls. Take Rannapo Route to Weatogue Road, which is 11 miles from Great Barrington.) Everything but the Ashley House is open year-round. Admission.

This is an extremely varied 294-acre natural site that is a delight to hike and explore. Even the youngest visitors will find rocks, 800 species of flowering plants, 53 species of ferns, numerous birds, and other natural objects lovely to look at and experience. A *cobble* is an old English name for an outcropping of rock, and this particular cobble, about 500 million years old, is made of limestone and overlooks the Housatonic Valley. Hike to the top of Hurlburt's Hill and look out over valleys where cows graze and rivers run, or follow the resident naturalist on a guided walk and learn about the natural history of the property. The Ledges Trail takes about a half hour to hike and is a good walk if you are traveling with young children. Another 4.5 miles of trail wind through woods along the river and lead to spectacular viewing areas at this designated National Natural Landmark. At the visitors center, changing displays offer views of local flora and fauna, and trail guides are available. This is also an excellent bird-watching site, so bring along the binoculars and let the kids enjoy nature close-up. The Colonel John Ashley House, built in 1735, is the oldest house in Berkshire County and the site of the drafting of the Sheffield Declaration, an early declaration of personal freedom that predated the Declaration of Independence. Some older children may enjoy the tour of the homestead, which includes a large tool collection of the last 200 years, as well as period furnishings and decorative items.

Facilities: Restrooms. Visitor center/museum is wheelchair accessible and easy for strollers to maneuver through.

Mt. Greylock Summit. 30 Rockwell Road, Lanesboro, MA 01237; 413-499-4262; www.mass.gov/dcr/parks. Visitors center open year-round; road to summit seasonal.

The highest point in the state of Massachusetts is the peak of Mt. Greylock, at 3,491 feet. Now a state reservation, it comprises 12,000 acres of protected land offering spectacular views, remote boggy areas, alpine and boreal forests, and more than 40 rare plant species. Mt. Greylock has appeared in American literature through the writings of Herman Melville, Nathaniel Hawthorne, and Henry David Thoreau. Today the mountain offers many activities to visitors, including occasional nature programs for children. There is a War Memorial Tower and Beacon at the summit, and kids will enjoy the drive to the highest peak in the state!

Facilities: Restrooms, gift shop.

Pleasant Valley Wildlife Sanctuary. 472 West Mountain Road (off US 7), Lenox, MA 01240; 413-637-0320; www.massaudubon.org. Open year-round. Admission.

This Massachusetts Audubon sanctuary covers 1,300 acres and contains a wealth of natural settings for animals and plants, plus 7 miles of well-marked trails. The short, easy-to-walk trails lead through forests, wildflower meadows, wetlands, around ponds, and to the summit of Lenox Mountain. The ponds here are usually active with beavers, bullfrogs, and the occasional leaping fish. Naturalists are often on hand to answer any questions. If you are in the area during the summer, you may want to take advantage of the summer day camp, which runs for one- and two-week sessions and includes many outdoor activities. In addition, sanctuary staff conducts an array of seasonal programs. Canoe trips are offered regularly on the Housatonic River and area lakes during certain months. Check the Web site or call for a catalog of programs.

Facilities: Restrooms. This site is not recommended for strollers or wheelchairs.

HORSEBACK RIDING

Undermountain Farm. 400 Undermountain Road, Lenox, MA 01240; 413-637-3365; www.undermountainfarm.com. (Located 1 mile from the center of Lenox.) Open year-round.

This picturesque riding facility consists of a collection of beautifully renovated Victorian farm buildings surrounded by 150 acres of pasture, forest, and hay fields. A large indoor riding arena, a spacious outdoor arena, and miles of riding trails provide ample terrain for all horse enthusiasts. There are pony rides for young children, and guided trail rides are available for all ages and levels of ability. Lessons may be scheduled as well. During the summer there is a day camp for children over the age of five.

Facilities: Restrooms.

ICE SKATING

Boys and Girls Club of Pittsfield Skating Arena. 16 Melville Street, Pittsfield, MA 01201; 413-448-8258. There are public skating sessions for hockey and figure skating. Call in season for a schedule. Admission.

Lansing-Chapman Ice Rink. 76 Latham Street, Williamstown, MA 01267; 413-597-2433; www.williams.edu/athletics. This indoor rink, on the campus of Williams College, has times for public use that vary by season. Make sure to call ahead. Admission.

Vietnam Veterans Skating Rink. 1267 South Church Street, North Adams, MA 01247; 413-664-8185; www.northadams-ma.gov. Call or check web site for schedule. This indoor rink, run by the city of North Adams, offers public skating sessions on weekend afternoons. Admission.

CANOEING, KAYAKING, AND RAFTING

Berkshire Outfitters. 169 Grove Street (MA 8), Adams, MA 01220; 413-743-5900; www.berkshireoutfitters.com. Open year-round.

You can rent flat-water, recreational one- or two-person kayaks here— as well as two-person canoes—and take them on your vehicle to wherever you want to go. For an additional charge, they will provide transportation for you and the equipment to and from nearby Cheshire Lake.

Crab Apple Whitewater, Inc. 2056 Mohawk Trail (MA 2), Charlemont, MA 01339; 413-625-2288, 1-800-553-RAFT; www.crabapplewhite water.com.

This family-owned and -operated outfitter has been in business for over 25 years. They offer a variety of full- and half-day trips on the Deerfield River in rafts or inflatable kayaks. For a fun, easy white-water rafting trip, ask about going out on the Fie Brook section of the river, a 10-mile trip and the perfect outing for families with young children. (Kids must be at least five years old to go on a river trip.) Calm sections of the river allow your guide to fill you in on local history and offer an opportunity to take in the beautiful scenery. There is a stop midway through the journey for a hearty riverside picnic lunch.

Wild 'n Wet Sport Rentals. Located at Matt Reilly's Restaurant on US 7, Pontoosuc Lake, Pittsfield, MA 01201; 413-445-5211. This informal establishment specializes in renting canoes and paddleboats on Pontoosuc Lake, a lovely place to get out on the water for a relaxed family outing. You are able to rent boats by the hour here.

Zoar Outdoor. 7 Main Street, Charlemont, MA 01339; 413-339-8596, 1-800-532-7483; www .zoaroutdoor.com.

Kayaking or rafting down the Deerfield River is a great way to see the Berkshires and to spend a hot summer day. This is also the place to call if you are interested in taking a "family kayak clinic"— learning the finer points of the sport with the kids. Clinics range from one to three days for beginner, intermediate, and advanced levels—all are led by certified instructors. In addition to offering classes and renting equipment, they have guided white-water raft-

Rafting down the Deerfield River is an adventurous way to experience the Berkshires. BERKSHIRE VISITORS BUREAU

ing trips and zipline canopy tours. Whatever you want to do, they will tailor an outing to suit your needs.

PARKS

The Berkshires region extends over hundreds of square miles of villages, parks, and forests; these areas offer a chance for young visitors to experience the outdoors firsthand. The following state forests offer the most facilities and activities for young children. The park season runs from

Memorial Day weekend through Columbus Day, dawn until dusk. There are day-use charges, and campsites are available by advance reservation for a fee. Each park has picnic tables, grills, and play areas—although they may be crowded on holidays and weekends. Unless otherwise noted, the sites are not wheelchair accessible. The Web site for all is www.mass.gov/dcr/parks.

Beartown State Forest. 69 Blue Hill Road, Monterey, MA 01245; 413-528-0904. The park is located off MA 23, midway between Great Barrington and Otis. This is a huge 12,000-acre reservation with a full offering of outdoor activities including camping, fishing, and hiking. The forest is open in the winter for cross-country skiing. There is a beautiful pond loop trail (1.5 miles of flat terrain) around Benedict Pond that is a great place to introduce children to hiking. The Appalachian Trail also runs through this forest for a couple of miles near Benedict Pond. Note that there is no lifeguard on duty at the pond and swimming here isn't recommended.

Mt. Washington State Forest. 413-528-0330. Take NY 23 to South Egremont and watch for signs. This park contains 4,169 acres, including Bash Bish Falls with its spectacular 60-foot cascade tumbling through a series of gorges and forest before dropping into a sparkling pool below. You can also hike on the numerous well-marked trails, which are converted to cross-country trails in the winter. The main attraction at this park is the falls, one of the state's most dramatic and its highest single-drop waterfall.

October Mountain State Forest. 256 Woodland Road, Lee, MA 01238; 413-243-1778. Take US 20 from Lenox to the entrance of the park. There are 16,500 acres here, making it the largest state forest. It is the perfect place for overnight camping, with nearly 50 campsites—or at least a full-day outing. At one time the park was a private game preserve, and there are several fishing spots and walking trails. Picnic areas are numerous. In the winter there are 25 miles of cross-country ski trails and plenty of space to feel alone in the woods!

Pittsfield State Forest. 1041 Cascade Street, Pittsfield, MA 01201; 413-442-8992. This park has thousands of acres including two spacious camping areas and two large picnic areas. There is also a swimming beach with a lifeguard on duty during the summer months. From April through November you can drive up to Berry Pond, one of the highest natural bodies of water in the state. Another highlight of this forest is the Tranquility Trail, a 0.75-mile paved wheelchair-accessible trail. In the northeastern corner of the forest is Balance Rock State Park, famous for its 165-ton limestone boulder seemingly precariously balanced on bedrock. This natural curiosity will especially intrigue the kids!

Sandisfield State Forest (York Lake). York Lake Road, Monterey, MA 01245; 413-229-8212 (summer months only), 413-528-0904 (rest of the year). Although the 300-foot beach on York Lake in this park is a popular site for swimming, there is no lifeguard on duty. Visitors may picnic, go boating (there is a boat launch ramp), hike, or camp overnight. The 1.5-mile Pond Loop Trail is a good choice for those with young children. During the winter, there are several miles of cross-country ski trails to explore.

Western Gateway Heritage State Park. 115 State Street, North Adams, MA 01247; 413-663-6312. Visitors center open year-round. This urban cultural park focuses on the era of railroads. Located in a former railroad yard, various exhibits tell the story of the Hoosac Tunnel, a wonder of engineering while it was built from 1848 to 1875; 200 men lost their lives during construction. The tunnel was dug 4.75 miles through Hoosac Mountain, linking Albany and Massachusetts. It is still used today and is the longest transport tunnel east of the Rockies. Kids will enjoy the audiovisual story of the park, and there are special events on-site throughout the year.

PICK-YOUR-OWN AND OTHER FARMS

Farms that welcome visitors are limited in the Berkshires. The following farms welcome guests and offer a chance to see fruits, vegetables, poultry, and maple syrup–making up close. If you are making a long drive to a pick-your-own farm, call ahead to make certain that the harvest is ready.

Blueberry Hill Farm. 100 East Road, Mt. Washington, MA 01258; 413-528-1479. This lovely farm is open during the summer months for blueberry picking, which makes a nice outing after a hike in nearby Mt. Washington State Forest.

Green River Farms. 2480 Green River Road, Williamstown, MA 01267; 413-458-2470; www.greenriverfarms.com. Farm store open year-round; hours vary seasonally for pick-your-own strawberries, corn, vegetables, and apples. There is a lot to do on this bustling farm and it makes a great place for a picnic lunch along the Green River. The petting farm includes rabbits, goats, and donkeys and there are sunset wagon tours available as well.

Lakeview Orchard. 94 Old Cheshire Road, Lanesboro, MA 01237; 413-448-6009; www.lakevieworchard.com. There are both sweet and tart cherries as well as raspberries to pick here in July. The apples are ready to be harvested in mid-August through October. The kids will enjoy visiting the cider mill on the premises and watching how the apples are pressed before sampling a refreshing drink. They also grow and sell plums, peaches, apricots, and nectarines—although they aren't available for pick-your-own.

Otis Poultry Farm. 1570 North Main Road (MA 8), Otis, MA 01253; 413-269-4438; www.otispoultryfarm.com. Open year-round. This farm has been in business since 1904 and kids will love the short tour of the poultry farm. Their store offers a wide selection of gourmet items, honey, maple syrup, fresh baked goods, and (of course) eggs and poultry.

Windy Hill Farm. 686 Stockbridge Road, Great Barrington, MA 01230; 413-298-3217; www.farmfresh.org. Located between Stockbridge and Great Barrington. Here you will find nearly two-dozen varieties of pick-your-own apples, so that everyone in the family will come away with their favorite type of fruit.

SKIING AND SNOWBOARDING

Bousquet. 101 Dan Fox Drive, Pittsfield, MA 01201; 413-442-8316; www.bousquets.com. Lift ticket fee.

This is the Berkshires' oldest ski center, dating back to 1932, and the atmosphere is old-time and family-oriented. Bousquet caters particularly to the beginner, novice, and intermediate skier, so you can expect to find gentle skiing (and snowboarding) on many of the 22 trails and slopes serviced by four lifts. There are ski classes (group or private) that take all ages, from toddlers on up. And there are snow tubing chutes for those who prefer a change of pace. During the summer, kids can enjoy a splash-down water pool, a miniature golf course, driving range, and go-carts.

Facilities: Restrooms, snack bar, restaurant, ski shop, nursery, rentals, lockers.

Butternut Basin. 380 MA 23, Great Barrington, MA 01230; 413-528-2000; www.skibutternut.com. Lift ticket fee.

There are 22 trails and 12 lifts here, but Butternut is a low-key place to learn to ski. The area itself is lovely to look at and offers excellent views of the Massachusetts and New York mountains. A separate beginner's slope is a perfect place for first-time slope sliders to take a tumble

The chair lifts at Butternut Basin provide great views. BERKSHIRE VISITORS BUREAU

or two. The Skiwee, Mini-Rider, and New Adventurer programs for children include those age 4–12 and range from beginners to advanced instruction. There is a half-day program for children aged 4–6. Children are divided into classes depending on their age, ability, and size. A full-service nursery tends to kids who prefer not to ski, and the staff has a full-day program guaranteed to keep them happy and busy while Mom and Dad are out on the slopes. Cross-country skiers will find groomed trails, and snowboarders will enjoy this area too. There is a snow tubing center as well.

Facilities: Restrooms, snack bar, restaurant, retail shop, nursery, rentals, lockers.

Jiminy Peak Mountain Resort. 37 Corey Road, Hancock, MA 01237; 413-738-5500; www.jiminypeak.com. Lift ticket fee.

This is a demanding mountain for skiers and snowboarders, and it's recommended for adults and children who are comfortable on the slopes. The mountain offers over 40 trails and slopes serviced by six high-speed chairlifts. A beginner's slope for those learning to ski and snowboard gets lots of afternoon sun. There are complete rentals and snowboard and ski lessons on-site, with extensive ski classes geared to all ages and abilities—but new, younger skiers may feel a bit overwhelmed at all the action on this large, busy slope. The children's program is excellent, with lessons and lunch: It includes a 3-Year-Old Program, a SkiWee Program (ages 4–6), and an Explorer's Program (ages 7–12). The Cub's Den welcomes children aged six months and older who prefer to remain indoors. Jiminy Peak is a full-service resort with all the amenities, and offering special overnight package rates for families. During the summer, visitors will enjoy the Alpine Slide, a coaster of wheels that wends its way down the slopes, the miniature golf course, and outdoor swimming pool.

Facilities: Restrooms, snack bar, restaurant, ski shop, nursery, rentals, lockers.

Kennedy Park. Main Street (US 7), Lenox, MA 01240; 413-637-5530. (The access point for this park is behind the Lenox House Restaurant (55 Pittsfield Road), just north of the village.) Free.

This 180-acre park has seven trails, formerly old carriage roads and bridle paths that are great for cross-country skiing. The roads wind in and out of what was once the site of a grand old hotel. Each trail is well marked with colorful blazes of paint, and the white novice trail is especially nice to try if the kids are new on skis. There are no facilities here, and you must have your own equipment. The scenery is spectacular.

Notchview Reservation. 83 Old MA 9, Windsor, MA 01270; 413-684-0148. (Located northeast of Pittsfield.) Admission.

This 3,000-acre preserve has about 12 miles of marked and maintained trails. Notchview has one of the highest base elevations (2,000 feet) among New England Nordic ski areas. The reservation's visitors center provides trail maps; several of them are suitable for young children and beginner skiers. Two trailside shelters offer rest stops and fantastic views.

Facilities: Restrooms.

Otis Ridge. 159 Monterey Road (off MA 23), Otis, MA 01253; 413-269-4444; www.otisridge.com. Lift ticket fee.

A small hill in comparison to other Berkshire mountains, Otis Ridge has 11 slopes and trails and five lifts (only one is a chair lift). However, I can't think of a nicer place to take kids who want to learn to ski without pressure from large classes or advanced instructors. The setup here considers careful ski instruction as the best way to manage younger skiers, and there is little of the competition found at larger slopes. Note that children must be at least 4 years old for group lessons. Only 800 lift tickets per day are sold here, so the trails never become too crowded. A ski camp is offered for children aged 8–16. The price of the lift tickets is very reasonable and this is an excellent place in the Berkshires for beginning skiers, with complete learn-to-ski packages available for day or weekend use. Note that there is no child-care service available here.

Facilities: Restrooms, cafeteria, ski school, ski shop, full equipment rentals, lockers.

Stone Hill Clark Trail System. Clark Art Institute, 225 South Street, Williamstown, MA 01267. Access to the trails is from the rear parking lot of the museum. Free.

The two cross-country "loop" circles here are the Pasture Loop (0.7 mile long) and the longer Stone Bench Loop (1.5 miles). These neighborhood-type ski trails are both good choices for outings with young children. And the Stone Bench Loop *does* have a stone bench where you can stop and take in the beautiful views of the nearby mountains!

SWIMMING

There are numerous places to swim in the Berkshires, from swimming holes to state forest preserves to private pools, but the following places offer some of the best kid-friendly water fun. Don't forget to check the state parks listings here for other swimming areas. Unless otherwise noted, each site charges an admission fee, and there are lifeguards on duty.

Lake Mansfield. Lake Mansfield Road, Great Barrington, MA 01230; 413-528-1510; www.lakemansfield.org. This 40-acre body of water, less than 1 mile from the downtown area, has a clean beach and designated swimming area. There are lifeguards on duty during the summer months. The playground, picnic area, and portable toilets make this a good spot to cool off after exploring Great Barrington.

Onota Lake at Burbank Park. Valentine Road and Lakeway Drive, Pittsfield, MA 01201; 413-499-9343. The Burbank Park area of this 617-acre lake has lifeguards on duty; it's a nice place for a family outing.

Sand Springs Pool and Spa. 158 Sand Springs Road, Williamstown, MA 01267; 413-458-5205; www.springspool.com. This is one of the oldest continuously running spas in the country, and it still soothes both adults and kids with its heated mineral waters. Facilities include a 50-by-75-foot pool fed by natural mineral springs, along with a heated toddler pool with a fountain, and oversized hot tubs fed by natural mineral springs.

Windsor Lake. Intersection of Bradley Street and Kemp Avenue, North Adams, MA 01247; 413-662-3047. This lovely lake has a large swimming area and may be crowded on weekends, but there are lifeguards on duty. During the summer months, there are free weekly concerts.

THEATER

Theater in the Berkshires is a summer event with professional entertainment, and children are particularly enchanted with many of the productions. Everything from comedy to Shakespeare is on tap, and it's a sure bet that if you are near a major town, you will be able to find a theater group in residence during July and August. The following theaters have all offered children's programming, but schedules change each year, so call or check the Web site for up-to-date information.

Barrington Stage Company. 30 Union Street, Pittsfield, MA 01201; 413-236-8888; www.barringtonstageco.org. Enjoy award-winning musicals, comedies, and dramas in a 520-seat state-of-the-art theater. They offer children's productions as well as a three-week Kids Act (summer musical theater camp) program for those young people interested in the performing arts. There are reduced ticket rates for children and students.

Berkshire Theatre Festival. East Main Street, Stockbridge, MA 01262; 413-298-5576; www.berkshiretheatre.org. This theatre was founded in the 19th century and has been going strong ever since. In the past, stars such as Katharine Hepburn, James Cagney, and Montgomery Clift (he started here as a 12-year-old actor) have appeared here. The wide variety of programs includes some for children and families, like *Annie* and *A*

An attentive young audience at the Inside/Out Stage at Jacob's Pillow.

Christmas Carol, as well as a range of dramatic offerings and Shakespeare that will appeal to older children who are fascinated by the theatrical arts.

Jacob's Pillow Dance Festival. 358 George Carter Road, Becket, MA 01223; 413-243-0745; www.jacobspillow.org. This is one of the best dance festivals in the country, and I recommend it for children interested in dance of any kind. There are special youth matinees featuring groups like the Dance Theatre of Harlem Ensemble that will appeal to older children as well as younger ones who can sit through an entire performance. A couple of the other performances have included the colorful costumes and vibrant music of the Magic of Creole troupe and Pilobolus (with its acrobatic dances). If you don't think the kids can sit through an entire show, watch a free performance of a work in progress at the Inside/Out Stage, or take the time to watch the dancers at work in the studios, some of which are open to the public.

Shakespeare and Company. 70 Kemble Street, Lenox, MA 01240; 413-637-3353, 413-637-1199; www.shakespeare.org. The theater here showcases a variety of works by the Bard throughout the summer. Some older children will enjoy these plays, especially if they have studied Shakespeare in school. However, most children will prefer the ongoing Bankside Festival on the premises outdoors by the theater. There is continual revelry, concerts, and impromptu entertainment—all free of charge. This is a wonderful way to introduce young people to Shakespeare.

Williamstown Theater Festival. 1000 Main Street, Williamstown, MA 01267; 413-597-3400; www.wtfestival.org. This nationally renowned festival presents dozens of performances every summer, with some of them moving to Off-Broadway. Offerings range from classics to modern plays that are performed in two theaters. There are also some free outdoor theater performances and a special program for youngsters called the Greylock Theater Project. A great way to spend a summer evening is watching one of their outdoor productions under the stars. Besides, the younger ones can fall asleep on the lawn when they get tired—and you can still enjoy the show.

Index

▼▲▼▲▼▲▼